FIFTH EDITION

Archery

STEPS TO SUCCESS

Kathleen M. Haywood, PhD
Catherine F. Lewis, MEd

HUMAN KINETICS

Library of Congress Cataloging-in-Publication Data

Names: Haywood, Kathleen author. | Lewis, Catherine, 1957- author.
Title: Archery : steps to success / Kathleen M. Haywood, Catherine F.
 Lewis.
Description: Fifth edition. | Champaign, IL : Human Kinetics, [2025] |
 Includes bibliographical references.
Identifiers: LCCN 2023040457 (print) | LCCN 2023040458 (ebook) | ISBN
 9781718221369 (paperback) | ISBN 9781718221376 (epub) | ISBN
 9781718221383 (pdf)
Subjects: LCSH: Archery.
Classification: LCC GV1185 .H38 2025 (print) | LCC GV1185 (ebook) | DDC
 799.3/2--dc23/eng/20231010
LC record available at https://lccn.loc.gov/2023040457
LC ebook record available at https://lccn.loc.gov/2023040458

ISBN: 978-1-7182-2136-9 (print)

The web addresses cited in this text were current as of September 2023, unless otherwise noted.

Acquisitions Editor: Diana Vincer; **Developmental Editor:** Anne Hall; **Managing Editor:** Hannah Werner; **Copyeditor:** Joan Little, Pendulum Editing; **Permissions Manager:** Laurel Mitchell; **Graphic Designer:** Julie L. Denzer; **Cover Designer:** Keri Evans; **Cover Design Specialist:** Susan Rothermel Allen; **Photograph (cover):** WhiteBaltzinger/iStock/Getty Images; **Photographs (interior):** © Human Kinetics, unless otherwise noted; **Photo Asset Manager:** Laura Fitch; **Photo Production Specialist:** Amy M. Rose; **Photo Production Manager:** Jason Allen; **Senior Art Manager:** Kelly Hendren; **Illustrations:** © Human Kinetics; **Printer:** Sheridan Kentucky

Human Kinetics books are available at special discounts for bulk purchase. Special editions or book excerpts can also be created to specification. For details, contact the Special Sales Manager at Human Kinetics.

Printed in the United States of America   10 9 8 7 6 5 4 3 2 1

The paper in this book is certified under a sustainable forestry program.

Human Kinetics
1607 N. Market Street
Champaign, IL 61820
USA

United States and International
Website: **US.HumanKinetics.com**
Email: info@hkusa.com
Phone: 1-800-747-4457

Canada
Website: **Canada.HumanKinetics.com**
Email: info@hkcanada.com

E9109

FIFTH EDITION

Archery

STEPS TO SUCCESS

Contents

Climbing the Steps to Archery Success

Get ready to climb a staircase, one that will lead you to become an accomplished archer. You cannot leap to the top or skip stairs; you get to the top by climbing one step at a time. The steps to archery success are arranged in order so that each step is an easy and safe transition from the previous one. This fifth edition allows you to progress to an intermediate stage in your preferred type of archery, be that traditional archery, competitive target shooting, competitive 3-D shooting, bowhunting, or bowfishing (new to this edition) by building a solid foundation of fundamental archery skills.

Archery is a sport that involves the use of many pieces of equipment. Your first step is to fit the equipment to your unique body structure and strength level. Even if you plan to learn on simple equipment and buy better equipment later, your equipment needs to fit when you are learning to shoot. Poorly fit equipment can cause beginners to develop flaws that become habits that are difficult to change later.

The next step is learning how to handle archery equipment safely. Shooters in any type of archery must be aware of the harm an arrow can do if they do not exercise care at all times.

The following step is to learn to shoot with good technique, first by mimicking shots and then by shooting arrows. The early emphasis is on building good technique and consistently executing that good technique. Just about any beginner can hit the bull's-eye once if he shoots enough arrows. The goal of the technique step is to learn how to hit the bull's-eye consistently. Even if your interest is bowhunting or bowfishing, your success on that one important shot is likely to come after hours of practice hitting your target consistently.

Subsequent steps allow you to refine your technique and adapt it to both your unique body structure and the type of archery you want to shoot. Accessories are added gradually at just the right time to improve your accuracy. Throughout the steps, you can engage in specific learning activities and practice exercises to advance your skill and break the monotony of the typical archery practice session.

Additional steps build your mental skills for shooting and teach you multiple ways to analyze your performance to correct the minor flaws that affect your accuracy. Upgrades in equipment can help improve your scores, but you need to be a critical consumer. The latest "new thing" will not always improve your shooting accuracy. You also will learn to adjust your equipment to achieve smooth arrow flight and maximize scores. Near the top of the staircase, you will learn to prepare and adapt your equipment for specific types of archery, especially competitive target archery and traditional archery, competitive 3-D shooting, bowhunting, and bowfishing.

Archery: Steps to Success provides a progressive plan for developing your shooting skills and building confidence in your ability to hit your mark. Whether you want to shoot in a recreational league or in a competitive tournament, to enjoy the bowhunting season or shoot 3-D rounds year-round, you will improve your performance and enjoy shooting more as you develop greater competence and learn more about archery and archery equipment. To help you do that, a new feature appears in the fifth edition: What Sport Science Says boxes present scientific research on an aspect of archery in layman's terms. These research results often provide the "why" behind an emphasis in technique or the addition of a shooting accessory.

As you go through the steps to success, you will follow the same sequence with each step:

1. Read the explanation of what is covered in the step, why the step is important, and the focus of the step, which may be on a skill, a concept, the use of equipment, or a combination of the three.

2. Study the photos and illustrations, which show exactly how to execute aspects of the shot.

3. Read the instructions for each exercise. Complete the exercise and record your score.

4. At the end of the step, review your performance and total your scores from the exercises. Once you've achieved the indicated level of success with the step, move on to the next step.

Make *Archery: Steps to Success* part of your successful climb to the top. Learn the fundamental form that provides a solid foundation on which to build your skill. Use a systematic and gradual approach to advancing your skills and using equipment accessories. You can specialize in a form of archery, but all successful archers and bowhunters use the same basic form. Consistency is the name of the game for archers. Even when you reach the top, the exercises in this book can keep your shooting sharp, and you can learn more about how archery equipment influences shooting. The tools for analyzing your performance can be used no matter what your level, experience, or type of equipment.

The reward for completing the steps to success is a lifetime of enjoying the many forms of archery. For some, the challenge of improving performance is enough. For others, spending hunting season in the woods is their desire. Those who like competition can choose from a variety of archery contests, such as Olympic-style outdoor shooting at long distances, 3-D animal target shoots, and indoor tournaments with 100 archers on the shooting line. You can even practice using one of the virtual reality archery games. Good luck on this step-by-step journey to developing the physical and mental skills necessary for accurate shooting. Enjoy your climb in *Archery: Steps to Success* to becoming a successful archer, and join legions of people throughout history who have learned to hit their marks!

The Sport of Archery

When you pick up a bow to shoot your first arrow, you are partaking in an activity dating back at least 20,000 years. The bow and arrow are pictured in drawings from that time on a cave wall in Spain's Valtorta Gorge. Other finds document the long history of archery: flint arrowheads from the period between 25,000 and 18,000 BC, arrow shafts from approximately 9000 BC, one-piece yew and elm bows from 8000 to 6000 BC, and a rock fresco of an Egyptian archer from approximately 7500 BC. In 1991, the preserved body of a man who lived around 3300 BC was found in the Alps. He carried a quiver of 14 arrows.

The bow and arrow were once critical to humankind's survival. The bow allowed humans to become proficient hunters, shooting prey from a distance. Prey provided various raw materials, such as hide, bone, and sinew, for tools, shelter, and clothing and added protein to the diet. Early bow designs reflected the materials available in the geographic region and the tools available for craftspeople. For example, early bows were selfbows made from a single piece of wood; the design eventually preferred was created by gluing together multiple pieces of wood. Bow designs also reflected the way bows were used. Short bows were easier to handle from horseback or chariots, and longbows were better for shooting distant targets from fortified encampments.

Empires rose and fell as a result of the use of the bow and arrow as weapons. The ancient Egyptians established the bow as a primary weapon of war around 3500 BC. They made bows almost as tall as themselves and arrowheads of flint and bronze. Around 1800 BC, the Assyrians introduced a new bow design: a short composite bow of leather, horn, and wood with a recurve shape. It was more powerful than the long-bow used by the Egyptians and could be handled easily on horseback. This bow gave the Assyrians an edge in battle over their rivals in the Middle East. The Hittites also used the short recurve bow in mobile warfare by shooting from the light, fast chariots they developed around 1200 BC. Middle Eastern superiority in archery continued for centuries as the peoples of the area successfully fought Europeans. The Mongols conquered much of Europe, and the Turks threw back the Crusaders, in part because of their superior recurve bows and better shooting technique.

In the Far East, the samurai warriors of Japan were known for their archery skills. They developed a bow about 7 feet (2 m) long called the yumi, which was made largely of bamboo. A unique feature of the yumi was the placement of the grip about two-thirds of the way down the bow. The shorter lower limb perhaps allowed the bow to be shot more easily from kneeling positions or horseback.

In the 11th century, the Normans developed a bow that they used to defeat the English (Anglo-Saxons) at the Battle of Hastings in AD 1066. In battles of the time, archers avoided carrying large numbers of arrows by reusing their enemies' arrows. The English positioned themselves behind a shield wall. The Normans gained an advantage by retrieving many of their arrows lying near enemy lines and shooting them in an arc over the wall.

After the Battle of Hastings, the Norman and Anglo-Saxon cultures were integrated. The English adopted the bow as their major weapon and then improved it. Their famous longbows were about 6 feet (1.8 m) long and very powerful. Longbowmen became the core of English armies that would dominate battles for centuries to come. Many ballads of the 13th and 14th centuries, such as the tales of Robin Hood, attest to the archery skill of the English. English kings would often require Englishmen to practice archery on Sundays and holidays or ban other sports that diverted time from archery.

Although the value of the bow as a war weapon declined swiftly after the invention of firearms in the 16th century, the fun and challenge of archery guaranteed its continued existence as a sport. King Henry VIII promoted archery as a sport in England by directing Sir Christopher Morris to establish an archery society, the Guild of St. George, in 1537. Roger Ascham published the book *Toxophilus* in 1545 to preserve much of the archery knowledge of the time and to maintain an interest in archery among the English.

Archery societies were founded throughout the 1600s, and the tournaments they held firmly established archery as a competitive sport. The Antient Scorton Silver Arrow Contest was first held in 1673 in North Yorkshire, England, and continues to be held today, with the Antient Silver Arrow awarded to the first archer each year who hits a 3-inch (7.6 cm) center on the target from 100 yards (90 m) with a recurve bow. Women joined the men in competition and were first admitted to an archery society in 1787. Contests were held in three major forms of archery: one that resembles today's target shooting to a vertically mounted target; one that was a precursor of clout shooting (long-range shooting to a large target laid out on the ground); and one called roving that resembles field shooting today, wherein archers walk along the countryside to shoot at various targets.

On the North American continent, Indigenous peoples relied on the bow and arrow for hunting. Their bows, however, were short and weak. European settlers brought their well-developed knowledge of bowmaking and kept alive the interest in target archery in North America. The first archery club on the continent, the United Bowmen of Philadelphia, was established in 1828.

The Civil War spurred greater interest in archery in the United States. When the war ended, the victorious Union prohibited former Confederate soldiers from using firearms, so some took up archery. Two veterans and brothers, Will and Maurice Thompson, learned archery with the help of Native Americans in Florida. Maurice wrote a book, *The Witchery of Archery,* that helped spread interest in archery across the country.

By 1879, the National Archery Association (NAA) had been founded and began holding national tournaments. In 1938, Ben Pearson established a company to mass-produce archery equipment. Enthusiasm for field archery (a target archery competition that simulates hunting) and bowhunting itself led to the establishment of the National Field Archery Association in 1939.

Archery first became an official Olympic event at the 1900 Paris Olympics, an appropriate sanction because the mythical founder of the ancient Olympic Games was Hercules, an archer. Archery was an event at the 1904 St. Louis Olympics and the 1908 England Olympics—and female archers were included in both games—but archery made only one more Olympic appearance over the next six decades.

The problem with early archery competitions was the lack of a universal set of rules. The host country could decide whether or not to offer archery competitions and select the rules to be used. To better organize competitive archery, Polish archers worked to establish an international governing body. As a result, the Fédération Internationale de Tir à l'Arc (FITA) was founded in 1931. FITA set up universal rules and designated particular rounds that would be shot in international competitions, including the Olympics. As a result, international competition grew and gained so much momentum in succeeding decades that archery was readopted for the 1972 Olympic Games. It has been a part of the Olympics ever since, and medals are now awarded to men and women in both individual and team competitions. Archery was one of the most popular 2012 Olympic events viewed on television. It was also one of the 21 events in the Paralympics held in London in 2012, and has remained a popular event at every Olympics and Paralympics since.

Technical advances of the mid-20th century in the design of bows and arrows and the availability of new materials increased shooting accuracy and, consequently, interest in archery. Two developments had a particular impact. In 1946, Doug Easton developed a process for manufacturing aluminum arrow shafts. The uniformity of aluminum arrows in weight and spine (stiffness) greatly increased the accuracy and enjoyment of shooting for many. Then, in the late 1960s, H.W. Allen of Missouri invented the compound bow. The early compound bow used eccentric (off-center axle) pulleys mounted in the tips of the bow limbs to reduce the holding (draw) weight of the bow at full draw length. With the compound bow, archers can hold longer, which gives them more time to aim, shoot more arrows, and shoot heavier poundage, all with less fatigue and more control. These types of bows became popular for target and field archery and especially for bowhunting.

Smaller inventions and improvements also boosted the accuracy and enjoyment of shooting throughout the 1900s. In 1937, bowsights were first used at an NAA tournament. In 1951, plastic vanes became an alternative to the feathers on arrows, and in 1961, the Hoyt Archery Company made bows with attached stabilizers. Release aids came on the scene in national competitions held in 1970.

With advancements in firearms and the development of video games with so much variety in content, you might think there would be little interest in archery today. In fact, quite the opposite! Interest in archery remains high as technology makes equipment accessible to people of any age, ability level, and size. The Crossroads Wounded Warrior Project in the United States introduces archery to wounded soldiers. Video technology and automatic scoring systems also have resulted in archery becoming an exciting spectator sport, whether in person or through the media, and even with long shooting distances. Advances in archery technology have drawn many to archery. They enjoy applying the latest advances to their equipment. Yet other archers enjoy shooting with the same type of equipment used hundreds of years ago, and traditional archery has a large following, too. Some archers enjoy both. Whether for target shooting, bowhunting, or bowfishing, archers now have many options and ways to shoot.

ARCHERY TODAY

Newly available and affordable materials such as carbon have led to the design of lighter and therefore faster arrows, more consistent performance of bow limbs, and more flexibility to interchange parts and accessories. Throughout the history of shoot-

Courtesy of Competition Archery Media.

Figure 1   Archery is popular with people of all ages and ability levels.

ing, new innovations in materials and technique have boosted interest and participation in archery. New archers today can use modern equipment and accessories to shoot with great accuracy. Even more important, advances in equipment make it possible for more shooters than ever before to hit their marks.

Archery is enjoyed today by thousands of people all over the world. It appeals to all kinds of people—men and women, children and older adults, and those with and without disabilities or injuries (figure 1). Another reason for the popularity of archery is the many ways to enjoy the sport, including target shooting, bowhunting, bowfishing, and even archery tag.

Target Archery

Target archery has been popular since the days of King Henry VIII of England. The challenge of hitting the mark is timeless. Today, many archers enjoy shooting recurve bows and using their fingers to hold and release the bowstring (Olympic style). Others enjoy shooting compound bows and using mechanical releases (figure 2). Some like to shoot with traditional equipment, just the bow and arrows, whereas others enjoy using every possible new product and innovation. Targets can be flat and circular, pictures of game animals, or 3-D foam animals.

When compound bows and release aids came onto the archery scene, there was an obvious need to provide separate competition categories for archers, because this equipment provides an advantage in precise shooting. Some archery associations chose to sponsor certain equipment categories and not others, and others were

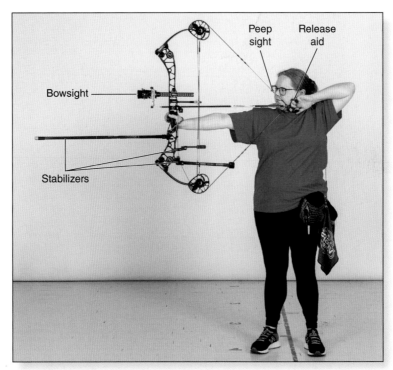

Figure 2   An archer using a compound bow, a peep sight, a bowsight extended from the bow, a release aid, and stabilizers.

founded to provide competitive opportunities for certain types of equipment. Often, these devices first became popular in the United States, and it took time for their use to spread around the world.

Today, target archers are lucky to have many choices in equipment styles and competitive formats. Those living in colder climates can often find indoor facilities with shooting distances of around 20 yards (18 m). Outdoors, target archers can shoot longer distances and classic competitive rounds in which all archers shoot from a line to concentric circle targets. Or, target archers can shoot field archery events in which they walk from target to target and shoot from varying distances to ringed targets.

As noted earlier, it would be easy to assume that interest in archery has waned as video games and other technologies have increased in popularity. On the contrary, books and movies that have included archery have made the sport more popular. *The Hunger Games* and *Brave* are examples. Also, video games have included versions of archery-like games, and these encourage players to try the real sport. A popular and growing program, National Archery in the Schools, brings archery to schools and is encouraging a new generation of participants. All of this proves once again that the simple challenge of hitting a bull's-eye is timeless.

Other Types of Archery

Bowhunting (figure 3) is a very popular activity today. Bowhunters enjoy the challenge of taking game as they help to control the size of game populations whose natural predators have dwindled. The amount of game taken during a season is usually regu-

Figure 3   Most bowhunters use compound bows, which are more compact than recurve bows, making use in the woods and from tree stands easier.

lated. Bowhunting seasons are often much longer than gun hunting seasons, offering bowhunters more opportunity to enjoy hunting.

The majority of bowhunters now use compound bows rather than recurve bows. Compound bows make bowhunting more humane for more hunters because a kill is more likely than a wound with the increased arrow speed as a result of the potential for heavier draw weight. The compound bow allows smaller people or those with disabilities to hunt with the necessary bow draw weight.

Bowhunting has become so popular that bowhunters often hold competitive rounds in the off-season. Hunting with a bow typically demands more practice than gun hunting, so off-season simulated hunting events give bowhunters opportunities for practice. Field archery simulates hunting in that the shooting distance and terrain vary from target to target. In some field archery rounds, paper animal targets are used instead of concentric ring targets. Silhouette or three-dimensional (3-D) foam targets shaped like animals are popular in hunting rounds. They are placed in wooded or grassy areas at unmarked distances. In hunting rounds, the equipment, especially the bowsight, might be limited to that typical for hunting.

Flight shooting is another type of archery enjoyed in some parts of North America. Arrows are shot for distance using bows and arrows designed for just this purpose. Today's flight bows shoot more than 900 yards (823 m).

Bowfishing is yet another way to enjoy archery (figure 4). From a boat or the shore, fish are shot with an arrow attached to fishing line. A special reel is mounted on the face of the bow. The breeds of fish taken include carp, gar, buffalo, sucker, redhorse, stingray, and skate. Most effective shots are taken through a depth of 4 feet (1.2 m) or less because water quickly slows an arrow.

Novelty shoots are occasionally held for enjoyment and variety. These sometimes take the form of clout shooting, in which a 48-foot (14.6 m) target is laid on the ground and shot at from 140 to 180 yards (128-165 m). Archery golf, which is similar to regular golf, involves shooting a flight arrow, an approach arrow, and a putting arrow at a 4-inch (10 cm) ball. In roving, archers in small groups take turns choosing and then shooting at a target to see who can come the closest.

Ike Carasquillo

Figure 4   A fishing bow is used to hunt fish in water 4 feet (1.2 m) or less deep.

Some parts of North America also have crossbow competitions. Technical advances in crossbow design and materials have made crossbows very accurate. Today's shooters aim at 60-centimeter (24 in.) target faces from distances as great as 65 meters (71 yd).

A number of virtual archery platforms are now available. For example, an archery game is available for the Oculus Quest and Quest 2 virtual reality headsets. Single-player games are available, but scores can be compared with those of other players on a leaderboard. AccuBow provides a special "compound" bow and a virtual reality app for a smartphone. The smartphone is mounted on the bow, but the phone can be mirrored onto a television. There is no arrow, but the bow can be dry-fired to make a shot. Target archery, bowhunting, and bowfishing scenarios are available. Cool Things Wonder Fitter comes with a recurve bow, an arrow, and an arrow tube that is mounted on the bow. The arrow is shot into the tube. An app for a smartphone is provided, and that app is also mirrored onto a television. The bow's magnetometer and gyroscope are calibrated, and the archer can then shoot an arrow in various games and scenarios. There are also virtual reality systems that use a target wall or stadium onto which a scene is projected. In TOXEVO – Virtual Real Archery, archers can shoot real arrows at moving targets. The system scores the shot, and scores can be compared with those of other connected archers. Sports Simulator is available in dedicated stadiums and includes archery as one of the available sports.

No matter which form of archery or what type of equipment you come to enjoy, no matter whether your archery setting is real or virtual, the same basic form and shot-to-shot consistency lead to shooting accuracy. The equipment and your physical and mental skills must come together to produce the perfect shot.

EQUIPMENT AND ACCESSORIES

Equipment is important to your success in archery. High-quality equipment that's fit to your size, strength, and interest can bring you success for many years. High-quality equipment is also expensive. The more knowledgeable you are about archery tackle, or equipment, the more likely you'll be to choose the type of equipment that matches your size and strength. At the same time, merely spending money on archery equipment is no guarantee of success. You should learn to be a critical consumer because someone will always be anxious to sell you the magic bow or accessory to make you a champion! If you need to improve and refine your technique, no amount of money spent on equipment will make a difference in your scores.

In this section, you will learn about basic archery equipment and accessories, including terms for various pieces of equipment and the advantages and disadvantages of each type. Information about advanced accessories is also included. You can read about these advanced accessories now or come back to this material later.

Choosing a Bow

Two major types of bows are commonly used today. One stores energy in the bow's limbs, and the other makes use of cams to store energy. The bows that store energy in the limbs can be straight or recurve. Every type of bow has advantages and disadvantages (table 1).

Straight-limb bows are the centuries-old traditional design (figure 5). Because early bowmakers had limited materials available, they simply attached a bowstring to the tips of a straight section of wood. The string was shorter than the bow, pulling the bow into an elongated C shape. When drawn, straight-limb bows do not provide much leverage, so they are either limited in the distance they can propel an arrow or require a great number of pounds of pull to draw.

Table 1   Advantages and Disadvantages of Bows

Type of bow	Advantages	Disadvantages
Straight-limb	• Inexpensive • Can be fitted for right-handed or left-handed archers	• Little cast • Not center shot
Recurve	• Greater cast • Greater arrow speed • Interchangeable limbs if take-down style	• Shooting distance requires heavy draw weight
Compound	• Holding weight is less than draw weight • Potentially faster arrow speed	• Must be fitted for archer's draw length

Also, straight-limb bows typically have a shelf for the arrow that is to the side of the bow's handle. It is more difficult to shoot accurately when the arrow starts off center. On the other hand, these bows can be made to allow archers to shoot the same bow either right- or left-handed. Archers who enjoy traditional archery often shoot straight-limb bows of laminated wood or laminated wood and fiberglass. Beginners sometimes are provided solid fiberglass straight-limb bows in class situations because they are inexpensive and can be used by right- or left-handers. Once archers learn the basics, they should graduate to another type of bow unless they want to participate in traditional archery activities.

The recurve bow design (figure 6) is more efficient than the straight-limb bow design. A recurve bow in its relaxed position has limb tips that are curved back, away from the archer. The bowstring lies across 2 to 3 inches (5-7.6 cm) of the limb. When the bowstring is drawn back, the curves straighten to provide leverage. When the string is released, the curves return to their original shape. This series of actions imparts more arrow speed than a straight-limb bow can impart. The length of the limbs is fitted to the archer's size to maximize the leverage that the limbs provide. This quality is called cast. The terms used to describe the various parts of both straight-limb and recurve bows are given in figures 5 and 6. Note that the back of a bow is the surface facing away from the archer.

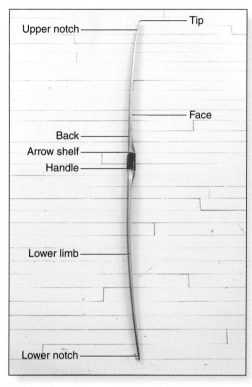

Figure 5   An unstrung straight-limb bow.

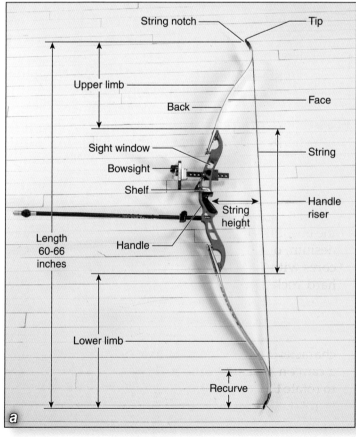

Figure 6   Various views of a recurve bow: *(a)* bow with major parts labeled.

(continued)

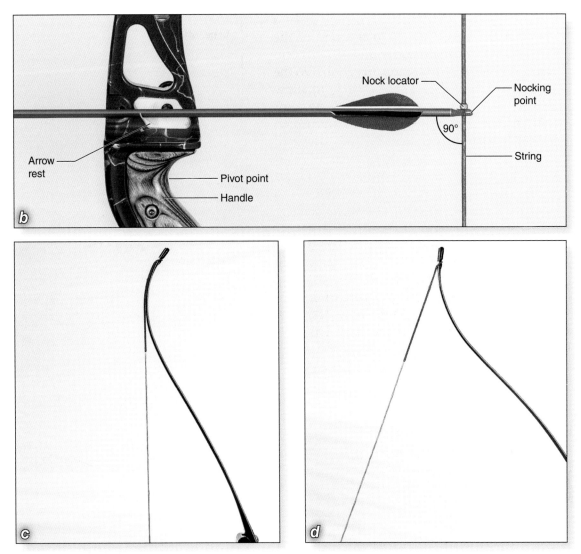

Figure 6   *(continued)* Various views of a recurve bow: *(b)* close-up of arrow rest and nocking point area; *(c)* bow limb in relaxed position; *(d)* bow limb in drawn position.

The recurve bows used in competition today consist of a metal handle riser section and removable limbs. Both can vary in size for numerous combinations to ensure that the bow fits the archer exactly. The metal handle riser can be made of aluminum, magnesium, or carbon. Limbs are typically composites of many materials, such as foam cores with carbon overlays, carbon and fiberglass laminations, or wood cores (often hard rock maple) with fiberglass and carbon laminations. Designers of bow limbs strive for an ideal combination of speed, stability, and smoothness when deciding what materials to use and how to combine them.

Compound bows also have a metal handle riser and composite limbs, but they are characterized by a cam mounted on one or both limb tips (figure 7). Some models have a cam on the lower limb and a round wheel on the upper limb. The energy required to rotate the part of the pulley with the long radius is greater than the energy required to rotate the part with the short radius. The pulleys are mounted so that the energy required to pull back the bowstring is greatest at mid-draw and the smallest at full

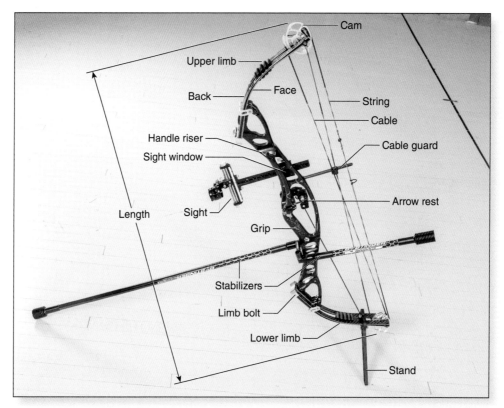

Figure 7   A compound bow. The wheels can be round, eccentric pulleys, or cams.

draw when the archer is holding to aim. When the archer releases the bowstring, this situation is reversed, and the energy applied to the arrow is increased. For example, an archer with a 40-pound (18 kg) compound bow of 60 percent let-off, or reduction, holds only 16 pounds (7.3 kg) of resistance at full draw. However, 40 pounds (18 kg) of thrust is imparted to the arrow.

A disadvantage of the compound bow for young people who are growing or for shooters who share a bow (such as families or instructional classes) is the need to fit the bow to the person's draw length so that the point of greatest weight reduction corresponds to the archer's full draw. A recent innovation in the manufacturing of compound bows addresses this disadvantage for youth. A light-poundage compound bow with a single cam (a round wheel mounted on the other limb tip), the Genesis, is now available (figure 8). The bow's poundage is typically 10 to 20 pounds (4.5-9 kg), and there is no let-off, or poundage reduction. Shooters with any draw length up to about 30 inches (76 cm) can use the bow. This compound bow is ideal for young people (whose draw lengths will increase with growth) and those in instructional settings. The poundage is adequate for short distances and allows beginners to focus on form.

Compound bows used primarily for hunting can look somewhat different from those used for target shooting (figure 9). Hunting compounds often have a handle riser shaped like an elongated C arching away from the shooter. This results in a shorter distance between the bowstring and arrow rest, permitting the use of a shorter arrow. Hunting compounds tend to be shorter from axle to axle compared to target compounds. These design features represent a speed-accuracy trade-off. Hunting compounds shoot faster arrows, but target compounds are smoother and permit the precise accuracy needed in competition. Both compounds can provide a significant reduction in the holding weight compared to the peak, or shooting, weight. The handle riser of target compounds also can have a "shoot-through" design, meaning that the

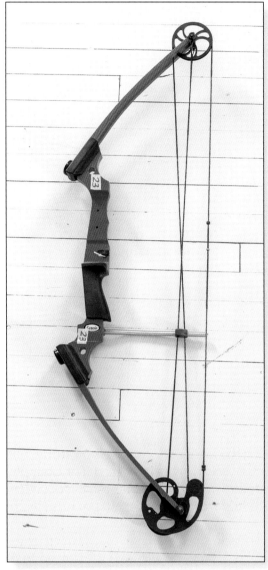

Figure 9 A compound bow designed for hunting. Note the different shape of the handle riser and different orientation of the limbs compared to the compound bow more suitable for target shooting in figure 7.

Figure 8 A light compound bow with a single cam.

handle's structure provides a center channel through which the arrow travels. The arrow can then be perfectly centered and travel straight to the target.

So which type of bow is right for you? Both modern recurve and compound bows make it possible to shoot with great precision. Your decision about which to use depends in part on what equipment rules are in place for the type of archery you wish to shoot. Because compound bows allow archers to shoot arrows with many more pounds of thrust than it takes to hold the bowstring at full draw while aiming, separate competitive divisions are usually held for compound bow shooters. Olympic-style divisions permit only recurve bows. If your interest is target archery, visit local archery clubs and ranges. Find out whether the competitive events in your geographical area include both divisions. This information might influence your decision.

Because most hunters use compound bows, this type of bow typically dominates competitive hunting events. Yet bowhunting with traditional equipment (a straight-limb or recurve bow but no bowsight or stabilizer) has many advocates who also shoot in simulated hunting events. In time, you may decide to have one bow that you use only for hunting and another for simulated hunting contests. Remember that you can still learn to shoot with a recurve bow even if you know that you eventually will buy a compound. You can attain a more precise fit in a compound bow once you have increased your strength and solidified your shooting form. We discuss fitting a bow to your size and strength in step 1.

Choosing Arrows

Arrows are made of at least four materials or their combinations: wood, fiberglass, aluminum, and carbon. Just as with bows, the various types of arrows have advantages and disadvantages (table 2). The basic terminology used to describe the parts of an arrow is the same for each type and is given in figure 10.

Expert archers, if given a choice between a high-quality bow with medium-quality arrows or a medium-quality bow with high-quality arrows, would always pick the latter. Quality arrows are extremely important to accurate shooting. Beginners can be

Table 2   Advantages and Disadvantages of Arrows

Type of arrow	Advantages	Disadvantages
Wooden	• Inexpensive	• Cannot be matched to each other • Not readily matched to archer's draw length and weight
Fiberglass	• Can be sized to draw length and weight • Can be matched better than wooden arrows	• Breaks easily
Aluminum	• Can be precisely manufactured • Wide range of sizes available • Durable • Arrow tips can be interchanged	• Can be expensive
Carbon and aluminum–carbon	• Fast • Strong	• Can be very expensive • Carbon layer breaks down if struck • Can require special adhesives

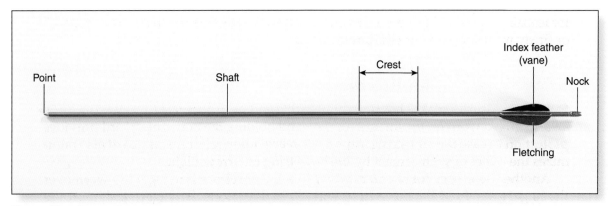

Figure 10   Parts of a target arrow.

hard on arrows, so you might want to start with inexpensive ones and later invest in the best quality you can afford.

Because they are inexpensive, wooden arrows are acceptable for beginning archers, but they are not very durable, and they warp easily. Because of differences in the pieces of wood used to make arrows, they cannot be closely matched. As a result, an archer might find variations in flight from arrow to arrow.

Fiberglass arrows are more durable than wooden arrows, and they can also be sized to fit archers of various arm lengths and strengths. Fiberglass arrows of a given size can be manufactured more consistently than wooden arrows. However, fiberglass arrows are brittle. Now that aluminum and carbon arrows are more economical and widely available, fiberglass arrows are not very common.

Aluminum, carbon, and aluminum–carbon arrows have become the arrows of choice because they can be manufactured in a wide assortment of spines (i.e., the bend-ability of an arrow). Most importantly, that spine can be reproduced so that archers have perfectly matched sets of arrows. Archers can match the spine of their arrows to their size and strength and to the bow to attain near-perfect flight. This means that the arrow travels through the air in the most aerodynamic way possible. Aluminum and carbon arrows can be customized for the type and weight of the tip and for the nock style, and they are still relatively durable.

Aluminum arrows are manufactured in a variety of sizes and using various qualities of aluminum alloy. Because you can straighten bent arrows and easily replace damaged arrow points, you can maintain a good set of aluminum arrows for quite some time. Those used for hunting can be fitted with an insert so you can switch back and forth between target tips and broadheads. Hunters install the target tips to practice but they install the broadheads with their sharp blades to hunt. Aluminum arrows fletched with feathers can be stripped and plastic vanes applied, or vice versa, so they offer much variety in setup. They are versatile, consistent, and durable.

Aluminum–carbon arrows are made of an aluminum core wrapped with carbon. Carbon and aluminum–carbon arrows are smaller and lighter than pure aluminum arrows. However, carbon and aluminum–carbon arrows are less durable than aluminum arrows. They are typically used by archers who shoot long distances in outdoor settings. These arrows tend to be impractical for archers who tightly pack their arrows into a target, which is typical when shooting short distances, because the carbon wrapping breaks down when struck. The rising popularity of carbon and aluminum–carbon arrows has led manufacturers to offer economical choices for these arrows so even beginners have a wide choice of arrow shafts.

You can begin shooting with economical arrows and later graduate to better arrows as your technique becomes routine. In step 1, you will find out how to select arrows for learning to shoot. In step 8, you will learn how to select arrows that can be "tuned," or finely matched, to your equipment setup.

Choosing Accessories

Several accessories make shooting comfortable and more accurate (see step 1). One is an arm guard worn on the forearm of the hand holding the bow. This guard provides protection in case the bowstring slaps the forearm upon release. This guard also mini-mizes the effect of such contact by the bowstring on arrow flight.

Another accessory for shooters who use a finger release is a finger tab worn over the fingers that hold the bowstring. This tab both protects the fingers and improves the smoothness of the bowstring's release.

A quiver is a handy accessory for holding or carrying arrows. It also minimizes injuries by keeping sharp arrow tips contained. Quivers come in a variety of styles (figure 11). Most archers use a belt quiver. If you're shooting outdoors, a ground quiver that is stuck into or set on the ground might be convenient. Hunters often use quivers mounted on the sides of their hunting bows for ease in traveling through wooded areas.

Figure 11   Two types of quivers: *(a)* belt quiver; *(b)* ground quiver.

An arrow rest (figure 12) is an important accessory. It is mounted on the side of the handle riser above the bow shelf. Some compound bows shot with mechanical releases have a handle riser with a window that places the arrow rest in the very center of the riser. You place the arrow on the arrow rest and keep it there until you shoot it. The advantage of shooting an arrow off an arrow rest over shooting an arrow off the bow shelf is that the arrow rest allows the arrow fletching to clear the bow more smoothly on its flight toward the target. This results in a smoother flight and consequently more accurate shooting. Arrow rests vary in type and cost. The most expensive ones are adjustable so that a bow can be precisely tuned for ideal arrow flight. For your initial experience in archery, a simple arrow rest will suffice. In step 1, you will learn how to install an arrow rest.

The bowsight is an attachment that places a marker, or aiming aperture, in the bow window. To aim, you line up the aperture with the bull's-eye rather than look at the relationship between the arrow and bull's-eye. With a bowsight, you can direct an arrow to the same place, horizontally and vertically, on every shot by controlling the elevation and left-right direction of your bow arm. If the arrow is not directed precisely to the bull's-eye, you can systematically adjust the bowsight by an exact amount for subsequent shots.

Figure 12   A simple arrow rest used with a cushion plunger and a collapsible arm.

A bowsight is attached to the bow so that the aiming aperture is visible to the archer at full draw in the bow window, which is to the left of the upper handle riser for a right-handed archer. Hunting sights usually have more than one aiming aperture, each of which is set for a specific shooting distance. Target sights have one aperture that is repositioned as the archer changes shooting distance.

The aiming aperture of a bowsight should be adjustable both horizontally and vertically. A vertical scale on the bowsight allows you to record the sight position appropriate for various shooting distances. If the present sight position is directing the arrow slightly high or low at a given shooting distance, a scale permits you to see exactly how a certain adjustment affects the arrow's landing spot. Manufactured sights also come with a scale, or you can purchase an adhesive paper scale or even a short metal ruler to mount on the sight.

Target sights for bows can be very simple, inexpensive devices, or they can be elaborate, precisely made tools that extend from the bow (see figure 2). The difference between sights is typically the ease and accuracy of moving the aperture and durability. The more expensive sights also can accommodate various types of aiming apertures, depending on the archer's preference.

Choosing Optional Accessories

Several additional accessories can improve your scoring accuracy even more. These include a bow sling, stabilizers, a kisser button, a peep sight, a draw check, and a release aid. Some of these accessories are governed by equipment regulations for competition, so you might want to research these regulations before buying an accessory.

The bow sling (figure 13) is a rope or strap that encircles the hand or fingers and the bow so the bow does not fall to the ground even if the archer releases their grip on the bow handle. A loose grip on the bow handle is an ideal part of sound shooting technique. A bow sling is inexpensive and allows the archer to relax the hand holding the bow without fear of dropping it.

Various types of bow slings are available. Some attach to the bow, and the hand is slipped through the strap when the archer takes hold of the bow. Others attach to the thumb and forefinger or to the wrist. The type of sling used is a matter of personal preference. All the types work well, and the expense is minimal considering the improvement in shooting accuracy that comes with a relaxed bow hand. You can begin using a bow sling right away or wait until you reach step 4.

A stabilizer (figure 14) is a metal rod with a weight on its end. High-quality bows come with inserts that allow one or more stabilizers to be attached to the face or back of the bow. Some attachments allow for additional stabilizers angling back and out, termed V-bars for the shape they make. A stabilizer improves shooting accuracy by reducing the tendency of the bow to turn, or torque, in the bow hand. Step 1 explains how to select one or more stabilizers for your bow.

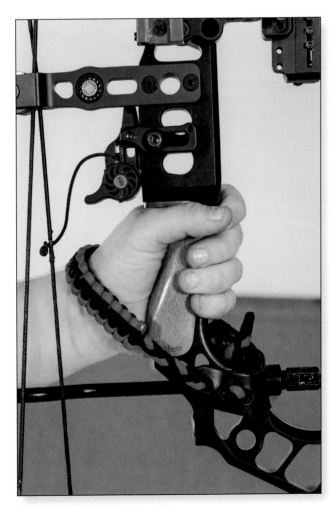

Figure 13   A bow sling.

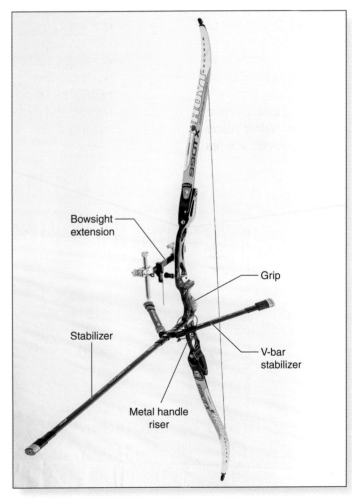

Figure 14   A bow with stabilizer and a bowsight extension attached.

The kisser button is a small, horizontal disk that is attached to the bowstring above the nock locator. The kisser button is set to touch between the lips at full draw. It aids archers in maintaining a consistent anchor. In step 6, you will learn how to position and use a kisser button.

The peep sight is a small plastic or metal disk with a hole in the middle that is inserted between the strands of the bowstring. It is always used with a bowsight. The archer looks through the peep sight when aiming. Its function is similar to that of a rear sight on a rifle. It improves aiming accuracy because the archer lines up the peep sight, the bowsight, and the bull's-eye. If you decide to use a peep sight, step 5 describes how to install one.

A draw check can be helpful to some archers. Even with a solid anchor position, the precise length of the draw may change slightly from shot to shot. A draw check eliminates any variation. There are several types of draw checks; the most common is a clicker. We discuss clickers further in step 8.

Shooting with a release aid (figure 15) is "cleaner" than shooting with a finger release. With a finger release, the bowstring rolls off the fingers when they relax to let the string go forward. This causes the string to deviate from a straight line forward, and of course, the arrow is attached to the bowstring. This string deflection is minimized when a mechanical release is used. Release aids are popular with hunters and target archers alike. When used properly, they result in more accurate shooting than is possible with the fingers. A single loop of rope or a small metal rod on the mechanical release holds either the bowstring itself, just below the arrow nock, or an added loop of string attached to the bowstring above and below the arrow nock called a D loop. In competitive events, archers using release aids are almost always placed in different divisions than archers releasing the bowstring with their fingers. Usually, archers using release aids shoot compound bows. Step 6 goes into more detail on shooting with a release aid.

Figure 15   Release aids can be triggered by the small finger, back tension, or the index finger.

TARGET ARCHERY COMPETITION

Unlike most sports in which a single set of rules governs play, competitive target archery can be shot in many types of rounds (formats for competition) or contests. For example, indoor contests are usually shot at a constant, short distance (20 yd, or 18 m) at a target of uniform size. Outdoor contests, though, are usually shot at various distances with targets of different sizes, depending on the distance. The number of arrows shot in a round also varies. Indoors, 30, 45, or 60 shots is typical, but 56 to 144 shots per round is common outdoors. Tournaments can consist of one round shot on one day or multiple rounds shot over two or more days. Sometimes, different types of rounds are shot in the same tournament.

Unless the round simulates hunting, a target of concentric circles is used. The closer an arrow lands to the center of the target, the more points are awarded. One thing is typical of all rounds: the score of individual arrows is totaled, and the archer with the highest point total wins the contest. In recent years, some archery tournaments have used head-to-head competition, sometimes after a traditional round to establish seedings, and a winner advances until a single archer is declared the champion. These formats are particularly exciting for spectators. The Olympic Games have adopted this format.

Competitive target archery is also shot with a variety of bows, although archers are often separated into classes within a tournament or into different tournaments based on their equipment. Archers shooting traditional, recurve, and compound bows might be separated into scoring groups. Those using finger releases are separated from those using mechanical releases. Men, women, youth, and archers with disabilities are usually placed in different scoring groups based on the ability to shoot heavier poundage, which generally translates to higher scores because the arrow travels in a flatter arc. These various classes might have additional limitations on accessories.

Bowhunting is a popular archery activity. Although some attempt gun hunting with little or no practice, bowhunters must take the time to set up their equipment and to practice shooting. A bowhunter with a reasonable chance of success when the opportunity arises is one who has spent hours in repetitive practice. Given the necessity of practice, bowhunters often participate in target events for those with bowhunting equipment. The targets may be concentric circles or animal likenesses with scoring zones superimposed. When bowhunters participate in these events alongside target archers, they usually know their shooting distance. Competitive rounds using three-dimensional (3-D) targets shaped like game are often laid out in wooded areas with the distances to targets unmarked to more accurately simulate hunting conditions.

SHOOTING RULES

The variety of archery associations, kinds of equipment, and types of rounds lead to variations in archery rules. You need to be familiar with the set of rules that govern any class, range, or contest in which you participate. Many of the rules are similar, however, and the following common archery rules for shooting and scoring provide a good foundation for your early experiences in archery. Later in this book, you will learn safety rules in more detail.

If you shoot with a class or at an indoor range, the shooting distance will be specified. If there is a shooting line (a straight line marked on the floor or ground), stand with one foot on each side of it when shooting.

An established number of arrows is shot and then scored multiple times in a round. This number of arrows is called an end. It is both discourteous to others while practicing and a rule violation in formal competition to shoot more than the designated number of arrows.

If you are shooting with a group, someone may be assigned to control shooting with a whistle. One blast signals the beginning of shooting. Two blasts indicate that archers may go forward to the target to score and collect their arrows. Three or more blasts are an emergency signal indicating that all shooting must immediately cease. If no one is controlling the shooting, be sure to wait until all archers have finished shooting before you go forward to retrieve your arrows.

Archery targets vary, depending on the round shot. Arrows in the official 5-colored, 10-scoring-ring target face count as follows from the center out: 10 points, 9 points, 8 points, 7 points, 6 points, 5 points, 4 points, 3 points, 2 points, and 1 point. If an arrow touches two scoring areas on the target face, the higher score counts in most contests. Any arrow missing the target face is scored a zero.

If an arrow drops from the bow as you are nocking, drawing, or letting down, you can reshoot that arrow provided that you can retrieve it without leaving the shooting line. If you cannot reach it, the arrow is considered shot. You can retrieve it when the signal to retrieve arrows is given. It scores no points.

If you shoot at an outdoor range, shoot from the same distance as any other archers already shooting when you arrive. If you can leave an unused target lane between yourself and other archers, you can shoot up to 10 yards (9 m) closer or farther to the target than the other archers.

ARCHERY RESOURCES

Archery is shot around the world. Many countries have archery associations, and archery periodicals are published worldwide.

INTERNATIONAL ASSOCIATIONS

World Archery Federation	**www.worldarchery.sport**
International Field Archery Association	**www.ifaa-archery.org**
International Bowhunting Organization	**https://iboarchery.com**

UNITED STATES

USA Archery (formerly National Archery Association)	**www.usarchery.org**
National Field Archery Association	**https://nfaausa.com**
United Foundation for Disabled Archers	**www.uffdaclub.com**
Archery Shooters Association Federation (promoting bowhunting and sponsoring 3-D target competitions)	**https://asaarchery.com**

USA Crossbow Inc.	**https://usacrossbow.org**
Physically Challenged Bowhunters of America, Inc. (PCBA)	**https://pcbainc.wordpress.com**
Bowfishing Association of America	**https://bowfishingassociation.com**

YOUTH ARCHERY

Junior Olympic Archery Development (JOAD)	**Contact USA Archery**
National Archery in the Schools Program (NASP)	**www.naspschools.org**

UNITED KINGDOM

The Grand National Archery Society (Archery GB)	**https://archerygb.org**
British Long-Bow Society	**www.thebritishlongbowsociety.co.uk**

CANADA

Federation of Canadian Archers (Archery Tir à l'Arc Canada)	**https://archerycanada.ca**

ITALY

Federazione Italiana Tiro con l'Arco	**https://fitarco-italia.org**

AUSTRALIA

Archery Australia	**https://archery.org.au**
Australian Bowhunters Association	**https://bowhunters.org.au**

KOREA

Korea Archery Association	**www.sports.or.kr**

ARCHERY PERIODICALS

- *The U.S. and International Archer,* www.usaarchery.org
- *Archery Magazine* (magazine of the National Field Archery Association in the United States), https://nfaausa.com/about/archery-magazine
- *Bow International* (quarterly publication for archers published in Worcestershire, UK), https://www.bowhunter.com

PREPARING YOUR BODY FOR SUCCESS

Archery is not as vigorous as most other sports, but archers must exert force by using the same back and arm muscles on every shot. Strength is an obvious advantage in shooting, as is muscular endurance. Increased strength allows you to shoot a bow of heavier poundage that shoots arrows in a flatter trajectory. Muscular balance and flexibility are advantages as well. Increased muscular endurance allows you to shoot long practice sessions without a breakdown in technique as you tire and helps you be just as competitive in the late ends of a tournament as in the early ends. Archers should use regular strength and flexibility exercises to prevent the overuse, imbalances, and injuries that can result from the repetitive motions of shooting. Remember that the arms and shoulders are not used symmetrically in archery.

It would be easy to assume arm and shoulder exercises are the only exercises needed to improve your shooting. Yet, precision shooting requires a stable base. Strong legs and core muscles are needed to maintain the stance, while upper-body muscles are used to draw the bow. A good strategy for archery is to use a general resistance (weight) training program to which additional arm and shoulder exercises are added. Three sessions a week with 2 to 3 sets of 12 repetitions per exercise is sufficient to improve your strength and muscular endurance. Be sure your resistance training routine works both sides of the body to compensate for the asymmetrical movements of the archery shot (see What Sport Science Says in step 11).

Following are exercises for the arms, shoulders, and upper back that benefit archers. You can use cable and weight stack machines, free weights and dumbbells, or a set of resistance bands or rubber tubing.

- Chest press or push-ups
- Single-arm rows
- High cable rows
- Single-arm lateral raises
- Shoulder shrugs
- Shoulder press
- Lat pull-downs
- Overhead triceps extension
- Biceps curls
- Chest fly
- Reverse fly

You can also mimic the archery shot with rubber tubing—both right- and left-handed shots. Other good exercise activities are rowing, swimming, and yoga.

Core exercises that promote a stable stance while drawing a bow are as follows:

- Crunches
- Leg raises hanging from a fixed bar
- Pelvic rotations on the floor
- Torso extensions from the floor
- Torso extensions from a bench
- Deadlifts
- From kneeling on hands and knees, single-leg extensions

An ideal way to maintain flexibility and muscular balance and to prepare for shooting is to develop a preshooting stretching routine. A few minutes of moderate to vigorous activity, such as jogging, rope jumping, walking, or jumping jacks, warms the muscles before you stretch. Try to do a stretch for each direction of movement in the upper-body joints. Stretch slowly into position and hold for 10 seconds. Repeat each stretch three to six times. Avoid bouncing or forceful twisting motions. Breathe normally. Rubber tubing stretch routines are particularly good. It is easy to carry the tubing with your equipment and use it regularly. After stretching, draw your bow several times without shooting. Ease the string back after drawing; do not release it without an arrow in place. If time permits, repeat your stretching routine after shooting, too. This is a good time to work on increasing your range of motion because the exercise of shooting increases blood flow to the muscles.

Acknowledgments

The new photos in this fifth edition of *Archery: Steps to Success* were only possible with the help of several people and organizations. First, we thank St. Louis Bow Hunters of St. Charles, Missouri, for letting us use their indoor archery range for the photo shoot. Second, we thank the archery team from Lindenwood University (St. Charles, Missouri) and their head coaches, Derek Schaub and Steve Wolk, for helping us recruit archers for the photos. Archers Hallie Sellers, Brianna Hayes, Ashton Probus, and David Hollenberg modeled everything we asked, from perfect shooting form to common errors. They took a true interest in helping us show a range of equipment and shooting styles. We wish them many 10 rings!

Fitting Equipment

You have probably seen young children trying to hit balls with baseball bats or tennis rackets that are too big for their bodies. That problem is obvious. Poorly fitted archery equipment might not be as obvious to the untrained eye, but it causes frustration all the same. Try as you might, you will not have much success with ill-fitted equipment, and continuing to use it might result in bad habits. Using ill-fitted equipment also can be dangerous.

Your first step to success in archery is to get equipment that is matched to your size and strength. The time and effort you put into perfecting your shot technique will yield better scoring results if your equipment is well matched to your body and set up properly. Buy the best equipment you can afford, but keep in mind that the most expensive equipment in the world will not give you better results if it is not matched to your size and strength. In fact, ill-fitted equipment can work against your efforts to learn good shooting form and refine your form. Be wary of using secondhand or borrowed equipment unless the exercises in this step indicate that the equipment is a match for you! Later in this step, you will learn how to set up your bow to shoot. With properly fitted and well-prepared equipment, you can feel confident about learning good shooting technique because you know you are getting the most out of your equipment.

Learning and practicing good archery technique is the first challenge. Expensive equipment will not produce substantially better results than basic but well-matched equipment will. Once your shooting technique is well practiced and your results are improving, custom-fit equipment can help you reach the next performance level. In this step, we stick to basic equipment. Later, we address choices you can make to obtain equipment that is custom fit and suitable for the type of archery you want to shoot.

In archery, energy is stored in the bow during the drawing of the bowstring. This energy is transferred to the arrow when the archer releases the bowstring. The more energy you can store in the bow, or the heavier the draw weight you can pull, the more energy can be transferred to the arrow and the faster the arrow can fly.

Contorting your body in all sorts of ways to use the heaviest draw weight possible may seem like a good idea, if it were not for a rather important thing—accuracy! To shoot accurately, you must be able to replicate your technique from shot to shot as precisely as possible. To achieve this consistency, you must use a draw weight that is in your comfort range. Draw weight is a function of the physical properties of the bow and the distance of the draw, which is in turn ultimately related to your arm length. For this reason, success depends on a bow matched to your size and strength.

Later, you will learn more about what happens to an arrow when the bowstring is released. For now, recognize that an arrow can vary in two ways: length and spine (stiffness and flexibility). For a given bow draw weight and arrow length (both related to your arm length), there is an optimum range of arrow spine. So, arrows also must be matched to your size and strength and to your bow.

FITTING YOUR BOW AND ARROWS

Determining the right bow for you involves several steps. First, you need to decide whether you will shoot right- or left-handed because bows are made either right-handed or left-handed. This text provides instructions for archers shooting right-handed. Those shooting left-handed should reverse them. Second, you need to determine your draw length and the bow best sized to you. The exercises later in this step will take you through this process.

Choosing Your Shooting Side

Choosing whether to shoot right- or left-handed might seem obvious. Most right-handed archers choose to shoot right-handed, using the left hand to hold the bow and the right hand to pull the bowstring. Certainly, right-handed archers with a dominant right eye should shoot right-handed, and left-handed archers with a dominant left eye should shoot left-handed.

If you are cross dominant, which means that you are right-handed but left-eye dominant, or vice versa, you have a choice to make. Here is why: An archer tends to line up the dominant eye with the target when aiming, but the most natural shooting form is to look down the shaft of the arrow to aim—that is, to aim with the eye on the same side as the string hand. An archer shooting right-handed with a left-dominant eye risks switching eyes to aim, using the dominant eye on some shots and the eye looking down the arrow on other shots. Obviously, this would detract from horizontal accuracy. You must choose to shoot on the side of your dominant hand or your dominant eye. If you are more comfortable shooting on the side of your dominant hand, you can learn to shoot with your dominant eye closed and aim with your nondominant eye, instead of drawing with your nondominant hand. For example, if you are right-handed and cross dominant, close your left eye to aim. If you do not, you might line up your left eye with the target and shoot your arrows to the left on some but not all of your shots. Fitting exercise 1 will help you determine your dominant eye.

If you are cross dominant and plan to use a bowsight, closing your dominant eye to aim with the other eye should prove successful. With a bowsight and sight settings for shooting various distances, you do not need the depth perception that shooting with both eyes open provides. Many archers use a peep sight, similar to the rear sight of a rifle, placed in the strands of the bowstring along with a bowsight. Only your aiming eye can see through the peep sight to line up the bowsight with the target.

Fitting Exercise 1   **Determining Eye Dominance**

When determining your hand preference for shooting, you need to know which eye is dominant. Place one hand over the other so that a small hole is created between your thumbs and fingers. Extend your arms toward a target. With both eyes open, center the bull's-eye or a small, distant object in the opening made by your hands (figure 1.1*a*). Slowly bring your arms toward your face while continuing to look at the bull's-eye with both eyes open. When your hands touch your face, the opening should be in front of the dominant eye (figure 1.1*b*). If the opening is in front of both eyes, you simply need to repeat with a smaller opening.

Figure 1.1   Determine eye dominance. *(a)* Put one hand on top of the other to make a small hole, centering the bull's-eye in the hole. *(b)* Bring hands to face, keeping both eyes open.

An alternative method is to assume the same position, but instead of moving your hands toward your face, keep your arms extended. With both eyes open, center the bull's-eye in the opening, and then close your left eye. If the bull's-eye or object remains in view, your right eye is dominant. If not, your left eye is dominant.

Success Check

- Keep the opening in your hands about the size of a nickel.

Score Your Success

Dominant eye:

_____ Right _____ Left

Determine dominant eye = 3 points

Your score _____

What Sport Science Says About Eye Dominance

You might think eye dominance is a small part of shooting, but sport scientists have researched eye dominance, hand dominance, and success in archery. Laborde and colleagues (2009) first examined beginning archers' accuracy, finding that those with the same side eye and hand dominance scored higher than those with cross dominance. These beginners did not use a bowsight. The researchers then obtained eye and hand dominance information from three groups of regular archery participants at three levels: local, regional, and national and international archers. These archers used a bowsight. A considerable portion of these regular participants (15%-19%) shot with a crossed pattern (shooting right-handed with a dominant left eye or vice versa). The use of a bowsight likely allowed these archers to be successful. They used their right eye to aim through the sight when shooting right-handed, even if their left eye was dominant. The situation was parallel for archers shooting left-handed. Research emphasizes that matching hand and eye dominance is important when shooting without a bowsight, but not as important when shooting with a bowsight.

Determining Draw Length

You need a draw length measurement to fit a bow and select your arrows. Draw length is the distance between the nocking point of the bowstring and the grip of the bow handle (the pivot point) at full draw. Your arrows must be longer than your draw length; otherwise, they will fall off the back of the arrow rest as you draw your bow. Your draw length also influences your bow selection, as you will see later, so an accurate draw length measurement is very important.

Fitting exercise 2 will help you determine your draw length. It is important to get an accurate measure of your draw length because ill-fitted equipment can work against establishing good shooting form. If you decide to purchase your own equipment after your initial archery lessons, remeasure your draw length at that time. If you are purchasing before you begin lessons, be sure to seek expert advice. Fortunately, most bows suitable for competition or for hunting can be adjusted a small amount to precisely match your draw length.

Fitting Exercise 2　Determining Draw Length

In this exercise, you will use two methods to determine your draw length. First, obtain a light-poundage bow and a long arrow. Stand about 8 yards (7 m) from a target. You won't actually shoot this arrow, but you should always be safe with a drawn arrow. If you are shooting right-handed, hold the bow in your left hand. Without the arrow, hook onto the middle of the bowstring with the first three fingers of your right hand. Raise the bow and pull the string back (keep your elbow high) until the string above your hand touches your nose. Be sure to stand erect and keep your head erect. Ease the string back. Practice this action several times, making sure your left arm is extended but does not push the bow away. Never release a drawn string without an arrow (i.e., dry-fire) because doing so can damage your bow.

Now, snap the arrow onto the bowstring beneath the nock locator, and place the arrow on the arrow rest of the bow. Pointing the bow toward the target, draw the string back with one finger hooked onto the string above the arrow and the other fingers below the arrow and hold. Have someone mark the arrow directly above the arrow rest (figure 1.2); then you can ease the string back. Measure from the nock slit to the mark. This measurement is your draw length.

Another way to determine your draw length is by using the Pellerite method (Pellerite 2001).

Stand with your back to a wall. Extend your arms and hands out to your sides at shoulder level. Have someone mark the tip of each middle finger. Measure this distance (i.e., your wingspan). If your wingspan is 71 inches (180 cm), your draw length is 28 inches (71 cm). For every inch (2.5 cm) your wingspan is less than 71 inches, subtract 1/2 inch (1.3 cm) from the 28-inch draw length. For every inch your wingspan is over 71 inches, add 1/2 inch to the 28 inches. Alternatively, you can divide your wingspan by 2.5 to get an estimate of your draw length.

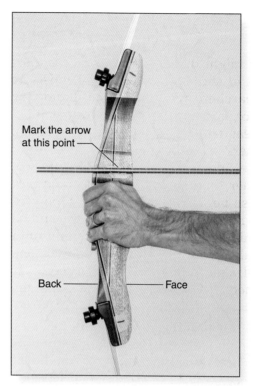

Figure 1.2 Determining draw length by marking the arrow.

Were the two measurements close to each other? One obvious difficulty with the first method is that you need to have good form to get an accurate measurement. This is not always the case with beginners. For a beginner, the Pellerite method is often more accurate.

Success Check

- Stand erect.
- Keep head erect.

Score Your Success

Draw length measured using a measuring arrow: _____ inches or centimeters

Draw length measured using the Pellerite method: _____ inches or centimeters

Determine draw length using both methods = 3 points

Your score _____

Fitting a Recurve or Straight-Limb Bow

If you will be shooting with a recurve or straight-limb bow, you need to select one that is the proper length and weight. First, use table 1.1 to determine your ideal bow length by using your draw length.

If your recurve bow has a handle riser and detachable limbs, keep in mind that bow length is a function of both riser and limb length. For example, a bow could be 68 inches (173 cm) in length by having a 23-inch (58 cm) riser and long limbs or a 25-inch (63.5 cm) riser and medium-length limbs. Shorter risers tend to make a bow shoot at a slightly heavier draw weight for a given limb length.

Next, choose a draw weight. Start with a light weight that you can pull and hold easily while developing good form. As you build strength and develop consistently good form, you can change to a heavier draw weight bow. Adult archers of average strength typically begin with a recurve bow with a draw weight of 20 to 25 pounds (9-11 kg). Stronger archers can begin with 25- to 30-pound (11-13.6 kg) bows. Lighter bows of 15 to 20 pounds (6.8-9 kg) are appropriate for young archers.

The draw weight printed on the bow or bow limbs is the draw weight at a standard draw length of 28 inches (71 cm), a draw that is 26-1/4 inches (66.7 cm) from the throat of the bow grip plus 1-3/4 inches (4.5 cm). The bow's stamped draw weight is not as important to you right now as remembering how draw length changes the actual shooting weight of your bow. If your draw length is shorter than the standard, the bow limbs will not deflect as far, and you will be shooting less weight than the weight printed on the bow. If your draw length is longer than standard, you will be shooting more weight than the printed weight. To estimate the actual draw weight you would shoot with a particular bow, add 2 pounds (1 kg) for every inch (2.5 cm) your draw length is above the standard, or subtract 2 pounds (1 kg) for every inch your draw length is below the standard. Select a bow accordingly. For example, if you want to shoot 35 pounds (16 kg) of draw weight and have a 30-inch (76 cm) draw, the bow you ideally select would be stamped 31 pounds (14 kg) at 28 inches (71 cm), with your 30-inch draw of that bow adding 4 pounds (1.8 kg).

For the early steps to success in archery, you will be shooting short distances to large targets without a bowsight. The goal at this stage is to learn good shooting form and refine it. You will not need a heavy bow to get the arrow to the target. Typically, it is better to learn good technique with a lighter-poundage bow and then transition to a heavier bow once you have established good form, strengthened the muscles used to draw and hold the bow, and want to shoot from longer distances.

Obtaining the appropriate bow length is also more important when you begin to shoot longer distances. Remember that energy is stored in the bow limbs during the

Table 1.1 Selection of Bow Length

Draw length (in.)	Bow length (in.)
24 or less	60-64
25-26	65-66
27-28	67-68
29 or more	69-70

drawing of the bowstring. Recurve bow limbs that are long cannot store very much energy if drawn by someone with a short draw length. The quality of getting the most energy storage in the limbs for bending them a given amount is called cast.

Archers want the most cast possible for their draw length, which is why bow length is important when fitting recurve bows. Shooting longer distances with a straight-limb bow requires a high level of muscle strength.

Most competition-quality recurve bows consist of a handle riser section and detachable limbs. Because limbs of different lengths can be used with the same handle riser, it is possible to custom fit the bow length to the archer.

Fitting a Compound Bow

Compound bows for competitive target shooting and for hunting must be fitted for draw weight, draw length, and axle-to-axle (axle of the cam) length. The holding weight of a compound bow, which is the force that is held at full draw, is a fraction of its peak weight, which is the force that is imparted to the arrow. Obviously, you can select a compound bow with a heavier draw weight than that of a recurve bow. You must have the strength to pull through the peak weight of a compound bow to reach the holding weight. The draw weight of a compound bow can be adjusted, and the range of adjustment varies with the bow. The archery shop where you purchase your compound bow should have a scale to measure the bow's peak weight and its holding weight at your draw length if you don't have the manufacturer's specifications. A staff person can also help you adjust the draw weight of your bow.

The size and type of the cam of a compound bow determines the point in the draw at which the holding weight is reached. This point is called the valley because it is the point in the draw with the lightest draw weight. Ideally, the valley should correspond to your draw length. Compound bows today have a range of draw lengths and allow adjustments, sometimes in increments of a quarter inch. This makes it easier to fit a compound bow, but your draw length must fall within the specified range for the bow so that the valley and your draw length match.

Bow length is a consideration when selecting a compound bow. Compound bows are measured from axle to axle; hence, bow length is often termed axle-to-axle length. The shorter the length, the more acute the angle of the string at full draw. Very short lengths (26-27 in., or 66-69 cm) are appropriate for young archers. Shorter adults with shorter draw lengths match well with shorter axle-to-axle lengths, while taller adults with longer draw lengths match well with longer axle-to-axle lengths. Short axle-to-axle bows tend to shoot faster arrows than longer compound bows do, but they are also easier to torque, or turn in the hand, which detracts from accuracy. We address torquing the bow on release later when we discuss bow hand grip.

The brace height of a compound bow also varies. Bows with shorter brace heights generally shoot an arrow faster than ones with a longer brace height, but they can be less forgiving of a flaw in your technique.

Quality compound bows can be very expensive. A good idea is to visit an archery pro shop and be fitted with a basic bow to use as you learn to shoot and build your strength. You can invest in better equipment later. The shop might even have a trade-up program. Many archers also learn to shoot with a recurve bow, even if they know they want to eventually shoot with a compound bow.

MISSTEP

Based on your draw length measurement, you select a bow that you can't pull all the way back to your face or, in the case of a compound bow, that causes you to lean back to get the bowstring to the valley.

CORRECTION

Your draw length measurement is either too short or too long. Perform fitting exercise 2, especially the wingspan measure, to reestablish your draw length and obtain the proper bow for that draw length.

Fitting Exercise 3   Finding Actual Draw Weight

The poundage given by a recurve bow manufacturer is the poundage at a standard 28-inch (71 cm) draw length. Your draw length is probably different; draw weight changes by approximately 2 pounds (1 kg) for every inch (2.5 cm) of difference from the standard draw length. To practice calculating draw weights, determine the actual, or shooting, draw weights for each of the combinations shown in table 1.2. (Answers appear at the end of this step.)

Table 1.2   Draw Weight Drill

Case	Draw length (in.)	Draw weight marked on bow (lb)	Actual draw weight
1	24	25	
2	29-1/2	30	
3	27-1/2	30	
4	30	35	
5	28	40	
Yours			

Success Check

- Add 2 pounds (1 kg) for every inch (2.5 cm) over the standard 28 inches (71 cm).
- Subtract 2 pounds (1 kg) for every inch (2.5 cm) under the standard 28 inches (71 cm).

Score Your Success

_____ Case 1 calculated correctly

_____ Case 2 calculated correctly

_____ Case 3 calculated correctly

_____ Case 4 calculated correctly

_____ Case 5 calculated correctly

Calculate all five cases correctly = 3 points

Calculate four cases correctly = 1 point

Your score _____

Choosing Arrows

Using arrows of proper length is absolutely critical from a safety perspective. Drawing an arrow past the arrow rest can be dangerous, and this situation is likely to happen if the arrow is too short for your draw length. On the other hand, an arrow that is too long does not fly well.

As a beginner, determine your arrow length by adding at least 3-3/4 inches (9.5 cm) to your draw length, as shown in figure 1.3. When you establish a more consistent form, you can use arrows just about 1 inch (2.5 cm) longer than your draw length.

Figure 1.3 FITTING ARROWS

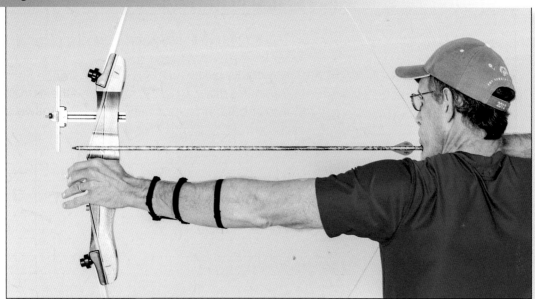

1. Beginning shooters add 3-3/4 inches (9.5 cm) to draw length.
2. Experienced shooters add about 1 inch (2.5 cm) to draw length.

3. Determine actual draw weight.
4. Choose shaft size.

Arrows also vary in shaft size. The rationale for determining the ideal shaft size is presented in step 8, Upgrading, Tuning, and Maintaining Equipment. For now, you can select the size of your arrow shaft from a reference table, such as the simplified one in table 1.3 for light-poundage bows. A pro shop or the arrow manufacturer's website will have a complete selection table, or even selector software or an online program that can be used to select shaft size. If you go to a website, you will be able to enter your information and obtain a short list of recommended arrow sizes. If you are learning with a bow that has a draw weight greater than those in table 1.3, you might want to visit a pro shop and get help making your selection. For a recurve bow, they will use information such as your draw weight, arrow point weight, arrow length, and limb type. For a compound bow, they will use your peak bow weight, arrow point weight, arrow length, release type, bow speed rating, and if the type of arrow you want uses inserts, the insert weight. You will need similar information for selecting hunting arrows.

Fitting Exercise 4   **Arrow Selection**

To determine a target arrow size in this exercise, first use table 1.3, a simplified target arrow selection chart. Note that this chart requires your arrow length, which is longer than your draw length. For this purpose, you can use the length given in table 1.7 as the arrow length. Assume that you are fitting arrows for a recurve bow. Move down column 1 to find the bow draw weight and then across to the designated arrow length to find an arrow group suitable for that poundage and length. Using table 1.4, find the arrow size and shaft type in that group. The size of an arrow shaft is printed on its side. Note that several sizes could be appropriate.

   To determine a hunting arrow size in this exercise, first use table 1.5. Read down one of the first three columns, depending on the bow type, to find the bow's poundage. Then, read across for the arrow length to find the arrow group suitable for that combination. Use table 1.6 to find the hunting arrow shaft type and size in that group.

Table 1.3   Simplified Target Arrow Group Selection Chart for Light-Poundage Bows

Recurve bow draw weight—finger release (lb)	CORRECT ARROW LENGTH (IN.)			
	23	24	25	26
20-24	Y1	Y2	Y3	Y4
24-28	Y2	Y3	Y4	Y5
28-32	Y3	Y4	Y5	Y6
32-36	Y4	Y5	Y6	Y7

Table 1.4   Target Arrow Sizes by Group

Group	Shaft type	Size
Y1	Aluminum alloy	1214
	Carbon	2000
Y2	Aluminum alloy	1413
	Carbon	1800
Y3	Aluminum alloy	1416
	Carbon	1600
Y4	Aluminum alloy	1416
	Carbon	1400
Y5	Aluminum alloy	1514 or 1516
	Carbon	1200 or 1250
Y6	Aluminum alloy	1516 or 1614
	Carbon	1150 or 1200
Y7	Aluminum alloy	1614 or 1616
	Carbon	1000 or 1070

Table 1.5 Simplified Hunting Arrow Selection Chart

BOW AND RELEASE TYPE POINT WEIGHT 75 GRAINS			CORRECT HUNTING ARROW LENGTH (IN.)			
Medium cam compound bow, release aid, calculated peak bow weight (lb)	Recurve bow, finger release, actual peak bow weight (lb)	Modern longbow, finger release, actual peak bow weight (lb)	28	29	30	31
55-59	50-54	71-76	F	G	H	I
60-64	55-59	77-82	G	H	I	J
65-69	60-64	83-88	H	I	J	J
70-75	65-69	89-94	I	J	J	K

Table 1.6 Hunting Arrow Sizes by Group

Group	Shaft type	Size
F	Aluminum alloy	2018
	Carbon	500
G	Aluminum alloy	2020
	Carbon	400
H	Aluminum alloy	2215 or 2117
	Carbon	400
I	Aluminum alloy	2413 or 2315
	Carbon	400
J	Aluminum alloy	2413 or 2219
	Carbon	340
K	Aluminum alloy	2514 or 2317
	Carbon	300

Determine the shaft sizes and types for each of the cases shown in table 1.7. (Answers appear at the end of this step.)

Table 1.7 Determining Arrow Shaft Size

Case	Specifications	Aluminum alloy shaft size	Carbon or aluminum–carbon shaft size
1	Recurve bow, finger release, 27 lb draw weight, target arrow length 24 in.		
2	Medium cam compound bow, release aid, calculated peak bow weight 68 lb, hunting arrow length 30 in.		
3	Recurve bow, finger release, 51 lb actual draw weight, hunting arrow length 29 in.		
4	Recurve bow, finger release, 33 lb draw weight, target arrow length 26 in.		
5	Modern longbow, finger release, 76 lb draw weight, hunting arrow length 28 in.		
Yours			

(continued)

Fitting Exercise 4   *(continued)*

Success Check

- Read across to your draw or arrow length.

Score Your Success

_____ Case 1 accurately identified

_____ Case 2 accurately identified

_____ Case 3 accurately identified

_____ Case 4 accurately identified

_____ Case 5 accurately identified

Arrow size(s) in all cases identified correctly = 3 points

Arrow size(s) in four cases identified correctly = 1 point

Your score _____

Fitting the Arm Guard and Finger Tab

The final step in fitting your equipment is to choose an arm guard and finger tab. An arm guard that covers the forearm of your bow arm (the one that holds the bow) should be sufficient. Some archers find that their particular body structure places the upper arm close to the path of the string upon release. To protect the upper arm, they choose a long style of arm guard that covers both the upper arm and the forearm. Arm guards are used by archers shooting all types of bows.

The finger tab covers the first three fingers of your draw, or string, hand (the one that pulls the bowstring). Finger tabs come in several sizes. Choose one that covers the fingers when you form a hook to pull the string but that does not have an excess of leather extending beyond the fingertips. Many archers like to shoot with a clothing shield so that their bowstring at full draw does not catch in a loosely fitting shirt. Figure 1.4 shows a properly fitted finger tab, arm guard, and clothing shield. Obviously, archers using a finger rather than a mechanical release use finger tabs.

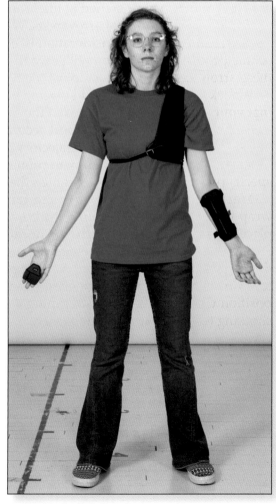

Figure 1.4   A properly fitted finger tab, arm guard, and clothing shield.

SETTING UP YOUR BOW AND ACCESSORIES

At the very least, you should have a nock locator on your bowstring before you begin shooting and an arrow rest mounted on your bow. You could also install a bowsight now, but because the initial steps emphasize good form and all shots will be at short distances to large targets, a bowsight isn't absolutely necessary. In step 5, you will learn how to install and use a bowsight.

Another helpful accessory is a sling. This is a strap that surrounds the bow and wrist or the bow and the thumb and forefinger. The strap prevents the archer from dropping the bow upon release of the string, given that a relaxed hold of the bow leads to more accurate shots than a tight grip on the bow handle. You will read about the grip in more detail in step 4, but for now, it is easy to use a sling. Put it on when you pick up a bow to shoot. It requires no further attention!

If you are using an inexpensive straight-limb bow, either fiberglass or a traditional long-limb bow of laminated wood, the bow handle might serve as an arrow rest. Some inexpensive recurve bows also are made with a shelf on which the arrow rests. Most other recurve and compound bows, though, are meant to have an arrow rest installed on them. Some of these bows have a cutout section in the handle riser. You must purchase an arrow rest and install it on the handle riser in the proper location, as shown in figure 1.5b. Installation exercise 2 will guide you in positioning such a rest. More expensive recurve and compound bows have a hole in the handle riser to ensure that the rest is installed at the proper location.

There are many types of arrow rests. Whether you are using a finger or mechanical release is an important consideration in choosing an arrow rest. Later, as part of the tuning process in step 8, you will learn the advantages and disadvantages of some of these arrow rests and how to adjust them precisely.

A nock locator guides you in placing your arrows on the bowstring. It guarantees that your arrows will be oriented at the same angle on every shot. Even slight variations in the angle can affect vertical accuracy because a small distance at the tail end of the arrow affects the arrow's trajectory to the target. A nock locator often is a small, C-shaped piece of metal lined with rubber or soft plastic to protect the bowstring. A special pair of pliers is used to tighten the locator on the string.

Metal locators are inexpensive and can be repositioned, but some archers simply wrap waxed dental floss around the bowstring to form a nock locator. Most archers place the locator so that the arrow is nocked right below it. The arrow sits at a perfect right angle if they shoot a mechanical release or slightly tail high if they release with the fingers, as shown in figure 1.5a. This preliminary placement should suit you well for your early archery experiences. Installation exercise 1 shows how to precisely position the nock locator when tuning a bow, something you should do once your shooting technique is well established.

Figure 1.5   SETTING UP EQUIPMENT

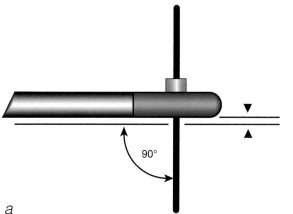

a

Nock Locator

1. Position bow square on string.
2. Mark corner of 90-degree angle on string.
3. Measure 1/2 inch (1.3 cm) up from mark.
4. Position lower edge of nock locator at point you have determined.
5. Clamp nock locator.

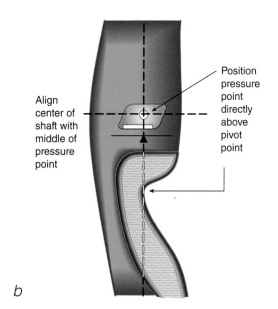

b

Arrow Rest

1. Align pressure point over handle pivot point.
2. Attach rest 5/8 inch (1.6 cm) above arrow shelf.

Installation Exercise 1   Nock Locator Setup

The first step in installing a nock locator is marking the point on the bowstring where the bottom of a nocked arrow forms a perfect 90-degree angle with the string. Bow squares are sold for this purpose, but you can substitute a large mechanical drawing triangle or a carpenter's L.

Position the lower edge of the nock locator 1/2 inch (1.3 cm) above the square if you are releasing with your fingers. This allows the arrow to clear the bow slightly tail high so that the arrow's fletching does not strike the bow handle. If you are using a mechanical release, position the nock locator so that the arrow is perfectly level or 1/4 inch (0.6 cm) high. Clamp the nock locator in this position (figure 1.6). Later, when you learn about fine-tuning a bow, you may want to adjust this position slightly.

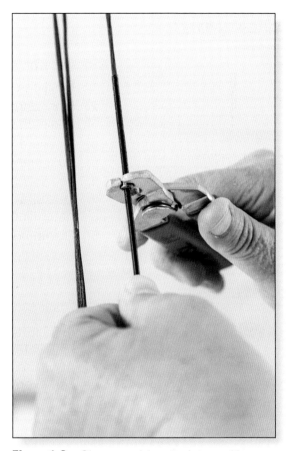

Figure 1.6 Clamp nock locator into position.

Success Check

- Place bow square so it gently sits on arrow rest (see figure 2.2 in step 2).
- Mark string at perfect right angle.
- Move up 1/2 inch (1.3 cm).

Score Your Success

Nock locator installed: _____ inches or centimeters above square

Install nock locator = 3 points

Your score _____

Installation Exercise 2   Arrow Rest Installation

To attach a self-stick arrow rest on a bow not tapped for a removable arrow rest, place the bow on a table. Align the pressure point of the rest over the pivot point (throat) of the bow handle. Position the rest 5/8 inch (1.6 cm) above the bow shelf to allow room for the arrow's fletching to clear the shelf upon release. Mark this place with several light pencil marks, peel the paper from the back of the rest, and press it into place.

If you are installing an arrow rest on a handle riser that is tapped for a removable arrow rest device, you likely will decide on the type of arrow rest based on whether you release with your fingers or with a mechanical release. If you release the bowstring with your fingers, you will probably use what is called a shoot-around rest. If you use a mechanical release, you will probably use a shoot-through rest.

(continued)

Installation Exercise 2   *(continued)*

With a shoot-around rest, you insert a cushion plunger into the hole tapped for that purpose (see figure 12 in The Sport of Archery). Place an arrow square (forming a 90-degree angle) on the bowstring with your bow on its side on a table, and align the center of the arrow shaft with the center of the plunger. Attach your arrow rest to the bow so the arrow sits in this position when the bow is held upright.

Attach a shoot-through rest in such a way that the launcher arms support a nocked arrow in a position so that it does not strike the handle riser upon release. Later, in considering fine-tuning, you will adjust the cushion plunger or launcher more precisely.

Success Check

- Align pressure point over pivot point.
- Place rest 5/8 inch (1.6 cm) above shelf.

Score Your Success

Arrow rest installed

Install arrow rest = 3 points

Your score _____

STABILIZERS

A stabilizer is a rod with a weight at the end that is attached to a bow's handle riser. The first stabilizer most archers use is mounted below the handle at a right angle to the long axis of the bow and pointed toward the target. Stabilizers minimize the torque, or turning, of the bow around its long axis as you release the bowstring and send the arrow on its way. The arrow can push slightly against the bow, especially when you hold and release the bowstring with your fingers. The arrow pushing against the bow can cause the bow handle to turn, affecting the flight of the arrow. Attaching a weight a distance from the bow's axis of rotation resists the turning. The resistance is a product of the amount of weight and its distance from the axis of rotation. Archers can get the same dampening effect from lighter weights farther from the axis and heavier weights closer to the axis.

Additionally, archers tend to grab the bow handle or push or pull it at release if they think their aim is slightly misdirected. These actions detract from accuracy, but stabilizers tend to dampen these movements by diminishing their effect. The weight of stabilizers simply adds to the inertia of the bow to movement. The weight also dampens small movements during aiming, allowing archers to settle on the bull's-eye.

As a novice archer choosing to use a stabilizer, you should first consider the amount of weight added to the bow itself. Whereas the weight of a stabilizer can dampen movements during aiming and release, too much weight can fatigue the shoulder muscles over a shooting session and have the reverse effect. Add a stabilizer to your bow now only if you are confident that you have the strength to hold your bow long enough to settle and aim every shot over your entire practice session. Begin with a single stabilizer with a light weight on the end. To use a stabilizer, you must have an insert on your bow so that the threads on the end of the stabilizer rod can be screwed into the insert. On bows that have a metal handle riser and wood, fiberglass, or composite limbs, these inserts are in the metal handle riser section.

As your muscular strength and endurance build with practice, you can later experiment with different types, numbers, and end weights. We will discuss stabilizers in more detail in step 10 for target shooting and step 11 for bowhunting.

ANSWER KEY FOR TABLE 1.2

FITTING EXERCISE 3. FINDING ACTUAL DRAW WEIGHT

Case 1: 17 pounds (8 kg)
Case 2: 33 pounds (15 kg)
Case 3: 29 pounds (13 kg)
Case 4: 39 pounds (17.7 kg)
Case 5: 40 pounds (18 kg)

ANSWER KEY FOR TABLE 1.7

FITTING EXERCISE 4. ARROW SELECTION

Case	Aluminum alloy shaft size	Carbon or aluminum–carbon shaft size
1	1413 or 1416	None
2	2413 or 2219	340
3	2020	400
4	1616	1000
5	2018	500

SUCCESS SUMMARY

You now know how to select a bow that fits you, to select arrows that fit you and are matched to your bow, and to select accessories that fit. You also know how to prepare your bow for shooting. The time spent selecting appropriate equipment and setting it up for shooting is a good investment in your success and enjoyment.

A properly fitted bow that matches your hand preference, draw length, and strength is more comfortable to shoot than a poorly fitted one and allows you to practice longer. Properly fitted arrows minimize your errors and increase your scoring success.

Score your success in moving through the exercises presented in this step. Enter your score for each exercise, and add them up to rate your success. If you scored at least 13 points, you can move to the next step.

Fitting Exercises

1. Determining Eye Dominance   _____ out of 3
2. Determining Draw Length   _____ out of 3
3. Finding Actual Draw Weight   _____ out of 3
4. Arrow Selection   _____ out of 3

Installation Exercises

1. Nock Locator Setup   _____ out of 3
2. Arrow Rest Installation   _____ out of 3

Total   _____ **out of 18**

Fitting and setting up equipment properly also contribute to safe shooting. Selecting arrows of proper length makes shooting safe for you. Installing a nock locator makes shooting safer for those around you because it minimizes vertical error, and consistently aiming with the eye over your arrow minimizes horizontal error. Because safety is a great concern in archery, you must now turn your attention to safety, even before you shoot.

Shooting Safely

When we were kids, the local police department gave a demonstration on the park archery range. A police officer filled a gallon (4 L) jug with sand and placed a balloon behind it. He fired a handgun into the jug. The sand stopped the bullet. An archer then shot an arrow into the jug. It passed through the sand and popped the balloon. The police officer made his point to would-be archers: An arrow can be lethal when shot from a bow.

In archery, safety should always come before shooting. In this step, you will learn how to shoot safely to protect both yourself and others. Safety rules apply before you shoot, while you shoot, and as you retrieve your arrows.

SAFE EQUIPMENT

The first step in safe shooting is choosing equipment that fits properly, as emphasized in step 1. Ill-fitted equipment can be a hazard to you and to others around you because it can cause you to shoot unsafely by using poor form or releasing the string before you have aimed. Shooting with equipment that is matched to your size and strength allows you to be in control of every shot. Choose a bow with a draw weight that you can draw easily and hold for at least several seconds without tiring.

Have an instructor or pro shop employee verify that your arrows are long enough for you. Do not lend your arrows to other archers or shoot arrows borrowed from another archer unless you know that the arrow length and spine are matched to the draw length and bow weight. Overdrawing a short arrow is dangerous because the arrow can shatter if it lodges behind the bow; the arrow can even embed itself in your arm (figure 2.1). If an arrow is too weak in spine, it is possible for a bow to shatter when the arrow is released. Each compound bow has a minimum arrow weight designated by the manufacturer. Determine this weight and choose an arrow that surpasses the minimum. In the absence of written instructions, check the bow manufacturer's website.

Once you have the proper equipment, you must routinely inspect it to ensure that it has not been damaged or become so worn that it is unsafe. Equipment failure during a shot can put you and others at risk of injury. Before every shooting session, inspect your equipment. This step is particularly important with older equipment, but it should be a regular part of your shooting preparation.

Figure 2.1 DANGEROUS PRACTICE: OVERDRAWING A SHORT ARROW

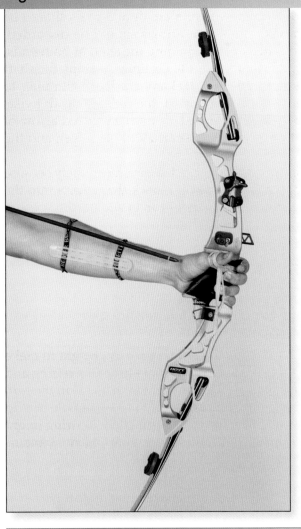

1. Ensure that arrows are of proper length (and weight for a compound bow).
2. Make sure bow weight is comfortable.
3. Ensure that bow limbs and arrows are free of cracks.
4. Make sure bowstring is intact.
5. Do not overdraw arrow!

Inspect your bowstring. If it is frayed or if any strand of the string is broken, replace the bowstring. Check the serving on your bowstring. The serving is the wrap that reinforces sections of the bowstring at the ends, where it loops and attaches to the bow limbs or a cable, and in the middle, where the arrow is nocked. If it is unraveling, tie it off, have it re-served, or replace the string. Next, inspect your bow. If there is a crack in the limbs, do not shoot your bow. Have an instructor or employee at a pro shop inspect it. A cracked bow could break at full draw and cause an injury.

Continue to inspect your bow. If the limbs are detachable, be sure they are properly seated in the riser. Look over the riser section to be sure there are no cracks, especially around the grip. Inspect the cables on a compound bow to be sure they are properly attached and seated. Examine the cams or pulleys and their axles to be sure they are secured and not bent.

Inspect your arrows. Each arrow should have a properly installed tip. With the arrow between your thumb and forefingers, move up and down the shaft as you rotate the shaft with your other hand. Feel and look closely for splits, cracks, dents, or any other indication of damage. Wood or fiberglass arrows with cracks should be broken into two pieces and discarded. Extremely bent aluminum arrows should be straightened before shooting, and cracked aluminum arrows should be discarded. Carbon arrows should get an additional inspection. Holding the shaft at both ends, flex it about an inch or two (2.5-5 cm). Repeat this four to six times, turning the shaft slightly each time. Discard the arrow if you hear or feel any cracks. Continuing to hold the shaft at the ends and twist it in both directions, if the carbon sheath twists easily, it is damaged, and the shaft should be discarded. Discard a cracked arrow of any material, even if the crack is small. Eventually the crack will get larger, and the arrow could shatter when released.

Inspect your arrows' nocks. Remove and replace cracked nocks immediately because a damaged nock can slip off the string before release. If a nock that inserts into the arrow shaft is loose, do not shoot the arrow until the nock can be replaced.

MISSTEP

Your bow dry-fires (the arrow falls to your feet on release).

CORRECTION

Inspect the arrow nock for cracks. Replace cracked nocks.

If you are shooting with a recurve bow, check the string, or brace, height to make sure it is at least 6 inches (15 cm; figure 2.2). Attach a bow square to the bowstring and set the arm of the bow square on the arrow rest. Read the length marked on the arm of the bow square at a point exactly above the deepest part of the bow handle or grip (pivot point). If the brace height is shorter than 6 inches (15 cm), the bowstring might slap your wrist. Step 8, Upgrading, Tuning, and Maintaining Equipment, explains how to adjust the brace height.

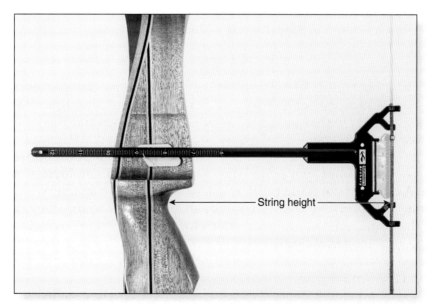

Figure 2.2 A bow square positioned to allow you to check the string, or brace, height.

If you are shooting with a compound bow, make sure that the cables and string assembly are routed and attached properly. If you are using a finger release with a compound bow, be sure to draw the bow with the back of the hand parallel to the bowstring. Turning the hand and placing a bend in the string could cause a cable to slip off the pulley or cam.

ATTIRE

Archery requires no particular uniform, but archers should avoid clothing that could catch the bowstring. When dressing to shoot, avoid baggy shirts, baggy sleeves, and chest pockets with buttons for trim. Remove pens, sunglasses, cell phones, and the like from shirt pockets (figure 2.3). Also avoid necklaces, dangling earrings, and pins. A bowstring could catch on any of these. If you have long hair, you may want to tie it back so that it does not become caught in the bowstring.

Wear shoes when shooting. If you drop an arrow on your bare foot or step on it in the grass, it could cause an injury. Wear an arm guard and use a finger tab. They protect you from abrasions and blisters.

Figure 2.3 DANGEROUS PRACTICE: ATTIRE

1. Wear shoes and close-fitting clothing.
2. Wear an arm guard and finger tab (unlike the archer pictured!).
3. Remove glasses, jewelry, and objects, such as pens, from pockets, and pull binoculars away from the bowstring.

Safe Equipment Exercise 1   Equipment Inspection

Develop an inspection routine that you conduct before every shooting session. Follow these steps:

1. Inspect bow limbs for cracks.
2. Inspect arrow rest for breakage or slippage.
3. Make sure bowstrings and compound bow cables are seated properly.
4. Inspect bowstring and its serving for fraying or breakage.
5. Check arrows for cracks in shafts or nocks, and make sure arrows' points are in place.

Success Check

- Cracked equipment is set aside.
- Bowstring and cable are properly seated.
- Bowstring and its serving are without frays.

Score Your Success

Safety inspection routine developed = 5 points

Your score _____

SHOOTING SAFELY

As you learn about the sport of archery, you must always be aware that you hold a lethal weapon in your hand when you shoot. Before shooting your first arrow, learn the safety rules and follow them rigidly. Keep safety in mind when shooting. Safety should always be a matter for conscious attention; never relegate it to the subconscious. Accidents often happen because people do not give their full attention to the task at hand. You must shoot with safety in mind.

Be sure to shoot outdoors only on a range designated for archery. Arrows that miss a target can travel a long way. They also can glance off hard objects, change direction, and travel a great deal farther to the side of the original trajectory than you might anticipate. Designated archery ranges provide a large safety zone around the target to allow for these possibilities. Because many private yards in municipalities border other yards and are not large enough for adequate safety zones, local ordinances usually forbid shooting in yards as well as city parks.

Most of the following safety rules point out in specific ways that a bow is a lethal weapon and that you must be very careful in its use. Anticipate dangerous situations. Ask yourself, what if _____? regarding potentially dangerous situations, and take steps to make your shooting safe before you begin.

Take your position on the shooting line when instructed to do so, making sure you straddle the line so that you and all shooters are standing in one straight line (figure 2.4). Nock your first arrow only after the signal to shoot is given (usually one whistle blast). Remember to only release the string from a full draw when shooting an arrow. Releasing without an arrow, or dry-firing, transfers the energy that would have gone to the arrow to your bow instead, possibly damaging it beyond repair.

Figure 2.4 SHOOTING SAFETY

1. Straddle shooting line.
2. Point arrow at ground or target.
3. Make sure area around and behind target is clear.
4. Shoot only at target.
5. Restart shot if arrow falls off rest.
6. Stop on emergency signal, usually three or more whistle blasts or a verbal command.

MISSTEP

You nock your arrow and then turn to talk to another shooter or a spectator.

CORRECTION

Be sure to keep your bow with a nocked arrow pointed at the ground or at the target (downrange). If you turn away from the target, remove your arrow from the bowstring.

Point a nocked arrow at the ground until the target area is declared clear and you are ready to draw the bowstring. Then, only point your loaded bow toward the target. Even an arrow released from a partially drawn bow can cause serious injury. Nock your arrow only at the nock locator.

If shooting on your own, check the target area to make sure it is clear at least 40 yards (37 m) behind and 20 yards (18 m) to each side of the target before each shot.

If an arrow falls off the arrow rest, restart the shot rather than attempting to replace the arrow at full draw. Otherwise, you may release the bowstring because of fatigue before getting the arrow into proper position.

Learn to shoot without holding the arrow on the bow with your index finger to avoid puncturing or scratching your finger. If you are shooting with a mechanical release, never draw the bow with your finger on the trigger of that release. You could accidentally trigger the release.

If any of your equipment falls forward of the shooting line when you are shooting in a group, rake it toward you with your bow or an arrow (figure 2.5) rather than crossing the shooting line to retrieve it.

Always shoot arrows toward the target; *never* shoot arrows straight up into the air. Shooting an arrow upward is very dangerous because you have no control over where it lands. Stop shooting immediately if you hear an emergency signal, which is often three or more whistle blasts.

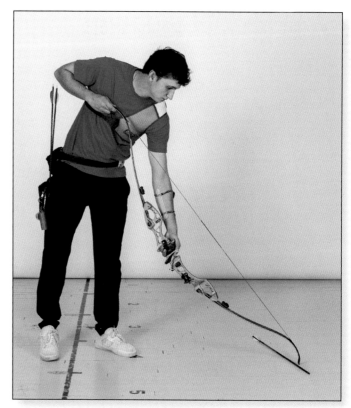

Figure 2.5 Use a bow to rake fallen arrows toward you. Do not cross the shooting line to retrieve any equipment that falls.

MISSTEP
You are ready to release when someone walks into the target area from the side or from the shooting line.

CORRECTION
You must let down (ease the string forward) immediately if someone walks into the target area or in front of the shooting line. Remind other archers to wait for the signal or for all other archers to finish.

RETRIEVING ARROWS SAFELY

It is tempting to think that the risk associated with archery is over once the arrows are shot. Yet, more archers are injured when retrieving and carrying arrows than when shooting. Not only do arrows have sharp points, but they also can cause injury by poking. The broadheads used for hunting deserve the utmost caution. They are razor sharp and can cause severe, life-threatening injuries. Adherence to the following rules should help prevent such injuries.

Step back from the shooting line when you finish shooting your arrows. However, if an archer next to you is at full draw, it is courteous to remain in place so that you do not distract the other archer.

Place your bow on a bow rack or in a designated area while you retrieve your arrows. Someone could trip over a bow left on the ground or floor.

Cross the shooting line to retrieve your arrows only when given the signal to do so (usually two whistle blasts). If no one is providing signals, move forward only after all other archers have stepped back from the shooting line to indicate that they have finished shooting.

If you suspect that one of your arrows has overshot the target, take your equipment with you to the target. You can place it in front of the target as a signal to anyone arriving to shoot that you are behind the target. This is particularly important in wooded areas and when you are shooting alone. With others, one archer could stand in front of the target while others search behind it.

Walk, don't run, to the target, and approach it with caution. Tripping into the nock end of an arrow can cause a serious injury, especially to your eyes.

Retrieve low arrows that landed in the grass short of the target as soon as possible on the walk to the target. If the fletching is embedded in the grass, pull the arrow forward and out of the grass to avoid damaging the fletching.

Be sure there is no one behind you as you pull your arrows from the target. Place one hand flat against the target face to prevent it from ripping, and then grasp the arrow shaft close to the target with the other hand. Twist the arrow back and forth to remove it. This twisting keeps the arrow from bending and prevents you from creating a large, forceful backward thrust that could strike someone nearby with the nock end of the arrow. Some archery ranges have a target line extending the width of the range and 2 yards (1.8 m) in front of the targets. Archers cross the line one at a time to retrieve their arrows, with the line keeping others at a safe distance.

To prevent eye and head injuries, use caution when retrieving notepads, pens, or other objects below the target. Be careful with arrows because the points are sharp. Carry them in a quiver or with the points in your palm (target points only).

What Sport Science Says About the Aerodynamics of the Arrow

Once gunpowder was invented, the armies of the world soon left the bow and arrow behind as a weapon of war. Yet we have stressed the importance of safety in handling the bow and arrow throughout this step. The arrow is not propelled by gunpowder, but it can be deadly. The aerodynamics of the arrow demonstrate why we should appreciate the damage a shot arrow might do if an archer is careless. Sport scientists have used a variety of tools to study an arrow in flight. For example, one research group (Miyazaki et al. 2013) used a wind tunnel to study arrow aerodynamics. They were able to suspend an arrow in the wind tunnel with a magnetic suspension system. They also used two high-speed cameras positioned 45 meters apart to study an arrow shot at 60 meters, both projected by a mechanical system and shot by an elite archer.

From their research and that of other sport scientists, we know quite a bit about arrow flight. We know that the typical velocity of a shot arrow is around 60 meters per second and that an arrow oscillates along its length and spins around its axis. The oscillation is the result of the archer's paradox, wherein the arrow flexes when the bowstring is released, rebounds in an equal and opposite reaction, and then continues this oscillation for its early flight. Oscillation makes the air flow around the arrow turbulent rather than laminar (smooth). We will say more about the archer's paradox in step 8. The arrow spins because of the aerodynamic effect of the fletching, and this plays a key role in stabilizing an arrow in flight. The arrow is an efficient projectile, and as such, the bow and arrow must be respected as a system to be handled with care.

MISSTEP

You are shooting alone, and you carry your equipment with you as you search behind the target for a lost arrow.

CORRECTION

Leave your bow in front of the target as a signal to other archers arriving to shoot.

Safe Shooting Exercise 1 Safety Test

You should demonstrate your knowledge of the safety rules of archery before shooting your first arrows. For your sake and the sake of others learning archery with you, you must know and obey the safety rules. Use the following questions to check your safety knowledge. The answers are on the next page.

1. What should you do if you find a crack in your bow limb?
2. What should you do if you find a crack in an arrow?
3. How do you inspect a carbon arrow?
4. What should you do if you find a crack in the plastic nock on your arrow?
5. How should you dress for shooting?
6. What should you check for on your bowstring?
7. How should you check a compound bow?
8. When is it safe to nock an arrow when shooting with a group?
9. When is it safe to nock an arrow when shooting on your own?
10. What does one whistle blast mean?
11. What do two whistle blasts mean?
12. What do three whistle blasts mean?
13. When is it permissible to step across the shooting line?
14. What should you do if your arrow falls off the arrow rest as you are drawing (pulling the bowstring back) or aiming?
15. When is it permissible to hold an arrow on the bow with your index finger?
16. What should you do when you finish shooting your arrows?
17. How should you approach the target?
18. When should you retrieve arrows that fall short of the target?
19. When should you retrieve arrows that land behind the target?
20. What should you check for before pulling your arrows from the target?

Success Check

- Review safety rules if you missed any questions.

Score Your Success

_____ percent correct (strive for 100 percent before shooting)

100 percent correct = 5 points

95 percent correct = 2 points

<95 percent correct = 0 points

Your score _____

ANSWER KEY

SAFE SHOOTING EXERCISE 1. SAFETY TEST

1. Do not shoot. Seek advice at a pro shop.
2. Break it into two pieces and discard it.
3. Hold the arrow at each end and bend it an inch or two (2.5-5 cm), repeating four to six times as you rotate the arrow; then twist it in both directions. If you hear, see, or feel any damage, discard the arrow.
4. Remove the cracked nock and replace it.
5. Wear close-fitting clothing and remove jewelry and items from pockets. Tie long hair back.
6. Check for fraying or a broken strand and a frayed serving.
7. Check for fraying and any cable not attached properly or seated in a pulley or cam. Check pulleys, cams, and axles to ensure that they are not bent.
8. After the signal (one whistle blast), it is safe to nock an arrow when shooting with a group.
9. After you check for a clear target area, it is safe to nock an arrow when shooting on your own.
10. It is permissible to nock an arrow and begin shooting.
11. It is permissible to cross the shooting line to retrieve arrows.
12. Stop shooting immediately. This is an emergency situation.
13. After two whistle blasts or when all archers have stepped back from the line, it is permissible to step across the shooting line.
14. Ease the string forward and start the shot over.
15. It is never permissible to hold an arrow on the bow with your index finger!
16. Step back from the line and place your bow in the designated area.
17. Approach the target at walking speed, watching for arrows that have landed in the grass.
18. On the way to the target, retrieve arrows that fell short of the target.
19. After positioning a fellow archer or your bow or quiver in front of the target, retrieve arrows that landed behind the target.
20. Check for archers or spectators standing in the way before you pull your arrows from the target.

SUCCESS SUMMARY

Every archer wants shooting to be an enjoyable experience. You should never place another archer in harm's way. Despite the inherent danger of the bow and arrow, shooting can be safe when you do two basic things: methodically and regularly inspect equipment, and anticipate unsafe shooting conditions so you can correct them before shooting.

For both exercises presented in this step, you can earn points to chart your progress. Enter your score for each exercise, and add them up to rate your success. If you scored at least 7 points, you can move to the next step.

Safe Equipment Exercise

1. Equipment Inspection   _____ out of 5

Safe Shooting Exercise

1. Safety Test   _____ out of 5

Total   **_____ out of 10**

Preparation is often a key to doing something well. You have prepared to shoot by obtaining equipment fitted to your body size and strength and by learning how to participate safely. Now you are ready to learn how to shoot. In the next step, you will begin by learning to draw and anchor your bow without an arrow. Once you are comfortable with the draw and anchor, you can safely learn to shoot your first arrows.

Shooting With Good Form

Some sports are fun to play and watch because you never know what's going to happen next. Wrestlers have an ongoing interchange of attack and counterattack; soccer players switch from offense to defense and back to offense within seconds; volleyball players dig the ball one minute and spike it the next.

Some sport skills are performed well only when they are executed the same way, correctly, every time. Like a great free-throw shooter whose every attempt looks like a replay of the one preceding it, a successful archer is a consistent archer. An archer's goal is to establish perfect form, called T-form, and then reproduce it on every subsequent shot.

Note that we're referring to consistency in technique, not outcome, at least at first. So don't be distracted by the flight of the arrow or scoring your shot. Because our emphasis is on form, we will demonstrate with simple equipment and a finger release. If you have advanced equipment or even a mechanical release, it is fine to use it as long as your equipment is fitted to your size and strength. We just want your attention to be on form during your early archery experiences and for you not to be distracted by equipment. The more consistent your form is, the more benefit you later will get from advanced equipment.

For now, you should learn the T-form shooting technique as taught in this step and practice it so that it becomes consistent and reliable. You will be using the same setup every time you take aim. You will also learn the secret to good shooting technique: back tension. If you think that working at good form sounds boring, just think how bored you'll be with bull's-eye after bull's-eye!

UNDERSTANDING T-FORM

The body's muscular structure can maintain good T-form alignment of the arms and trunk with less effort than in other positions. Muscle groups on opposite sides of the limbs and trunk pull evenly in T-form. Archers who assume bent positions at full draw are pulling more with one muscle group than another. They may find it difficult to assume that exact position on subsequent shots, especially when they are fatigued or nervous.

Remember that, in shooting archery, you maintain your position for several seconds to aim while holding the bow up and the bowstring back against many pounds of resistance. The nervousness you may feel from wanting to shoot well in a contest or the excitement you may feel as a deer approaches also can cause a breakdown in your form. You need a shooting style that is easy to reproduce, even under pressure. You need good form that is well practiced so that you can use that good form by habit and not conscious thought.

It is also easier to visualize placing your body into a T shape than placing it in a bent shape (figure 3.1). You can create an exact visual image of the straight lines and right angles of the T. If your body or limbs are in a bent position, you can more easily adjust to a straight position than you can to a different degree of bend. You can monitor your form more easily when your goal is T-form.

You may see other archers experiencing some degree of success shoot-

Figure 3.1 Visualizing T-form.

ing without T-form. This success might be short-lived. In the long run, archers with T-form are more comfortable and relaxed and shoot more accurately than archers without this alignment. Practicing T-form and making it a habit are well worth the effort in your early experience with archery.

MIMICKING A T-FORM SHOT

The best way to learn the basic T-form shot is to first mimic it without actually shooting an arrow. Mimicking gives you the chance to make the motions of shooting habitual and gradually get used to the equipment. Mimicking contributes to safe shooting, too. You can make sure you are handling the bow and arrow safely and are not overdrawing the arrow.

Take a stance with your bow arm side toward the target, feet shoulder-width apart, and weight even. Check your stance by imagining a straight line going through the toes of each foot. If this line would continue toward your target, you are in good position (figure 3.2a). If it would not, adjust your position. Stand straight and keep your shoulders square over your feet and your head square on your shoulders. Avoid twisting your trunk.

Hold the bow at the handle straight up and down in front of you. Form a hook with the middle three fingers of your string hand. Hook the bowstring in the end joint of the fingers with one finger above the nocking point and two below it (figure 3.2*b*).

Raise and extend your bow arm at shoulder level toward the target, keeping your string hand in place on the bowstring. Look over your front shoulder. Draw the string by pulling your elbow back in one fluid motion. The shoulder blade of the drawing arm should move toward your spine. Remember, you will need to exert enough muscular force to overcome the draw weight of the bow. Continue drawing to your anchor position. The anchor position is the place at which the string touches the tip of your nose and your top finger touches under the side of your chin. This is the safest anchor position for a beginning archer. Rotate your bow elbow down and out. Hold this position for a few seconds, noticing how it feels, and then slowly ease the string forward to the bow's relaxed position (figure 3.2*c*). Never release a bowstring unless there is an arrow in the bow because dry-firing might damage the bow. Relax before repeating the process.

Figure 3.2 MIMICKING T-FORM

Stance

1. Position your bow arm side toward target.
2. Align feet and keep weight even.
3. Stand straight.
4. Keep bow in front.
5. Make sure shoulders are square.
6. Keep mouth closed and teeth together.

(continued)

Figure 3.2   *(continued)*

Draw and Anchor

1. Set bow in V of thumb and index finger.
2. Set string hand hook.
3. Look over front shoulder.
4. Raise bow toward target.
5. Rotate bow forearm down and out.
6. Relax string hand and wrist.
7. Use muscles in back of string shoulder.
8. Draw string elbow back at shoulder level.
9. Position string on nose and forefinger on jaw.

Ease Down

1. Concentrate on target.
2. Ease string forward.

MISSTEP

The bow arm's elbow turns in toward the anticipated path of the bowstring.

CORRECTION

Make sure your bow hand is directly behind the bow handle, and then rotate your forearm down and out.

MISSTEP

The string arm's elbow bends, and then the back muscles are used to draw the bowstring.

CORRECTION

Think first of using the back muscles and then moving the elbow back to draw the bowstring.

Using the muscles of the back is important for good shooting. Starting the draw by rotating your string-side shoulder blade and moving your elbow back ensures good back tension. With back tension, you will be able to develop consistent form and resist tiring. Drawing with the back muscles places the two arms in a straight line pointing to the bull's-eye. In step 6, we discuss how back tension also makes for a smoother release.

You might be tempted to skip mimicking, but remember that learning T-form before you start worrying about where the arrow will go will reap benefits later. When an archer shoots with a draw position based on straight lines and right angles, accuracy is sure to follow. Some world-class archers mimic their shots as a warm-up before their shooting sessions, so don't be afraid to make mimicking a regular part of your archery practice.

Mimicking Exercise 1   Bow Arm Practice

It is helpful to practice rotating your elbow down and out while there is pressure against your hand. Approach a doorjamb and extend your bow arm. (If you are outdoors with nothing to lean against, you can have a partner provide resistance.) Place the heel of your hand against the doorjamb (thumb toward ceiling), and lean against the doorjamb slightly (figure 3.3a). Rotate your forearm around and down without moving your hand so that your forearm is vertical (figure 3.3b).

(continued)

Mimicking Exercise 1   *(continued)*

Figure 3.3   Bow arm practice: *(a)* Press heel of hand against doorjamb; *(b)* rotate forearm down without moving hand.

Be sure to keep your bow shoulder down, not hunched. You can check your position by bending your arm at the elbow. If your hand is at chest level, your elbow position is correct. If your hand is at face level, your elbow position is incorrect. Repeat nine more times. The more you practice, the more habitual good form becomes.

TO INCREASE DIFFICULTY

- Hold bow and extend it toward target.
- Hook bowstring with string hand and rotate elbow down.

TO DECREASE DIFFICULTY

- Hold bow arm out to the side at shoulder level, palm down. Keeping arm in place, rotate hand to vertical position. Your bow arm should be in proper position. Relax, and then try to achieve this position while performing this exercise.

Success Check

- Level shoulders.
- Keep hand vertical.
- Rotate elbow down and out.

Score Your Success

10 repetitions with correct form = 3 points

5 to 9 repetitions with correct form = 1 point

Your score _____

Mimicking Exercise 2   Looking in a Mirror

Standing diagonally in front of a mirror with a bow, practice setting your bow hand and a relaxed hook with your draw hand fingers. Raise the bow and draw by moving your elbow straight back at shoulder level. Keep your draw wrist straight and relaxed. Be sure to anchor with the bowstring touching the middle of your nose. Check your position for T-form by looking in the mirror; move just your eyes, not your head. Slowly ease the string back. Repeat nine more times.

TO INCREASE DIFFICULTY

- Repeat this exercise, drawing with your eyes closed so you can focus on the feel of T-form before you check the mirror.

TO DECREASE DIFFICULTY

- Perform this exercise without a bow or with a bow much lighter in poundage than your shooting bow.

Success Check

- Keep shoulders level and head erect.
- Move draw elbow back at shoulder level.
- Touch nose with string.
- Touch chin with forefinger.

Score Your Success

10 repetitions with correct form = 3 points

5 to 9 repetitions with correct form = 1 point

Your score _____

MIMICKING WITH AN ARROW

The next step is to mimic T-form with an arrow (figure 3.4). Take your stance as before. Nock an arrow just below the nock indicator on the string. The index (odd-colored) feather or vane should be toward you. Place the shaft on the arrow rest. Form your string hand hook and place one finger above the arrow and two below it. Draw to your anchor position as before. Remember not to go past your anchor position because you might pull the arrow off the arrow rest. Hold this position for a few seconds, and then ease the bowstring forward. Rest, and then repeat this mimic until you are comfortable handling the bow and arrow. Although the intention here is to mimic and not actually shoot an arrow, you should always practice in front of a target butt—the backstop for arrows—just in case you accidentally release the string.

MISSTEP

The arrow falls off the rest during the draw.

CORRECTION

Keep the wrist and first knuckles of the draw hand straight throughout the draw without cupping your hand. Use the hand only as a hook, moving the arm straight back with the back muscles. Keep the bow vertical.

Figure 3.4   MIMICKING T-FORM SHOT WITH ARROW

Stance

1. Position your bow arm side toward target.
2. Align feet and keep weight even.
3. Stand straight and square to target.
4. Nock arrow against nock locator.
5. Position index feather or vane toward you.

Draw and Anchor

1. Set bow hand; then set draw hand.
2. Put one finger above and two fingers below arrow.
3. Raise bow toward target.
4. Rotate bow forearm down and out.
5. Relax hands and keep back of draw hand flat.
6. Tighten back muscles and move draw elbow back.
7. Place chin on hand, with string touching chin and nose.

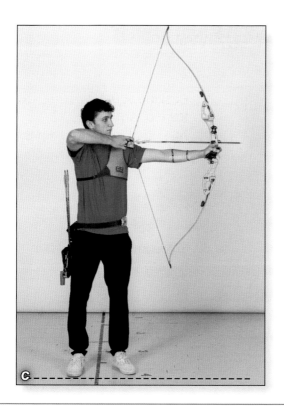

Ease Down

1. Align string and arrow shaft.
2. Keep bow level, pointed toward target.
3. Ease string forward.

Mimicking With Arrow Exercise 1   Partner Check

For this exercise, you will need a partner who is somewhat familiar with T-form. Mimic six shots with an arrow. Your partner should watch you from the side and back and try to catch you varying from T-form. You will probably find it more difficult to maintain form on your later arrows as you tire.

TO INCREASE DIFFICULTY

- Mimic 10 shots in a row.

TO DECREASE DIFFICULTY

- Mimic three shots in a row.

Success Check

- Keep bow arm and draw arm at shoulder level.
- Anchor (string touches nose).

Score Your Success

6 repetitions with consistent form = 3 points

3 to 5 repetitions with consistent form = 1 point

Your score _____

Mimicking With Arrow Exercise 2   **Mirror Exercise**

Standing diagonally in front of a mirror with a bow, practice nocking your arrow and setting your bow hand with a relaxed hook with your draw hand fingers. Raise the bow and draw by moving your elbow straight back at shoulder level. Keep your draw wrist straight and relaxed. Be sure to anchor with the bowstring touching the middle of your nose and chin. Check your position for T-form by looking in the mirror; move just your eyes, not your head. Slowly ease the string back. Perform six repetitions.

TO INCREASE DIFFICULTY

- Mimic the shot with your eyes closed after you set your draw hand hook, and then open them to check the mirror.

TO DECREASE DIFFICULTY

- Mimic the shot with a bow much lighter in poundage than the one you use.

Success Check

- Keep shoulders level and head erect.
- Move draw elbow back at shoulder level.
- Make sure string touches nose.
- Make sure forefinger touches jaw.

Score Your Success

6 repetitions with consistent form = 3 points

3 to 5 repetitions with consistent form = 1 point

Your score _____

Mimicking With Arrow Exercise 3   **Bow Hand Check**

Obtain two small dot stickers or pieces of colored tape. Place one on the middle of the bow handle just above where you place your hand. Take your bow hand position and place the second sticker on your hand right below the other dot on the bow. Mimic two ends of six arrows each (12 repetitions). Before drawing for each shot, take your bow hand position and check to see whether the stickers are aligned (figure 3.5).

Figure 3.5   The stickers should align.

Success Check

- Make sure the centerline of your arm intersects the center of the bow.

Score Your Success

12 repetitions with the stickers aligned = 3 points

8 to 11 repetitions with the stickers aligned = 1 point

Your score _____

EXECUTING THE T-FORM SHOT

Once you are comfortable mimicking T-form with an arrow, you need only add the release to shoot an arrow. Stand close (10-15 yd, or 9-14 m) to a target butt. You can place a large target face or just a paper plate on the target butt for a focus point. At first, don't worry about where your arrows land.

Remember your safety rules. When you are sure the area behind and to the sides of the target butt is clear, take the stance you learned in the mimicking stage (figure 3.6a). Set your bow and string hands just as before. Draw and anchor (figure 3.6b). Now, tighten your back muscles and simply relax your fingers to release the string (figure 3.6c). Keep your bow arm up and your head still. The bow will do the rest!

Figure 3.6 **T-FORM SHOT**

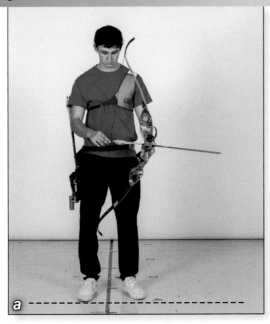

Stance

1. Position your bow arm side toward target.
2. Align feet and keep weight even.
3. Stand straight and square to target.
4. Nock arrow against nock locator.
5. Keep index feather or vane toward you.

(continued)

Figure 3.6   *(continued)*

Draw, Anchor, and Aim

1. Set bow hand; then set draw hand.
2. Place one finger above and two fingers below arrow.
3. Raise bow toward target.
4. Rotate bow forearm down and out.
5. Relax hands and keep back of draw hand flat.
6. Tighten back muscles and move draw elbow back.
7. Make sure string touches nose and forefinger touches jaw.
8. Align string and arrow shaft, and level bow.
9. Tighten back muscles.
10. Maintain relaxed bow and draw hands.
11. Count to three.

Release and Follow-Through

1. Relax draw hand to release string.
2. Draw elbow recoils on release.
3. Keep bow arm up, toward target.
4. Maintain head position.
5. Make sure draw hand finishes over rear shoulder.

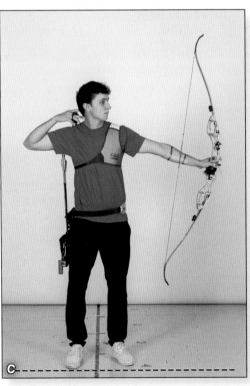

MISSTEP

The hips slide forward or the front shoulder scrunches up during the draw or while aiming.

CORRECTION

Stand straight and use the back muscles to draw by moving the draw elbow back. If you cannot make this correction, the draw weight of your bow may be too heavy. Switch to a bow that is lighter in draw weight while you learn good form.

After you have practiced the basic shot enough that you are comfortable drawing and releasing, add a predraw aim to your routine. A predraw aim places the bow arm high enough that the arrow tip aligns with a spot about 18 inches (46 cm) below the target center. After anchoring, align the bowstring (which appears fuzzy when your aiming eye is focusing on the target butt) and the arrow shaft. Check the bow limbs through your peripheral vision to ensure that the bow is vertical. These two additions give you consistency in aiming your arrows vertically and horizontally.

T-Form Exercise 1   Release Mimic

Without equipment, form your string hand hook. Hook it into the forefinger of your bow hand and anchor it under your chin (figure 3.7). Tighten your back muscles, leaving your draw hand relaxed. Now relax your fingers to "release." Your draw hand should be carried back toward your rear shoulder by your back tension. Practice six consecutive releases. You can do this exercise anywhere, anytime.

Success Check

- Keep string hand wrist and first knuckles straight.
- Tighten back muscles.
- Relax string fingers.

Score Your Success

Complete 6 repetitions, developing muscle tension only in the back = 3 points

Complete 3 to 5 repetitions, developing muscle tension only in the back = 1 point

Your score _____

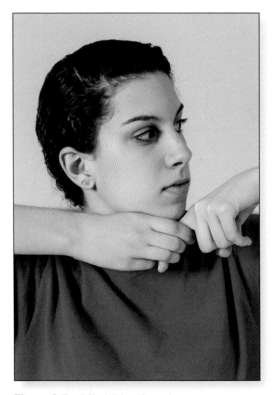

Figure 3.7 Mimicking the release.

T-Form Exercise 2   Grouping

Experienced archers know that grouping arrows is more important than shooting occasional bull's-eyes. You can always change your aiming point to center the group around the bull's-eye. This exercise emphasizes consistency by having you evaluate the grouping of your arrows. Using T-form consistently should lead to grouping. Shoot an end of six arrows from 10 yards (9 m) at an empty target butt. You don't need a target face. Take a tape measure to the target. Wrap the tape around all of your arrows to obtain the smallest measurement possible. Record the length of tape needed to surround your arrows.

TO INCREASE DIFFICULTY

- Shoot with your eyes closed. For safety, have a friend watch for safety hazards and make sure your bow is pointed toward the target butt.
- Move back to 15 yards (14 m).

TO DECREASE DIFFICULTY

- Shoot only four arrows per turn.

Success Check

- Relax bow hand and arm.
- Maintain follow-through position until arrow hits target.

Score Your Success

Length of tape needed to surround arrows is 35 inches (89 cm) or less = 3 points

Length of tape needed to surround arrows is 36 to 60 inches (91-152 cm) = 2 points

Length of tape needed to surround arrows is more than 60 inches (152 cm) = 1 point

Your score _____

T-Form Exercise 3   Hit or Miss

Our emphasis has been on establishing good form rather than scoring shots. If you are anxious to see how accurately you can shoot now, even without using an aiming sight, place a 2 feet by 2 feet (60 × 60 cm) piece of paper on the target butt. To establish a standard, shoot an end of five arrows from a distance of 10 yards (9 m) and note how many land on the paper. This is your standard for this exercise. Now shoot four more ends.

TO INCREASE DIFFICULTY

- Draw a tic-tac-toe pattern on the paper with a broad marking pen. Randomly write point values in the squares. Record the number of points earned by arrows landing in the squares. Arrows touching a line take the higher point value.
- Use a smaller piece of paper.

TO DECREASE DIFFICULTY

- Use a larger piece of paper.

Success Check

- Relax draw hand to release.
- Maintain T-form.

Score Your Success

Four ends with the same number as or more hits than your standard (first) end = 3 points

Two or three ends with the same number as or more hits than your standard end = 2 points

One end with the same number as or more hits than your standard end = 1 point

Your score _____

T-Form Exercise 4   Balloon Pop

Blow up six balloons and mount them on a target butt. Shooting an end of five arrows from a distance of 10 yards (9 m), try to pop as many balloons as possible. Repeat the exercise four times, replacing balloons as needed for each end.

TO INCREASE DIFFICULTY

- Use fewer balloons.

TO DECREASE DIFFICULTY

- Use more balloons.
- Place balloons closer together on the target butt.

Success Check

- Use proper T-form.
- Relax bow and string hands.

Score Your Success

Pop five balloons or more = 3 points

Pop three or four balloons = 2 points

Pop two balloons = 1 point

Your score _____

What Sport Science Says About T-Form

In this step to success, we emphasize T-form, especially starting the draw by moving the elbow back first and using the muscles in the back, behind the string shoulder, to draw the bowstring. Novice archers often begin by bending the elbow, thus using arm muscles to begin the draw. What does sport science say about muscle activation in the archery draw? Simsek and colleagues (2018) studied muscle activation during the draw and release. They placed electrodes over nine forearm, shoulder, and back of the shoulder muscles in 27 archers with different levels of expertise. Electromyographs (EMGs) were recorded just prior to and after the release of the bowstring. Six shots were measured.

The researchers found that novice archers activated their forearm muscles during the draw. Novice and intermediate archers alike used distal (forearm) muscles more than elite archers, who used shoulder and back muscles more than distal muscles. In fact, the researchers found that active use of the shoulder and back muscles and less use of the forearm muscles minimized horizontal oscillation of the bowstring after release. Less oscillation contributes to more accurate shooting. Sport science confirms that novice archers who work to use T-form can take a larger step toward shooting success.

DEVELOPING A MENTAL CHECKLIST

A mental checklist is a helpful way to proceed through shot setup. It reminds you to attend to the necessary aspects of shot preparation and leaves you little time to think about other things or be nervous. If you tend to repeat the same form error, your checklist can include a specific reminder to avoid that error.

A mental checklist helps you methodically and precisely prepare every shot in the same way. Your checklist points can vary on a daily basis with shooting conditions. For example, an archer shooting at a target on a sloping hillside often unwittingly cants the bow. The addition of a mental checklist reminder to level the bow helps the archer check for a level bow on every shot at this target.

Begin the development of your personal checklist by identifying the keys to success pertinent to your shooting style. Figure 3.8 gives a skeleton list of the keys to success. It assumes that some of the simplest aspects of shooting have already become routine for you. Remember, a mental checklist is highly personalized. It can reflect your unique shooting style and address the bad habits into which you tend to fall. Adapt this checklist for yourself. Feel free to add anything you tend to overlook or do incorrectly.

MISSTEP

You overlook important steps in your shot preparation. You make the same mistake on the majority of your shots.

CORRECTION

Practice your mental checklist without shooting. Next, practice it while mimicking shots. Then, shoot several ends with a written checklist, as in mental checklist exercise 1.

Figure 3.8   **MENTAL CHECKLIST**

Stance
1. Assume stance.
2. Nock arrow.
3. Set bow hand.
4. Set draw hand hook.

Draw and Aim
1. Raise bow and then draw.
2. Anchor.
3. Level bow.
4. Steady bow.

(continued)

Figure 3.8   *(continued)*

Release and Follow-Through

1. Tighten back muscles.
2. Relax draw hand to release.
3. Keep bow arm up and steady.

Mental Checklist Exercise 1   Learning Your Checklist

Copy the keys to success that you have chosen for your personal check- list onto a long, narrow sheet of paper that you can attach to the face of your upper or lower bow limb. As an alternative, copy the list with large lettering onto a large index card and lay the card on the ground in front of you (figure 3.9). (Anchor it on a windy day when shooting outdoors.) Use your written checklist for your next two practice sessions; then see whether you can recite your checklist to a friend without reading it. When you can do so, shoot without the writ- ten list, but remember to mentally go through your checklist on every shot.

Figure 3.9   Write out your checklist and anchor it to the ground in front of you if outdoors.

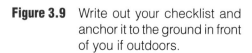

Success Check

- Say every point on your checklist.

Score Your Success

Recite all points = 3 points

Recite all points but one = 1 point

Your score _____

Mental Checklist Exercise 2   **Rehearsing Aloud**

Shoot four ends of five arrows each at 15 yards (14 m). On each arrow, recite the items on your checklist aloud as you perform them up until you anchor. Reciting the checklist aloud reminds you to attend to each item. Go through the items during the anchor and aim silently. After you release the bowstring, recall aloud your cues for maintaining follow-through.

Success Check

- Include every point from your checklist.
- Push other thoughts out of your mind.

Score Your Success

Complete 18 to 20 shots, remembering every step = 3 points

Complete 15 to 17 shots, remembering every step = 1 point

Your score _____

SUCCESS SUMMARY

You have been practicing the archery shot with T-form, which stresses straight lines and right angles. The sooner you make T-form a habit, the sooner you will achieve success in hitting your target!

The practice exercises in this step provide a variety of ways to make T-form a habit, so by now you should be comfortable getting a shot off. Following the mental checklist you created should improve your consistency from shot to shot and keep you shooting safely. This checklist also keeps your mind focused on the task at hand and gives negative thoughts little opportunity to invade your mind.

You probably noticed that the more consistent your T-form became, the more your arrows grouped rather than scattered on the target. An experienced archer can group arrows even when blindfolded, just by relying on the feel of habitually practiced T-form. See how close you are getting to meeting this goal.

For each of the exercises presented in this step, you can earn points to chart your progress. Enter your scores and add them up to rate your success. If you have 23 or more points, you likely have practiced sufficiently to advance to the next step. If you have fewer than 23 points, repeat some of the exercises to increase the number of repetitions you have practiced and the number of points you have earned before moving on.

Mimicking Exercises

1. Bow Arm Practice   _____ out of 3

2. Looking in a Mirror   _____ out of 3

Mimicking With Arrow Exercises

1. Partner Check   _____ out of 3

2. Mirror Exercise   _____ out of 3

3. Bow Hand Check   _____ out of 3

T-Form Exercises

1. Release Mimic   _____ out of 3

2. Grouping   _____ out of 3

3. Hit or Miss   _____ out of 3

4. Balloon Pop   _____ out of 3

Mental Checklist Exercises

1. Learning Your Checklist   _____ out of 3

2. Rehearsing Aloud   _____ out of 3

Total   _____ **out of 33**

In this step, we stressed that accurate shooting begins with learning good form—T-form—and then using it repeatedly to execute the archery shot. It is possible that variations of the square stance and bow hand position you learned in this step are better for your body structure. In step 4, you will have an opportunity to try some variations so you can decide what works best for you.

Refining Technique

ew sports can take as many forms as archery—target shooting, field shooting, distance shooting, bowhunting, and bowfishing. You are probably anxious to try one or more of these forms. As you choose a specific type of archery, you will need to individualize your T-form to be the most compatible with the goal of that style of archery. For example, getting a shot off quickly is more important in bowhunting than in target archery. Establishing an anchor position quickly becomes crucial to success in bowhunting.

You may want to create a personal shooting form to accommodate your body shape and structure. For example, you might choose a certain bow hand position because it is the most comfortable and consistent for your arm and wrist, or a certain stance because you have a larger chest than the average shooter. Refining the more detailed aspects of your shooting style will take your performance to a higher level. Practice exercises must emphasize exact positions and the replication of each aspect of your refined form. In this step, you will refine two parts of your shooting style: stance and bow hand position. Then, you will have an opportunity to reinforce your use of back tension in the draw and hold with your refined stance and bow hand position.

STANCE

In the basic T-form, you take a stance with feet about shoulder-width apart and toes along an imaginary line that goes straight to the target. This is known as the square stance, and it is a good stance for beginners because it is natural, easy to establish, and easy to duplicate. However, every archer also has a unique natural stance—a stance that feels most comfortable. Your body build may dictate the stance that is best for you. You must experiment to find the stance that enables you to naturally direct the bow straight to the target without drifting right or left.

The three basic archery stances are square, open, and closed. Each has advantages and disadvantages (table 4.1). The square stance (figure 4.1a) places the toes on a straight line to the target. The open stance (figure 4.1b) moves the rear foot up across this imaginary line and turns the forward foot outward, a position that opens the body to the target. The closed stance (figure 4.1c) moves the front foot up across the imaginary line. You will need to determine whether to open or close your stance and by how much.

Table 4.1 Advantages and Disadvantages of Various Stances

Type of stance	Advantages	Disadvantages
Square	• Natural position • Easy to duplicate	• Small base of support in front-to-back plane • Body can sway, especially in windy conditions • Minimizes string clearance, especially for large-chested shooters
Open	• Provides stable base of support • Minimizes tendency to lean away from target • Provides more string clearance than other stances	• Promotes tendency to twist upper body to face target • Promotes tendency to use arm more than back muscles to draw
Closed	• Provides stable base of support • Promotes good alignment of arm and shoulder in direct line to target	• Minimizes string clearance; string may strike body or clothing • Promotes tendency to lean away from target or overdraw

Figure 4.1 **STANCES**

Square

1. Feet are shoulder-width apart.
2. Toes are aligned.
3. Body is erect and shoulders are square.
4. Weight is even.

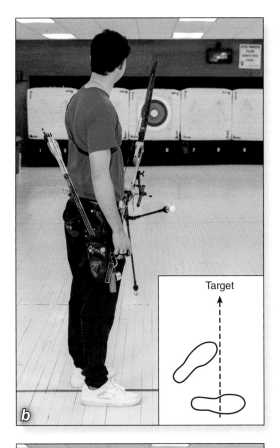

Open

1. Front foot turns outward.
2. Rear foot is forward 6 inches (15 cm).
3. Body is erect and shoulders are square.
4. Weight is evenly distributed.
5. Line to target intersects middle of rear foot and toes of front foot.

Closed

1. Front foot is forward 6 inches (15 cm).
2. Body is erect and shoulders are square.
3. Weight is even.
4. Line to target intersects toes of rear foot and middle of front foot.

MISSTEP

You feel tension in your draw arm when using the open stance.

CORRECTION

You might be opening your shoulders too much and need to square them to the target enough to use your back muscles to draw.

If you are planning to shoot target archery, you should strive to use an identical stance from shot to shot and from session to session. Three or four archers often shoot at the same target butt, so you might not always be able to stand directly in front of your target. You must learn to adapt so that an imaginary line through your stance points to the target even if you are standing slightly to the right or left.

If you are planning to shoot field archery or to hunt, you likely will experience uneven footing at times. You will have to adapt to the lay of the land. In this step, you might first want to determine your preferred stance so that you can assume that stance whenever possible. Then, practice shooting with various stances while striving to maintain the alignment of your shoulders toward the target.

Stance exercise 2 will help you find your natural stance. Once you find this natural stance, you may want to use foot markers to promote consistency until you can assume that exact stance from shot to shot without an aid. If you are outdoors, take your stance and then insert two golf tees into the ground in front of the toes of each shoe. You can accomplish the same thing indoors with two pieces of tape or a light chalk mark.

MISSTEP

Your foot position varies from shot to shot or from end to end.

CORRECTION

Use foot markers: golf tees outdoors; chalk or tape indoors.

Stance Exercise 1   Impact-Variation Exercise

This exercise demonstrates how stance influences the accuracy of shooting. With a square stance, shoot an end from 12 yards (11 m). Note and place a small mark at the center of your arrow grouping on the target face. Now, shoot an end with a closed stance. Again, mark the center of your arrow grouping. Shoot a final end with an open stance and mark the center of your arrow grouping. Note the relationship between your markers.

Success Check

- Body is erect.
- Weight is evenly distributed.

Score Your Success

Demonstrate the influence of stance on arrow groupings = 3 points

Your score _____

Stance Exercise 2   Alignment Check

This exercise helps you determine which stance provides the best alignment to the target for you. Attach a bowsight to your bow, or simply tape a toothpick onto the back of the bow so that one end extends into your line of sight and can be used as a sight. Stand approximately 15 to 20 yards (14-18 m) from the target. Without actually shooting an arrow, come to full draw and aim at the bull's-eye. Close your eyes and count to three. Open your eyes and note whether your bow has drifted to the left or right. If it has drifted to the right, open your stance a little; if it has drifted to the left, close it a little (if you are left-handed, transpose these directions). Repeat this process, changing your foot position approximately 1 inch (2.5 cm) at a time until you find a stance that does not result in drifting. When you have found the position that results in no drift, add a cue to your mental checklist from step 3 to remind yourself to use this stance on every shot.

Success Check

- Weight is evenly distributed.

Score Your Success

Perform three successive draws without drifting = 3 points

Your score _____

Stance Exercise 3   Golf Tee Exercise

With two golf tees in hand, take a stance on the shooting line directly in front of the target. Push the golf tees into the ground at your toes. Now move behind the shooting line. Sight down the golf tees to see whether an imaginary line through your stance goes straight to the target. Repeat this exercise by moving several steps up the shooting line and then several steps down the line from your first position, assuming the positions you might have if shooting in a group of four archers at one target. Sight down the tees for each position. You must learn to take the correct stance even if you cannot stand squarely in front of the target.

Success Check

- Stand with feet shoulder-width apart.
- Stand with shoulders square to target.

Score Your Success

Imaginary line through golf tees intersects bull's-eye in all four positions = 3 points

Imaginary line through golf tees intersects bull's-eye in three positions = 2 points

Imaginary line through golf tees intersects bull's-eye in one or two positions = 1 point

Your score _____

What Sport Science Says About Stance

Postural stability is important to performance in all precision-aiming sports. Minimizing movement, especially during aiming, is associated with consistent and repeatable shots that ultimately improve accuracy. Sport scientists have studied postural stability, often using a force platform or force plate. Sport scientists also have used cameras that can digitize the movements of the limbs along with force plates. When a shooter stands on a force plate, changes in their center of pressure on the plate can be quantified in terms of direction and distance. For example, if a shooter leans away from the target, the center of pressure would move toward the rear leg. The bigger the lean, the more the center of pressure moves. While we might think it is possible to stand perfectly still, in fact, we always sway at least some. The more stable a shooter is, the less the shooter sways and the less the center of pressure moves.

Sport scientists have learned several things about postural stability in archery. First, they found that greater stability is associated with higher-scoring shots and less stability with lower-scoring shots (Sarro, de Castro Viana, and Leite de Barros 2021). Second, greater stability after arrow release also is associated with higher-scoring shots (Spratford and Campbell 2017). Third, sport scientists observed that elite archers sway less than beginning archers (Simsek et al. 2019) and that body sway is synchronized with the bow arm to allow steady aiming in higher-scoring shots (Sarro, de Castro Viana, and Leite de Barros 2021). Finally, experienced archers rely more on proprioception (feel) than vision to achieve postural stability (Wada and Takeda 2020).

The research of sport scientists on postural stability tells beginning archers that it is important to have a stable and consistent stance. With attention to this detail, beginning archers establish a good base of support. With practice and training, postural stability improves to allow more accurate shooting.

BOW HAND POSITION

You can use one of several bow hand positions: the low wrist, the high wrist, or the straight wrist. Each wrist position has advantages and disadvantages (table 4.2). With each bow hand position, archers strive to maintain a relaxed bow hand to resist the push of the bow on the bow arm as the bowstring is drawn. Archers choose the hand position that best allows them to maintain a relaxed hold, given their strength and bone and muscle structure. If you have not yet used a finger or bow sling, do so now (see The Sport of Archery). With a sling, you are not as tempted to grip the bow out of fear of dropping it as you would be without a sling.

Any movement of the bow as the arrow is clearing the arrow rest can cause a deviation in where the arrow lands. Consider the fact that pushing the tail end of an arrow just one degree off center can make it land far from the bull's-eye. You want to avoid any movement of the bow at the time of release. If your bow hand is tense or grips the bow tightly, you are more likely to move upon release than you would if your bow

Table 4.2 Advantages and Disadvantages of Wrist Positions

Wrist position	Advantages	Disadvantages
Low	• Allows wrist to relax backward completely • Does not require great wrist strength	• Promotes tendency to grab bow if wrist and fingers are not relaxed
High	• Minimizes area of hand contacting bow handle • Minimizes bow torque • Minimizes tendency to grab bow on release	• Difficult to maintain over long shooting session without great strength • Promotes tendency to move wrist at release with fatigue
Straight	• Consistent from shot to shot • Makes deviations in position easy to feel	• Difficult to maintain over long shooting session without great strength • Pressure against skin web between thumb and forefinger promotes tendency to wrap fingers around bow

hand were relaxed. Archers who take a grip in which the hand is not directly behind the bow handle also have a tendency to bend the wrist during the draw. Usually, these archers can't maintain the wrist position through the shot. The wrist moves, affecting the arrow's flight.

Many archers also have a tendency to grab the bow as they release the string, even if the bow hand is relaxed during the draw and aiming. This turning of the bow, or torque, can still affect the tail end of the arrow as it clears the arrow rest. Also, beginning archers sometimes anticipate the release so that the bow is moving throughout the release of the bowstring. Only dedicated practice in relaxing the bow hand throughout the shot and follow-through can help you overcome these flaws that detract from accuracy.

Another reason for maintaining a relaxed bow hand is that your two hands tend to mirror each other in tension level. If your bow hand is tight, your string hand tends to be tight as well. If your bow hand is relaxed, your string hand tends to be relaxed, too, resulting in a cleaner release of the string or the trigger of a mechanical release.

Each of the three bow hand positions puts the wrist at a different height in relation to the bow hand. The low position (figure 4.2a) places your arm below your bow hand. The high position (figure 4.2b) places your arm above your hand. The arm and hand form a line in the straight position (figure 4.2c). In the low and straight positions, the hand is placed so that the pressure is along the inner side of the thumb muscle (the web of the hand). An easy way to find the low position is to extend your bow arm toward an imaginary target with your hand up, as if to signal someone to stop. From this position, simply relax the fingers without changing the wrist angle, and you have the low wrist position with the fingers forming a 45-degree angle with an imaginary vertical line.

Figure 4.2 **WRIST POSITIONS**

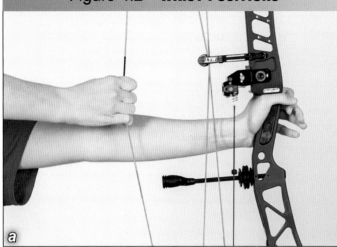

Low Wrist

1. Hand is on bow, pressure is along inner side of thumb, knuckles are at 45-degree angle.
2. Bow rests on base of thumb.
3. Centerline of arm intersects center of bow.
4. Wrist is relaxed backward as bow is drawn.
5. Hand and fingers are relaxed.

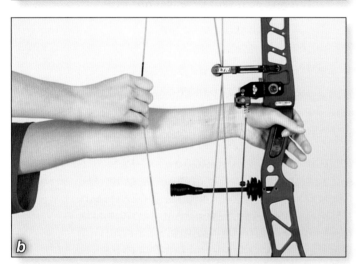

High Wrist

1. Centerline of arm intersects center of bow.
2. Wrist is higher than hand.
3. Pressure of bow is on small area of hand.
4. Hand and fingers are relaxed.

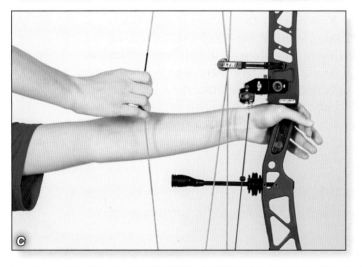

Straight Wrist

1. Centerline of arm intersects center of bow.
2. Wrist is level with hand.
3. Pressure of bow is on web of hand.
4. Hand and fingers are relaxed.

MISSTEP

Your bow hand is so tense that you either grip the handle tightly and your knuckles turn white or you extend your fingers and lock them into position.

CORRECTION

Relax the fingers of your bow hand. If you are afraid of dropping the bow, use a bow sling.

MISSTEP

You hold the bow handle to the side.

CORRECTION

Be sure to center your hand behind the bow and relax your fingers; the imaginary line down the center of your arm should intersect the center of the bow.

Regardless of which wrist position best minimizes torque and bow movement for you, the three positions have common features. First, an imaginary line running down the center of the bow arm should intersect the center of the bow. This alignment brings the line of pressure closest to the line of pressure exerted by the bowstring, making torque easier to control. Second, your hand and fingers must be completely relaxed so that the bow jumps forward upon release (and is caught by the bow sling) rather than turning to the right or left. As a result, the bowstring should travel in a straighter line as it accelerates the arrow, and the arrow should clear the bow without interference.

You may find that your physical strength and structure lend themselves to a particular bow hand position, yet most successful archers use a straight or low grip. The low grip position in particular allows the wrist bones to resist the force of the draw and transfer that force up the arm muscles to the shoulder and back. This is the most efficient shooting form and the one that best resists fatigue.

The shape of the bow's grip can determine a particular bow hand position, but it is best for your ideal wrist position to dictate your handle of the bow rather than the other way around. Some bows are made with removable handgrips, so you can install the handgrip shape that allows you to use your preferred bow hand position. Experiment with the various bow hand positions to determine the best one for you. Once you find your preferred position, if your bow has interchangeable handgrips, install the one for your preferred bow hand position.

Hand Position Exercise 1   Choosing a Bow Hand Position

This exercise provides an opportunity to try the various bow hand positions. Shoot six arrows from approximately 15 yards (14 m) with a high wrist. Then do the same with a straight wrist and then with a low wrist. Make sure the centerline of your arm intersects the center of the bow (figure 4.3). That is, the pressure of the bow against your hand, wrist, and arm is straight to your shoulder, despite the upward or downward angle between the hand and wrist. Changing your bow hand position might change where your arrows land on the target, but you need not be concerned about that now. Merely note how comfortable the bow hand position feels and where the arrows land (in a smaller or bigger group) on the target. The bow hand position that produces the tightest group and feels the most comfortable is probably the one you should use. Add a cue to your mental checklist to remind yourself to use this bow hand position on every shot.

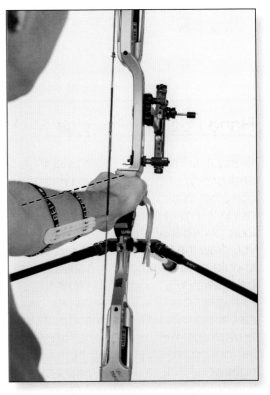

Figure 4.3   The arm line intersects the center of the bow.

Success Check

- Centerline of arm intersects center of bow.
- Hand and fingers are relaxed.

Score Your Success

Shoot three ends using each of the three wrist positions = 3 points

Shoot one or two ends using one of the three wrist positions = 1 point

Your score _____

Hand Position Exercise 2   Consistency Check

Obtain two small pieces of tape or two dot stickers. Place one on the middle of the bow handle just above where you place your hand. Take your bow hand position and place the second sticker on your hand right below the other dot on the bow (see figure 3.5). Shoot two ends of four arrows each from approximately 15 yards (14 m). Before drawing for each shot, take your bow hand position and check to see whether the stickers or pieces of tape are aligned.

Success Check

- Centerline of arm intersects center of bow.

Score Your Success

Dots align on 5 to 8 shots = 2 points

Dots align on fewer than 5 shots = 1 point

Your score _____

Hand Position Exercise 3 Torque Check

Without an arrow, take your stance and grip your bow as usual while an observer watches from a yard or so down the range in front of you as you look toward the target (figure 4.4). As you draw the string back, the observer should note whether the back of the bow always faces the target or turns to the right or left. The observer can also watch a stabilizer attached to the bow to see whether it points right or left during the draw. If the bow turns right or left, change your hand position on the handle until you can draw without torquing the bow, making sure you have a relaxed grip. Repeat for five draws.

Success Check

- Draw straight back.
- Draw close to bow arm.

Score Your Success

Five draws without torquing the bow = 3 points

Three or four draws without torquing the bow = 1 point

Your score _____

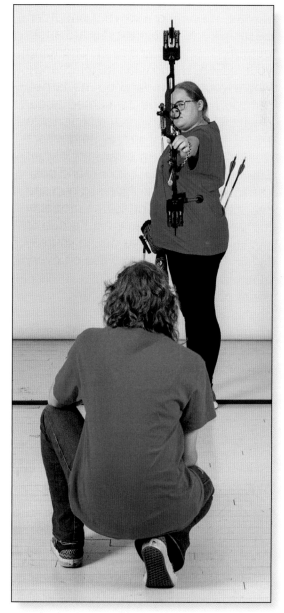

Figure 4.4 A partner checks your alignment from in front.

61

BACK TENSION

As you refine your shooting form for your body structure and the type of archery you want to shoot, one thing must not change: You must use your back muscles to draw and hold. Your draw must begin with the elbow moving back, and your draw-side shoulder blade should rotate and slide toward your spine. The tension in the muscles between your spine and shoulder blade should be maintained through the release. Back tension is crucial to an accurate shot, no matter the equipment or type of archery.

Slight variations in your stance and bow hand position should not have changed your back tension. This is a good time to make sure you are using back tension in your draw and hold. If you find that you are now drawing and holding without good back tension, you might have changed your stance or bow hand too dramatically, or you might not be aligning your shoulders to the target.

Larry Wise (2004), an archery champion, coach, and author, pointed out that it is easier to repeat a shot founded on back tension. The back muscles are short and easier to control than the arm muscles. Shot after shot, it is easier to reproduce the use of the back muscles than the same combination of arm muscles. When the back muscles are used, the arm muscles can relax. Using back tension also is less fatiguing than using arm muscles for drawing and holding.

The back muscles used in the archery shot are the draw- or string-side rhomboid muscles, assisted by the levator scapulae and the trapezius. When the draw is executed with these muscles, the draw-side shoulder blade, or scapula, moves toward the spine, and having rotated upward as you raised your bow arm with the string hand set, the shoulder blade now rotates down toward the spine as you draw. Stressing *elbow back* in the early steps to success was a way to encourage the use of the back muscles rather than starting the draw by flexing at the elbow and thereby relying on the arm muscles to hold the bow's tension. This initial movement of the elbow back results in the upper draw arm and elbow rotating around the shoulder with the elbow slightly higher than the shoulder line at full draw. Another result is that the draw-side forearm is aligned in the same plane as the arrow, another feature of T-form.

The tension developed in the back muscles during the draw should continue as you anchor and settle the sight on your aiming spot. In step 6, we discuss anchoring and releasing in detail, but several methods of releasing are founded on continuing to increase back tension to trigger the release. This promotes the most consistency possible from shot to shot over long practice and shooting sessions.

The exercises in this section give you an opportunity to check your back tension and establish the habit of using the back muscles on every draw. You might want to do some of these exercises periodically to stay in the habit of using the back muscles to draw and hold and relaxing the arm muscles.

Back Tension Exercise 1   Shoulder Blade Movement

It is easy to overlook how much shoulder blade movement accompanies arm movement because we don't easily observe the shoulder blade moving. You can demonstrate to yourself how the shoulder blades move in several ways. First, sit on the floor with your back against a wall and raise both arms out in front of you. Without letting your back move away from the wall, extend and raise your arms several more inches (7-8 cm). Now, slide your arms back toward the wall, without bending at the elbows, and then reach forward again, keeping your back in contact with the wall. Note how the shoulder blades slide forward around the rib cage as you reach forward and then slide back around the rib cage toward your arms as you retract them.

You can next demonstrate shoulder blade movement for yourself with a movement more like the draw of a bow. Stand comfortably where you have room around you. Mimic setting your bow and string hands on an imaginary bow, and then extend your bow arm. Move your string hand back, starting with the elbow back movement (elbow slightly above the plane of the shoulders), and feel your draw-side shoulder blade slide around your rib cage toward your spine. Move your string hand forward and feel your shoulder blade slide away from your spine. Repeat this several times, focusing on the feel of the shoulder blade movement.

Success Check

- Focus on shoulder blade sliding around rib cage.

Score Your Success

Demonstrate shoulder blade movement while sitting = 1 point

Demonstrate shoulder blade movement while mimicking draw = 1 point

Your score _____

Back Tension Exercise 2   Drawing With Back Tension

In this exercise, have a friend help you feel for shoulder blade movement as you draw your bow. Without an arrow, take your shooting position. Have your friend stand behind you and put a hand over your shoulder blade with a slight amount of pressure. Set your bow arm and string hand, extend your bow arm, and draw and hold for about three seconds before easing the string back. Focus on the feeling of tension in your back muscles while you hold. The pressure of your friend's hand should make you more aware of shoulder blade movement and the use of your back muscles to draw and hold. Repeat this for three sets (ends) of six draws each.

Success Check

- Feel shoulder blade move under slight pressure of friend's hand.

Score Your Success

Perform three ends of mimicked shots with a light touch on your shoulder blade = 3 points

Perform one or two ends of mimicked shots with a light touch on your shoulder blade = 1 point

Your score _____

Back Tension Exercise 3   Using a Training Aid

You can increase the strength of your back muscles and practice using them to draw and hold without using your bow. This allows you to focus on back tension without worrying about the sighting process or scoring. Although there are training aids made specifically for archers, you can also use exercise bands or resistance tubing to mimic the archery shot. Choose a beginning resistance level that allows you to use good T-form. Over time, as this level becomes easier, you can move up one level of resistance. Exercise bands are easy to grasp at the right length to mimic the draw, yet exercise tubing with handles allows you to mimic the bow hand and string hand positions (for a finger release) if you can adjust the handles to a workable length.

Using bands or tubing, draw and hold for about three seconds, for six repetitions. Rest and repeat up to six ends. On every draw, be sure to focus on the use of your back muscles and on relaxing your arm muscles. This is a good exercise to use periodically for conditioning, and it can be done away from the shooting range.

Success Check

- Focus on tension in back muscles and relaxing arm muscles.

Score Your Success

Perform three ends of drawing with exercise band or resistance tubing = 3 points

Perform two ends of drawing with exercise band or resistance tubing = 2 points

Perform one end of drawing with exercise band or resistance tubing = 1 point

Your score _____

SUCCESS SUMMARY

You have been refining and individualizing your archery shot while maintaining T-form. The exercises in this step provided opportunities to find the stance and bow hand position most comfortable for you. Chart your progress in individualizing and "grooving" your form by noting your exercise scores.

Recall that you developed a mental checklist in step 3. Add steps to your checklist to remind yourself to use the stance and bow hand position you determined to be the best for you.

For each of the exercises presented in this step, you can earn points to chart your progress. Enter your score for each exercise and add them up to rate your success. If your total is at least 18 points, move on to the next step. If it is less than 18, repeat some of the exercises with the goal of scoring higher.

Stance Exercises

1. Impact-Variation Exercise   _____ out of 3

2. Alignment Check   _____ out of 3

3. Golf Tee Exercise   _____ out of 3

Hand Position Exercises

1. Choosing a Bow Hand Position   _____ out of 3

2. Consistency Check   _____ out of 2

3. Torque Check   _____ out of 3

Back Tension Exercises

1. Shoulder Blade Movement   _____ out of 2

2. Drawing With Back Tension   _____ out of 3

3. Using a Training Aid   _____ out of 3

Total   _____ **out of 25**

Steps 3 and 4 stressed the value of T-form and adapting your form according to your body structure. Once you can consistently repeat the archery shot with good form, you can achieve even more accuracy by using a bowsight. A bowsight allows you to direct the arrow at the same place from shot to shot. In step 5, you will learn how to install and adjust a bowsight and how to use it to aim your shot. Combining consistent form with the use of a bowsight will improve the accuracy of your shooting.

Aiming and Sighting

At the 1993 World Target Championships, archer Park Kyung-Mo found himself shooting against a former world champion in the semifinal match. From 70 meters, he shot his first two arrows into the 10 ring, which is the inner part of the gold bull's-eye. The next arrow was a 9, landing in the outer part of the bull's-eye, but the remaining nine arrows all landed in the 10 ring. Park Kyung-Mo's score of 119 out of 120 possible points took first place.

Many years of practice helped Park Kyung-Mo win his match, but undoubtedly, such accurate shooting at a long distance would be very difficult without a bowsight. A bowsight helps you direct your bow in a consistent direction from shot to shot. Once archers establish sight settings for various distances, a bowsight allows them to step up to a new distance and hit the bull's-eye with the very first arrow! Although some archers enjoy the challenge of shooting barebow (without a bowsight), most target archers and bowhunters use a sight. In this step, you will learn how to choose, install, and use a bowsight. A short discussion of aiming without a bowsight is included in case you would like to explore traditional archery.

With a bowsight, you can direct your arrows to the same spot on your target from shot to shot. You can reproduce the alignment used on any one shot because you align an aiming aperture on the bowsight with the bull's-eye. If your arrows hit outside the bull's-eye, you can use the bowsight as a calibrated means of adjustment for subsequent shots. You can adjust the bowsight both horizontally and vertically; you must establish through trial and error just how great an adjustment is needed. When you change shooting distance, move the bowsight vertically—down for a greater distance, up for a shorter distance. This adjustment changes the height of your bow arm and, consequently, the trajectory of the arrow. The horizontal adjustment allows you to accommodate slight changes in shooting form that direct the arrow to the right or left and to adjust for shooting conditions, including wind.

SELECTING AND INSTALLING A BOWSIGHT

The bowsight is an attachment to the bow that places a marker or aiming aperture in the bow window to the left of the upper bow limb for a right-handed archer. You line up the aperture with the bull's-eye to sight rather than looking at the relationship between the arrow and the bull's-eye. The bowsight helps you direct an arrow to the same place horizontally and vertically on every shot by dictating the elevation and left-to-right direction of your bow arm. If your arrows are not landing around the bull's-eye, the sight gives you a systematic way to adjust until your sight setting is zeroed in on the bull's-eye.

You have many choices when selecting a bowsight. Bowsights can be very simple, inexpensive, handmade devices, or they can be elaborate, precision-made tools (figure 5.1). Simple sights do a good job of directing the arrow as you desire. The difference between expensive and inexpensive sights is typically the ease and accuracy of moving the aiming aperture. The style of archery you want to shoot also influences your choice of bowsight.

Purchased sights typically come in two types. One is permanently affixed directly to the handle riser on the back side of the bow (away from the archer) and along the bow window. The other type attaches to the side of the handle riser and is easily removed. It is either attached to a mounting bracket or screwed into an insert placed there for that purpose. This is typical of bows with metal handle risers. This arrangement makes it easy to change from one sight to another, to vary the distance the sight extends from the bow, or to remove the sight for transport.

There is an advantage to choosing a sight that extends out from the bow. The farther the sight extends from the bow, the more precise sighting can be. If the distance from the eye to the aiming aperture is short, a small error in sighting at the moment of release causes a larger error in where the arrow lands. That same error in sighting with an extended bowsight has less effect. Yet, the farther out the bowsight is, the more accentuated any bow arm movement appears to the archer during sighting. Target archers undoubtedly like to extend the bowsight away from the bow. Distances of about 6 to 9 inches (15-23 cm) are typical. New archers should probably keep the sight close to the bow so as not to accentuate bow movement during sighting. With increased strength and endurance and consequently steadier aim, the sight can be extended farther out.

Sights made for bowhunting can also extend out from the bow. Bowhunters, though, must take into account the ease of transporting their equipment through wooded areas, up to tree stands, and so on, so they typically extend the sight just 2 to 6 inches (5-15 cm) from the bow handle.

Target archers typically choose a sight that accommodates one aiming aperture. This aperture can be adjusted up or down, directing the bow lower or higher, and left or right. Because target archers have time to change a sight setting between shots, one aiming aperture is sufficient. Bowhunters, on the other hand, not only don't have the time to adjust a sight, but they also don't know ahead of time how far their game will be from their location. Sights for bowhunting typically accommodate three to five aiming apertures, or pins, each set for a specific distance. The heavier the draw weight a bowhunter shoots, the fewer pins are needed because the arrow trajectory is relatively flat at shorter shooting distances. Many bowhunting sights have lighted aiming pins to better sight in wooded areas or low-light conditions. A circular housing protects the lighted pins from damage.

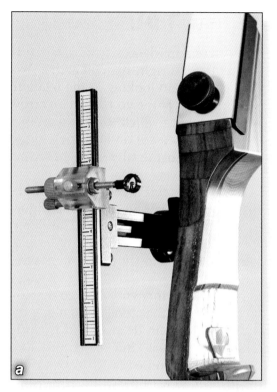 

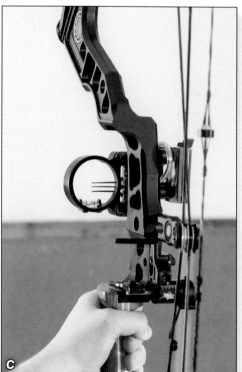

Figure 5.1 Bowsights: *(a)* inexpensive target sight from a front view; *(b)* tournament-quality bowsight from the archer's view; *(c)* bowhunting sight from the archer's view.

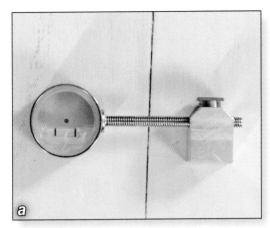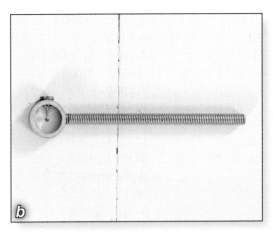

Figure 5.2 Two aiming apertures: *(a)* aperture with a dot and a level; *(b)* aperture with a drop-pin.

You have several styles of aiming apertures to choose from (figure 5.2). Examples of apertures that are aligned with the middle of the bull's-eye include a simple post with a small, round ball on the end, a ring with crosshairs, a ring with a post, and a magnifying lens with a dot or circle in the center.

Many archers prefer an open ring. They find that it is natural to center the target's ring inside the aiming ring. Some magnifying lenses have a circle at the center instead of a dot; like the open ring, the circle allows the archer to center the bull's-eye.

Aiming apertures can incorporate a level so that you know you are holding your bow level, but some competition categories restrict the use of levels as well as magnifying lenses. Most bowsights accommodate the use of various types of aiming apertures. Start with one that is simple, such as a post or an open ring. You can try other types later. It is probably best to delay using a magnifying or scope sight. Although these make the bull's-eye appear larger, they also accentuate your movements while aiming. Some archers react to this by trying to force the bow to remain still, which typically has the opposite effect on steadying aim!

Installing Exercise 1   Making a Simple Bowsight

Making your own sight is a good way to demonstrate how this simple accessory can improve your accuracy. Obtain a piece of felt or foam about 5 inches (13 cm) long, plastic tape, and a long, straight pin with a ball head. If you find self-adhesive 1/2- or 3/4-inch (1.3-1.9 cm) insulating foam, you won't need to tape it on your bow. Position the felt or foam on the back of your bow (the side away from you) along the sight window above the arrow rest. Place a piece of plastic tape along the felt or foam so you can mark every half centimeter on the tape with a permanent marker (figure 5.3). Stick the straight pin into the foam or felt so it is visible in the sight window. The pin serves as your aiming aperture. You can move the pin vertically and horizontally to adjust your sight setting. The marks help you note how far you have moved the pin and what locations on your sight correspond to various shooting distances.

Now, shoot two ends of five arrows each. Stand approximately 12 yards (11 m) from a backstop without a target face. Place a small, paper circle about 4 inches (10 cm) in diameter on the backstop as a target. On the first end, remove the pin from your handmade sight and aim at the circle as you have been. On the second end, replace the pin about two-thirds of the way up the bow window. On every shot, align the pinhead with the circle. Don't worry about hitting the circle; just focus on aiming there. On each end, note how tightly grouped your arrows are on the target backstop.

Success Check

- Align pinhead with aiming spot.

Score Your Success

You can earn points for both of the following:

Install and then shoot with a bowsight = 1 point

Shoot a tighter arrow group than without a bowsight = 2 points

Your score _____

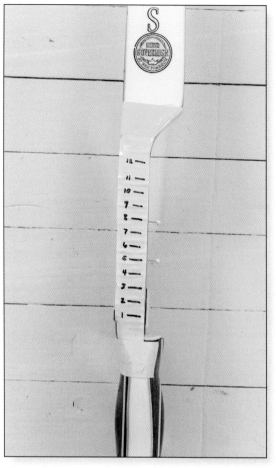

Figure 5.3 A handmade target sight with a pinhead as an aiming aperture.

PEEP SIGHTS

A peep sight (figure 5.4) is a small round or oval disk with a hole in the middle. It is placed between the strands of the bowstring at eye level. A peep sight acts as a rear sight, precisely aligning the bowstring and the tail of the arrow with the bowsight and target. Sighting is more precise when two locations between the archer's eye and the bull's-eye are aligned than when just one is aligned.

Obviously, a peep sight improves aiming accuracy. However, not all archers use peep sights. If you will be competing in archery tournaments, check to see that peep sights are allowed in your anticipated classification. Also, peep sights can be bothersome. They must be positioned so you can look through the small opening. Archers who tend to twist the bowstring when positioning their fingers, and even those who use mechanical releases, sometimes find that the peep sight rotates. Devices that hold the peep sight in the desired orientation are available. Yet, it is time-consuming to set up these devices, and it is an additional step to anchor in such a way that you can see through the peep sight. It is more difficult to get a shot off quickly when using a peep sight. If you are a beginning archer, you might want to wait to use a peep sight until your shooting form and shot setup are established and routine. You can add a peep sight later when it won't be a distraction from the other aspects of good shooting.

To install a peep sight, first place it between the strands of the bowstring above the nock locator at about the height of your aiming eye. Draw to your anchor and note whether you can look through the peep sight to see your bowsight. Ease the bowstring back and slide the peep sight up or down as needed. You may have to turn either the peep sight or the bowstring so the peephole is fully open to your eye. This is a process of trial and error.

Once you have the peep sight at the correct height, mark the bowstring at this location. You might also want to measure and record the distance between the peep sight and your nock locator. Tie the peep sight into the string so that it will not move. There are several methods for doing this, but they require practice to do well, so you may want to take your bow to a pro shop and have an expert tie in your peep sight.

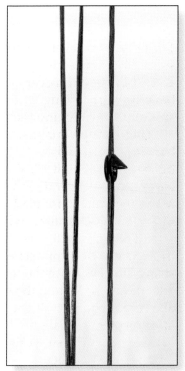

Figure 5.4 The peep sight. This style has a hood to reduce glare.

Installing Exercise 2   Installing a Peep Sight

You might not want to use a peep sight for shooting at this time. Yet it is good to see what is involved in using one should you decide to add it at a later time. Obtain a peep sight and install it as directed. You might have to draw several times and adjust the height of the peep sight after each draw. When you have the correct height, stand 12 yards (11 m) in front of a target. Without an arrow, draw and look through the peep sight to align the sight aperture with your aiming spot on the target. After a count of two, ease the string back. If the peep sight was turned and you could not look through it, try twisting the bowstring or taking the peep sight out and reinserting it at another angle. Be sure to merely hook onto the bowstring with the fingers of your draw hand rather than twisting the string with your fingers as you draw and hold. Twisting the string can turn the peep sight so that you cannot see through it. Perform five draws, aligning the sight aperture through the peep sight and letting down to rest after each draw. If you would like to continue using the peep sight, clamp or tie it in. If not, you can remove it after the exercise.

Success Check

- Keep back of draw hand flat.
- Looking through peep sight, align sight aperture with bull's-eye.
- Allow sight to settle on bull's-eye.

Score Your Success

Aim through the peep sight for five draws = 2 points

Aim through the peep sight for one to four draws = 1 point

Your score _____

USING A BOWSIGHT

The principles of using a bowsight are the same whether you have a simple, handmade sight, a hunting sight, or a sophisticated tournament sight. You aim the sight aperture at the bull's-eye on every shot. Your shooting form is basically the same as what you have been practicing, but you need to add several steps to your shot sequence that are related to aligning the bowsight.

After taking your stance (figure 5.5a), nocking your arrow, and setting your string hand or release aid, look at your target. Pick out a small area, such as the center of the bull's-eye or the hit zone of an animal or animal target. Focusing on a smaller target leads to more accurate shooting than focusing on a large area. This is the aiming phase of aiming and sighting. Once you look at your target (i.e., begin aiming), you should maintain visual contact with it until your arrow hits the bull's-eye.

You should next extend your bow arm and draw (figure 5.5b). Remember that if the eye opposite your string hand is dominant, you may need to close it so that your string-side eye, with the string in front of it, is used for aiming and sighting. Until you anchor and settle into the shot, the aiming aperture on your bowsight can be slightly above your target. When your form feels comfortable and right, slide the aiming aperture down to align with your aiming spot. Only one item in your visual picture can be in focus. Using this method to aim and sight, you will likely keep your target (aiming spot) in focus.

Level the bow by using the level mounted on your sight or by checking that the bow limbs are vertical in your peripheral vision. Your eye should bring the bull's-eye into focus, permitting the aperture and bowstring to blur slightly.

Aligning your eye, the sight aperture, and the target is necessary, but recall that the tail end of the arrow is attached to the bowstring. Ideally, you want to align the string, too! The arrow is automatically aligned with the line of aim if you use a peep sight because it is in the center of the bowstring. If you decide not to use a peep sight or to wait until later to use one, you must adjust your head position so that you see the string running down the middle of the bow limbs and handle. For a right-handed archer, the string should be just to the right of the aperture.

Wait to release until the sight aperture is steady in the middle of the bull's-eye. This usually takes several seconds. When the aperture is steady and aligned, tighten your back muscles and relax your string hand to release the string (figure 5.5c). You will be able to hold the sight more steadily as you practice and develop greater muscular strength and endurance. However, archers can rarely stop the aperture "dead" in the bull's-eye; attempting to do so usually results in too much tension in the bow and string hands. You can shoot very accurately if the aperture is steady and oscillating around the bull's-eye. It does not need to be perfectly still.

MISSTEP

Some of your arrows land to the right or left of the bull's-eye, and you are not using a peep sight.

CORRECTION

Align the bowstring with the middle of the bow limbs and just to the right of the sight aperture on every shot.

MISSTEP

Your arrows horizontally spread across the target.

CORRECTION

If you shoot with both eyes open, recheck for your dominant eye to ensure that it is on the same side as your string hand. If it is not, try closing your bow-side eye.

Figure 5.5 SHOOTING WITH A BOWSIGHT

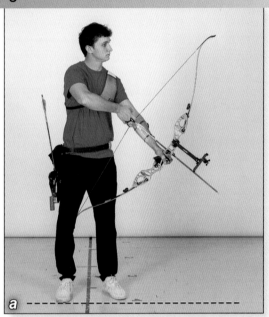

Stance

1. Assume stance.
2. Nock arrow.
3. Set bow and string hands.

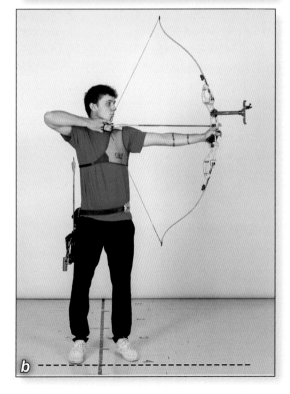

Draw and Aim

1. Focus on target (aim).
2. Draw and anchor.
3. Close eye opposite string side, if necessary.
4. Slide aperture down to align with aiming spot.
5. Level bow.
6. If using a peep sight, look through opening.
7. If not using peep sight, adjust head to see string bisecting bow and aligning just to right of aperture.
8. Focus on bull's-eye.
9. Steady sight aperture in center of bull's-eye.

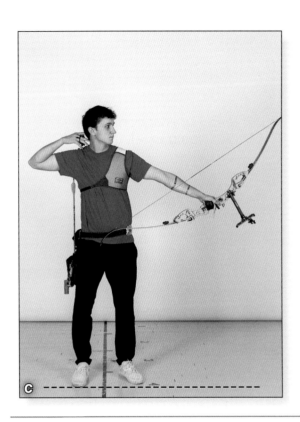

Release and Follow-Through

1. Tighten back muscles.
2. Relax string hand to release.
3. Keep bow arm up.
4. Keep head steady and focus on bull's-eye.

Sighting Exercise 1   Aligning and Aiming Mimic

Some archers tend to release the bowstring as soon as the sight is on the bull's-eye instead of steadying the aperture and aiming. Without using an arrow and from 20 yards (18 m), practice drawing, sliding the aiming aperture down to your aiming spot, aligning your string and sight, steadying your aperture, and aiming. Aim for a count of at least three, and then ease the string back. Remember that steadying means settling the aperture so that it oscillates in small movements around the bull's-eye; it does not necessarily mean stopping the aperture dead in the bull's-eye. Complete 10 repetitions.

Success Check

- Level bow.
- Align bowstring on every shot.
- Let sight aperture settle on bull's-eye.
- Focus on middle of bull's-eye.

Score Your Success

Complete 9 or 10 repetitions with sight settling on bull's-eye = 3 points

Complete 5 to 8 repetitions with sight settling on bull's-eye = 2 points

Your score _____

Sighting Exercise 2   Aiming Mimic on a Three-Spot

Here is another way to practice align-ing your string and sight aperture and aiming. Obtain a three- or four-spot target face (figure 5.6). This is a target face that has the inner rings of a larger target printed three or four times on one face. Very accurate archers who rarely have a shot land in the outer rings use this type of target face.

Figure 5.6   Three-spot target face.

Draw and align your string and sight aperture on the upper or upper-left bull's-eye. Aim and allow the sight aperture to settle on the bull's-eye. Count to two, and then move to another bull's-eye. Check your string alignment; then, again aim at this bull's-eye, settle, and count to two. If you tire, let down, rest, and repeat this exercise. Otherwise, continue to move to another bull's-eye. Do six sets of aiming.

Success Check

- Align eye, bowstring, sight aper-ture, and bull's-eye.
- Focus on bull's-eye.
- Let sight aperture settle.

Score Your Success

Complete 5 or 6 sets, settling on at least two bull's-eyes = 3 points

Complete 2 to 4 sets, settling on at least two bull's-eyes = 2 points

Your score _____

ADJUSTING THE AIMING APERTURE

You establish the proper horizontal and vertical position of the aiming aperture for a given shooting distance by trial and error. If you have aimed the sight at the bull's-eye but the arrows land elsewhere, you must adjust the aiming aperture.

After you shoot several arrows, observe their location on the target face. Move the aperture in the *direction of error* (figure 5.7). For example, if the arrows group low, move the sight aperture down. Sighting through a lower aperture results in your holding your bow arm and, consequently, your bow, higher. If the arrows group high, move the sight aperture up. If the arrows group left, move the aperture left. Be sure to make adjustments to the left or right with the bowsight oriented to the target. It is easy to become confused when you turn the bow around!

Figure 5.7 **AIMING APERTURE ADJUSTMENT**

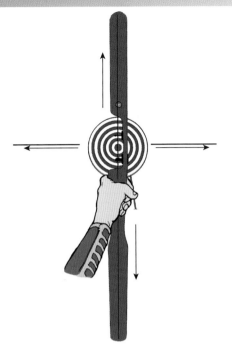

1. Move bowsight up if arrows group above bull's-eye.
2. Move bowsight down if arrows group below bull's-eye.
3. Move bowsight left if arrows group left of bull's-eye.
4. Move bowsight right if arrows group right of bull's-eye.

MISSTEP
Your arrows group farther from the bull's-eye after a sight adjustment.

CORRECTION
Move your sight in the direction of the group of arrows with your bowsight oriented toward the target.

MISSTEP
You aim the sight aperture off center to compensate for your sight setting.

CORRECTION
Aim at the center of the bull's-eye on every shot and patiently move your sight until you have a good sight setting.

When a sight setting is off, some archers are tempted to aim outside the bull's-eye to compensate rather than adjust the position of the sight. Aiming off center is less desirable than moving the sight, unless sight movements are restricted by the rules for a particular class or style of competitive shooting. Consistently finding any position on a target other than the center of the bull's-eye is almost impossible. Don't hesitate to move your sight. That is why it is adjustable! However, if you feel that you varied from T-form on a particular shot, don't make a sight adjustment based on where that arrow landed. Wait to analyze the position of an arrow shot with good T-form.

If you move to a longer distance, you need to move your bowsight down so that your bow arm is directed to give your shot a higher trajectory. Naturally, if you move closer, you need to raise your sight. How far you move your sight for a given change in distance is established first by trial and error. Thereafter, you can keep a written record of the setting for a particular distance. Target archers often carry a written table of their sight settings for given shooting distances.

Changing distances does not necessitate a horizontal adjustment of your sight. Small errors in the position of your sight, though, have a more apparent effect at longer distances. For example, if your arrows fall on the right side of, but still in, the bull's-eye when you shoot from 20 yards (18 m), they likely would fall to the right of, but outside, the bull's-eye at 50 yards (46 m). Therefore, some horizontal adjustment of your bowsight might be necessary as you change distances.

Target archers typically use a bowsight with a single aperture that slides up and down the sight. A scale on the sight enables archers to establish a chart of sight positions corresponding to various distances. Bowhunters do not have the time to reposition their sights for a given distance, even if the game is nice enough to stand still! A hunting sight usually has four- or five-pin apertures of different colors that can be positioned to correspond to the distances the archer is likely to shoot. The hunter estimates the distance to the game and selects the appropriate pin to use in aiming. If a bowhunter estimates being a distance that is between those corresponding to two sight pin settings, those two pins can "frame" the aiming spot. For example, a bowhunter might have a 30-yard (27 m) sight pin set and a 20-yard (18 m) sight pin set but estimates the target game to be 25 yards (23 m) away. The hunter would then put the space halfway between the pins into alignment with the aiming spot.

Adjusting Exercise 1   Sight Adjustment Practice

In this exercise, you practice designating the direction of sight adjustment. The location of a group of arrows is stated in terms of a clock face. Fill in the directions of sight adjustment that you need to bring subsequent shots to the center of the target. For example, for a group at four o'clock, move the sight aperture right and down. Answers appear at the end of this step.

1. For a group at six o'clock, how would you move the aperture?
2. For a group at eight o'clock, how would you move the aperture?
3. For a group at one o'clock, how would you move the aperture?
4. For a group at three o'clock, how would you move the aperture?
5. For a group at eleven o'clock, how would you move the aperture?

Success Check

- Orient bowsight toward target, as when shooting.
- Adjust in direction of arrow group.

Score Your Success

Five adjustments correct = 5 points

Three or four adjustments correct = 3 points

One or two adjustments correct = 1 point

Your score _____

Adjusting Exercise 2   **Sighting In**

Shoot from a short distance of 15 yards (14 m), using an 80-centimeter (32 in.) target face. Shoot six arrows using an initial sight setting with the aperture high on the sight bar. Note where the six arrows land and adjust your sight. Continue shooting and adjusting until your arrows group around the bull's-eye. Record the location of this sight setting by the rule or scale on the bowsight in table 5.1. Now move to 20 yards (18 m) and repeat this process. (With a bowhunting sight, work to set the next pin.) When you have established a sight setting, record it. Continue this process, moving back in 5-yard (4.6 m) increments to a distance of 35 yards (32 m). You can anticipate the needed sight adjustment by moving your sight down a small amount each time you increase your distance from the target. If time permits, repeat this exercise, moving from long to short distances and testing the sight settings in table 5.1.

Table 5.1   Sight Adjustments

Yards	Sight setting
15	
20	
25	
30	
35	

TO INCREASE DIFFICULTY

- Move to 40 yards (37 m) and record your sight setting adjustment.

Success Check

- Move your sight down as you move back.
- Move your sight left or right as needed.
- Make sight corrections after shots with good form, not bad.

Score Your Success

Establish all five sight settings = 5 points

Establish four sight settings = 4 points

Establish three sight settings = 3 points

Establish two sight settings = 2 points

Establish one sight setting = 1 point

Your score _____

Adjusting Exercise 3   **Subtraction**

This exercise is done with a partner. Place an 80-centimeter (32 in.) target on the target butt. Each of you should place a piece of tape around the tail end of one of your arrows. Shoot six arrows from 30 yards (27 m), using your 30-yard (27 m) sight setting. On each of four ends, total your five unmarked arrows. Then, subtract the value of your marked arrow from your opponent's score. (A sample is shown in figure 5.8.) Record your scores in table 5.2.

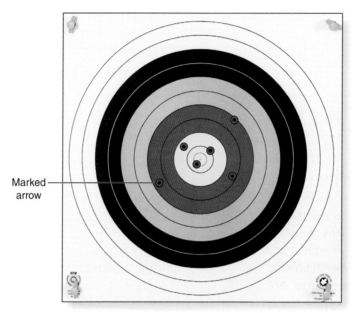

Marked arrow

Figure 5.8   Sample result of subtraction exercise.

Table 5.2   Scores for Subtraction Exercise

End	Total of five arrows	Minus points for marked arrow	Your points	Partner's points
1		–		
2		–		
3		–		
4		–		
Total				

TO INCREASE DIFFICULTY
- Shoot from 35 yards (32 m).

TO DECREASE DIFFICULTY
- Shoot from 25 yards (23 m).
- Use a larger target.

Success Check

- Align bowstring on every shot.
- Let sight aperture settle in bull's-eye.
- Focus on middle of bull's-eye.

Score Your Success

Outscore your opponent on three ends
= 3 points

Outscore your opponent on two ends
= 2 points

Outscore your opponent on one end
= 1 point

Your score _____

What Sport Science Says About Aiming

Sport researchers have addressed several aspects of aiming. One is the stability of the bow arm. If the bow arm is not steady, the aiming aperture will never settle on the target. Bow arm stability likely is related to a stable stance. Even if the bow arm is stable relative to an archer's trunk, the bow and sight move if the body sways. Two research studies looked at the relationship between bow arm stability and stance. We mentioned the Sarro, de Castro Viana, and Leite de Barros (2021) study in step 4. In addition to finding that smaller body sway was associated with more accurate shots, they found a correlation between body sway and bow arm movement. For the highest-scoring shots of their skilled archers, body and bow arm sway were synchronized and minimized during aiming. Quan and Lee (2016) attached accelerometers to the bodies and limbs of middle school archers. Accelerometers detect orientation; for example, an accelerometer autorotates the screen of your smartphone. The researchers recorded movement during the aiming phase of the shot. The arrows' accuracy was most affected by the motion of the forearm of the bow arm and the lower leg on the bow arm side. These research findings emphasize how important it is for archers to both establish a stable, consistent stance and use T-form that aligns the bow arm with the trunk for accurate shooting. This minimizes movement and allows the aiming aperture to settle on the target before release.

Researchers also studied the relationship between accurate aiming and a period of extended gaze fixation on the target, called the *quiet eye*. A group of researchers (Gonzalez et al. 2017) measured quiet eye durations in expert and novice archers while shooting and while playing an archery-like computer game. They measured eye movements by placing electrodes on the skin near the eye. In both cases, expert archers had longer gaze durations than novices. Likely, expert archers are maintaining focused attention on aiming. This suggests archers should quickly fix their gaze on their target and focus their attention on that target.

BAREBOW AIMING AND SIGHTING

As we said earlier, some archers enjoy the challenge of shooting without a bowsight, trying to hit their mark without an aid. Even though barebow or traditional archers do not use a bowsight, they still aim. Just as with sight shooting, archers shooting barebow must select a small aiming spot and maintain visual contact with this spot throughout the shot.

There are several methods that barebow archers can use to shoot accurately, even without a bowsight. One is known as gap shooting. After coming to full draw and settling into the shot, a gap shooter attends to the gap seen between the aiming spot on the target and the arrow tip. The closer the archer is to the target, the farther below the aiming spot the arrow tip is positioned, so the gap is relatively wide and below the aiming spot. As the archer moves away from the target, the gap narrows. At a certain distance, the aiming spot and arrow tip coincide. Moving even farther back means the arrow tip must be above the aiming spot, so the gap is above the aiming spot and widens as the archer continues to move farther from the target.

Some gap shooters learn to match the size of the gap between the aiming spot and the arrow tip to various distances. If they can accurately estimate their distance from the target, they can methodically adjust the gap to hit their mark.

The second barebow shooting method simply builds a feel for a shot based on experience and repetitive practice. Barebow shooters trust their bodies to have established the feel of a shot when they spot their target some distance away. You might hear archers call this instinctive shooting for this reason. Typically, barebow shooters using this method practice extensively at one distance, likely starting with a short distance, to establish this feel before moving to another distance.

Point-of-aim shooting is another barebow method. By trial and error, archers find a place, either on the target butt or on the ground (e.g., a stone or change in coloration of the grass), to aim the tip of the arrow at a given distance from the target. Something to consider about this method is that you are focusing on this point and not at all on the bull's-eye! That is, you are not aiming at the spot you want to hit, and some archers find this disconcerting.

Face walking and string walking are other common means of aiming without a bowsight. Remember that your anchor determines the position of the tail of your arrow and, consequently, the direction in which it is launched. Changing your anchor position up and down changes the direction in which the arrow is launched. With bowsight shooting, your anchor position should be as consistent as possible from shot to shot, but a barebow archer could intentionally change the anchor position, "walking" up or down his or her face, to systematically change the orientation of the arrow. This is known as face walking. Barebow archers using this method determine the anchor position on the face corresponding to a certain distance through practice. Face walking, of course, is not as accurate as sight shooting because it is difficult to find and use an exact anchor location for all possible distances. Nevertheless, many archers learn to shoot very well using this method.

Similarly, archers can vary the placement of their string hand on the bowstring but anchor in the same position. This also has the effect of changing the launch angle of the arrow; it is known as string walking. Most string walkers place all three fingers below the arrow rather than one above. Not only can they vary how far below the nocking point they set their string hand, but they can also count the wraps of serving on the bowstring to measure how far below the nocking point they set their hand. They place the tip of the arrow in the bull's-eye on every shot but determine through practice what string hand placement corresponds to a given shooting distance. Again, string walking is not likely to be as accurate as sight shooting, but archers who perfect the method can score very well.

Barebow Exercise 1   Gap Versus Instinctive Shooting

If you have a bowsight installed, remove the sight from your bow or remove the aiming aperture for this exercise. Shoot three ends of six arrows each from a distance of 10 yards (9 m), first by attending to the gap between your aiming spot (the center of the bull's-eye) and the arrow tip. At this distance, the gap likely will be below the aiming spot. Once you score well, try to reproduce the gap used on that shot on your subsequent shots. Record your score on each end. Then, shoot an additional three ends of six arrows, feeling your bow arm elevation and adjusting it from shot to shot based on your previous arrow. Record your score on each end, and then compare your scores to determine which method was more accurate.

TO INCREASE DIFFICULTY

- Add another set of three ends of six arrows each at 15 yards (14 m).

Success Check

- Maintain visual focus until arrow hits target.
- Keep bow arm up until arrow hits target.

Score Your Success

Shoot three ends with each barebow aiming method = 3 points

ANSWER KEY

ADJUSTING EXERCISE 1. SIGHT ADJUSTMENT PRACTICE

1. Down
2. Left and down
3. Up and right
4. Right
5. Up and left

SUCCESS SUMMARY

After learning to use a bowsight in this step, your shooting should be more accurate than before, especially at longer distances. Don't forget to update your mental checklist from step 3 for aiming and sighting with a bowsight. Consider the points for aiming and sighting listed in figure 5.5. Select cues from that list to add to your checklist. As you practice and some of these steps become habits, you can continue to refine your mental checklist.

Of course, simply having a bowsight does not mean that you will always hit the bull's-eye. Continue to refine your basic T-form. Make sight adjustments only after well-executed shots.

For each of the exercises in this step, enter the points you earned. Total your points to rate your success in learning to use a bowsight. If you have earned at least 19 points, you can move to the next step. Otherwise, repeat some exercises and earn additional points.

Installing Exercises

1.	Making a Simple Bowsight	_____ out of 3
2.	Installing a Peep Sight	_____ out of 2

Sighting Exercises

1.	Aligning and Aiming Mimic	_____ out of 3
2.	Aiming Mimic on a Three-Spot	_____ out of 3

Adjusting Exercises

1.	Sight Adjustment Practice	_____ out of 5
2.	Sighting In	_____ out of 5
3.	Subtraction	_____ out of 3

Barebow Exercise

1.	Gap Versus Instinctive Shooting	_____ out of 3
Total		**_____ out of 27**

While watching experienced archers, you might have noticed that they anchor in a different position than you have been using. The anchor position you learned in step 3 is a basic one, and many archers continue to use it. Other archers deviate from that position, sometimes because they find another position more comfortable and sometimes because of the type of archery they wish to perfect. In the next step to success, you will make one final adjustment in your shooting to put all of the basics in place to score well. You will decide on a preferred anchor position and whether you want to shoot with a mechanical release or continue to use your fingers to release the bowstring.

Anchoring and Releasing

To this point, you have been using an under-chin anchor point with a finger release. You certainly can continue to use this anchor position with a finger release, adapt it slightly, or change to using a mechanical release. Some equipment lends itself to the use of a mechanical release, and the type of archery you want to shoot might warrant a change to a release. A solid anchor position is important for release shooting, too.

The decision of whether to change your anchor and release can be determined by your body shape, the accessories you want to use, and the type of archery you wish to shoot—bowhunting, Olympic-style target archery, or professional target archery, for example. Keep this in mind as we review your choices, beginning with various anchor positions for finger shooters and moving on to various types of mechanical release aids.

The purpose of all anchor positions is consistency in both the draw length (which ultimately influences the amount of thrust imparted to the arrow and thus vertical accuracy) and left-to-right alignment in aiming (which ultimately influences horizontal accuracy). The more precise the anchor position, the better. Archers who draw but do not anchor on any part of their bodies cannot be sure they are aligned, either vertically or horizontally, the same way on every shot. Likewise, even if archers anchor on their faces or chins, if they let the anchor vary from shot to shot, they cannot be assured of accurate alignment.

In general, the more points on the face or neck the draw (string) hand and bowstring touch, the more precise the anchor position will be. There is a trade-off between establishing a very precise anchor and shooting quickly, such as in hunting or in difficult weather conditions like extreme cold. Additionally, the numbers and types of accessories archers wish to use—or are allowed to use by competition rules—can influence the anchor positions they use. Peep sights and kisser buttons are good examples. As a first step, we will learn how to install and adjust a kisser button to various anchor positions.

KISSER BUTTONS

A kisser button (figure 6.1), a small, plastic disk attached to the bowstring, is an inexpensive accessory that helps you position your anchor consistently from shot to shot. The kisser button is positioned on the bowstring so it is between your lips when you anchor—hence, its name.

If an archer tends to let the string hand float at full draw (that is, not come to an identical anchor position from shot to shot), the kisser button will not be aligned between the lips on each shot. The archer can adjust to align the kisser button and ensure a consistent anchor position from shot to shot.

Some archers tend to let the jaw drop on some shots rather than keeping the teeth together. If the string hand is anchored on or under the jaw, this results in the tail end of the arrow being higher or lower from shot to shot. A kisser button helps archers realize they have dropped the jaw on a shot because the button does not touch both lips.

You can install a kisser button now if you want to try it out or plan to shoot in a competitive classification that allows one and you believe it will help you. To position the kisser button properly, slide it onto the bowstring approximately 2 inches (5 cm) above the nock locator. Draw the string back until it touches your nose. Feel for the kisser button. Ease the string back. If the kisser button is above or below your lips, adjust it and draw again. Repeat these adjustments until the kisser button touches between your lips. You may then want to repeat coming to full draw several times, making sure you are using the anchor position you want. Once you are satisfied with the location of the kisser button, mark its place on your bowstring and record its distance from your nock locator.

In this step, you will experiment with anchor positions, which will require that you move your kisser button. Variations in anchor position or the use of a mechani-

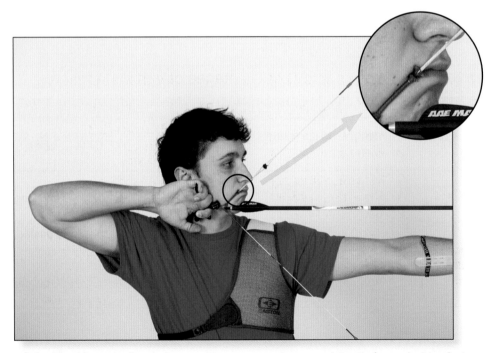

Figure 6.1   The kisser button helps position your anchor consistently from shot to shot.

cal release can affect the position of the kisser button. Once you have decided on the anchor position you will use from now on, you can clamp down the kisser button so it does not move. For a nominal cost, you can buy a small clamp that you can squeeze down over the end of the kisser button with a pair of nocking pliers.

Kisser Button Exercise 1   Installing a Kisser Button

Have your bow ready and obtain a kisser button. Adjust the position of the kisser button as explained previously. Now shoot three ends of five arrows each, and note how many times the kisser button is in the correct position when you first anchor.

Success Check

- Bowstring touches nose.
- Kisser button touches both lips.

Score Your Success

14 or 15 shots anchored correctly = 3 points

10 to 13 shots anchored correctly = 2 points

Your score _____

ANCHOR POSITIONS

Now we will review three general types of anchor positions (table 6.1). The first is the under-chin, low anchor position you have been using thus far. We will discuss this anchor position in more detail, along with a slight variation of it. The second is the side-of-face, high anchor position. Finally, we will consider the anchors used by archers who use mechanical releases.

Table 6.1 Advantages and Disadvantages of Various Anchors

Type of anchor	Advantages	Disadvantages
Under chin	• Multiple "touch points" • Prevents overdrawing	• Takes time to position • Less comfortable for some archers
Side of face	• Can be established quickly • Allows barebow archers to sight down arrow shaft	• Not as precise • Sometimes leads to plucking of bowstring
With mechanical release	• Very accurate • Allows elbow to be aligned with arrow at release	• Takes time to set and position • Scoring standards in competition are very high • Release aid must be adjusted and set for each person

Using the Under-Chin Anchor

The under-chin, low anchor position is probably the anchor most target archers use, but it may not be the one best suited for your body structure or the type of archery you prefer.

In the under-chin anchor, the string always touches the tip of the nose and the chin. The bowstring therefore crosses the mouth, offering archers the opportunity to use a kisser button if allowed and gain an additional touch point for this anchor. As mentioned earlier, the kisser button is positioned between the lips where the bowstring crosses the mouth. It is a good check against opening the jaw, which causes a vertical variation in the anchor position and the orientation of the arrow. Remember that the knuckles of the index finger on the draw hand touch the underside of the jaw.

There are two variations of the under-chin anchor. In one, the bowstring touches the tip of the nose, the center of the lips, and the center of the chin. Placing the string in the center of the chin necessitates tipping the head, which is an uncomfortable position for some archers. Archers with large hands or short necks sometimes find this version of the under-chin anchor difficult to use. Archers also need time to position this anchor, which is a disadvantage in bowhunting. It might be difficult to use a peep sight with this anchor, yet this can be a very precise anchor with three touch points centered on the face. Archers with relatively short arms sometimes prefer this anchor, and it does result in the shortest draw length any archer would use.

In the more popular variation of the under-chin anchor, archers bring the bowstring to the tip of the nose or sometimes slightly to the side of the nose, the mouth, and the side of the chin. Hence, the head can be more upright, and the draw hand can be tucked under the jaw more to the side of the neck (figure 6.2). If a kisser button is used, it is placed between the lips in the corner of the mouth. The precision of the touch points might not be quite as fine as with the centered version of the under-chin anchor, but using a peep sight with this version is easy, and most archers shooting in classifications that allow peep sights use them with this anchor position. This anchor position also results in a slightly longer draw length than with the centered version. Remember that a longer draw with a given bow, especially a recurve bow, provides a little more thrust.

Figure 6.2 **UNDER-CHIN ANCHOR**

Setup and Draw
1. Set a deep hook.
2. Keep back of hand flat and wrist relaxed.
3. Move draw elbow back.
4. Draw straight to face.

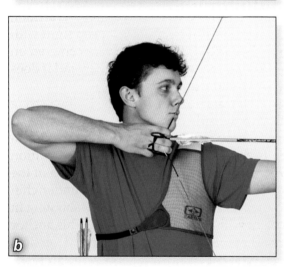

Anchor
1. Feel teeth together.
2. Touch string to nose and side of chin.
3. Touch kisser button, if used, to lips.
4. Keep draw hand firmly in contact with jaw.
5. Center target in peep sight, if used.

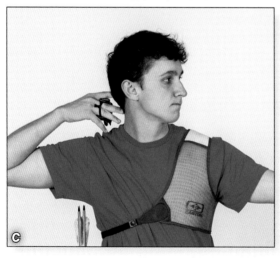

Release and Follow-Through
1. Aim.
2. Increase back tension.
3. Move elbow up and back (1/2 in., or 1.3 cm).
4. Allow explosion of release.
5. Maintain follow-through.

MISSTEP

You move your head forward to meet the bowstring.

CORRECTION

Keep your head erect, imagine T-form alignment, and bring the bowstring to your face for consistent shooting.

MISSTEP

You draw with your fingertips and have a cupped string hand.

CORRECTION

Set your string hand hook deep, at least in the first joint, and relax your hand to keep the hand and wrist flat.

A slight variation of this popular anchor position is to touch the string slightly to the side of the nose instead of the tip of the nose. This might be more comfortable for some archers, but it potentially sacrifices some precision in reproducing the draw length unless a draw check accessory is used.

With any anchor, your draw should be straight back in the plane intersecting the target, not out to the side and then back to your face. The anchor position should be firmly in contact with the face or jaw and identically positioned on every shot. Make the draw come to your face rather than tipping your head to meet your draw hand. When you use proper back tension, the follow-through of the release will always be back over the rear shoulder, no matter what type of anchor you use. Keep in mind that the rear position of the arrow influences the trajectory of the shot. Varying the trajectory by varying the anchor from shot to shot sends each arrow to a different place on the target. Once you select your anchor position, keep it and perfect it.

This is a good time to check your string hand hook. Set your hook so that the string is in the first joint of the fingers or even deeper. This will help you keep your hand and wrist flat (extended) and relaxed throughout the shot. Holding the string with your fingertips tends to cup the hand and put more tension in it. This typically causes more oscillation of the bowstring as it travels forward after the release. Go deeper to keep the back of the hand flat and relaxed. If you held the handle of a heavy briefcase in the first or second joints of your fingers, the weight would straighten your hand and wrist. This stretched, straightened position is what archers desire for their string hands. The more relaxed the hand, the better the bowstring clears the hand at release and the less the bowstring oscillates.

Most archers do not hold equally with all three fingers. They tend to hold either more with the top two fingers and lightly with the bottom or more with the bottom two fingers and lightly with the top. Don't worry about trying to hold equally with all three fingers. You can do whatever is most comfortable, but keeping your string hand relaxed is the key. As with all things in archery, it is important to do the same thing on every shot. The string hand hook should be set the same way on each shot, and the draw to anchor should be executed the same way on each shot.

What Sport Science Says About Releasing

The release is an important part of the archery shot because it can affect arrow flight. Archers commonly believe that the more smoothly the bowstring leaves the string hand and the less the bowstring is deflected as it rolls off the fingertips, the straighter the shot. There are two schools of thought on how archers should "make" the release happen. The first maintains that archers should relax the flexor muscles on the palm side of the hand and forearm. The second maintains that archers should both relax the flexor muscles and contract the extensor muscles on the back of the hand and forearm.

Researchers have examined the release to determine if one of these methods is associated with more accurate shooting than the other. They typically do this by placing an electrode on the skin over the underlying muscle to record electrical activity in the muscle via an electromyograph (EMG). A case study (Ertan et al. 2011) of an elite, world-top-20 archer documented her release as relaxation of the flexor muscles without involvement of the extensor muscles. The researchers also found that her release minimized bowstring deflection. Another study (Ertan et al. 2003) found that beginning and elite archers relaxed the flexor muscles and contracted the extensor muscles. A third study (Martin, Siler, and Hoffman 1990) recorded 15 skilled archers and found that eight archers used the first method (flexor relaxation only), while seven used the second (flexor relaxation and extensor contraction). It appears that archers use both methods, and neither has been linked to higher scores compared to the other. Researchers agree, though, that consistency is very important to accurate shooting regardless of which method of release is used (Horsak and Heller 2011). In *Steps to Success*, we urge beginning archers to keep the string hand relaxed throughout the shot. This minimizes the chance of making the common beginner error of pulling off or plucking the bowstring on release and causing a large deflection of the string.

Under-Chin Anchor Exercise 1   Mimicking With Eyes Closed

Work with a partner. Take only your bow and assume your stance, bow hand hold, and hook. Raise the bow and draw to an under-chin anchor with your eyes closed. Feel for the proper position, hold for a count of three while maintaining relaxed hands, and then ease the string back. This exercise establishes your feel for the proper anchor position. Repeat the draw and anchor 10 times, and have your partner look for consistency on every shot. (Your partner can use the Success Check as a guideline.)

Success Check

- Hook is deep.
- Head is erect.
- String touches nose.
- String touches chin.
- Kisser button, if used, is between lips.
- Draw hand is flat and relaxed.
- Index finger of draw hand is under jaw.

Score Your Success

10 repetitions with correct form = 5 points

8 or 9 repetitions with correct form = 3 points

6 or 7 repetitions with correct form = 1 point

Your score _____

Under-Chin Anchor Exercise 2   Sight-Setting Check

If you have made a slight change in your under-chin anchor, you need to check your sight settings. Start at 15 yards (14 m). Shoot until you attain an accurate sight setting. Move back to 20 yards (18 m), and then move back to 25, 30, 35, and 40 yards (23, 27, 32, and 37 m), shooting until you have an accurate sight setting. There is likely to be more difference in your setting at a longer distance than at a shorter distance.

TO INCREASE DIFFICULTY

- Add 45- and 50-yard (41 and 46 m) settings.

TO DECREASE DIFFICULTY

- Start at 10 yards (9 m) and stop at 30 yards (27 m).

Success Check

- Touch string to nose.
- Touch string to chin.
- Touch kisser button to lips.

Score Your Success

Attain new sight settings for 6 to 8 yardages (distances) = 3 points

Attain new sight settings for 5 yardages (distances) = 2 points

Your score _____

Using the Side-of-Face Anchor

Although the under-chin anchors are very precise, they do take time to position properly. Some archers prefer to anchor on the side of the face (figure 6.3). The common way to do this is to draw back to the side of the face and position the tip of the index finger in the corner of the mouth. The draw hand is thus tight against the face, providing a consistent "touch" on the face. Sometimes the thumb is tucked under the jaw. This anchor position can be set very quickly, which is why it is popular with bowhunters. A kisser button is not used, but a peep sight can be used.

Traditional-style archers also like this anchor position because the tail end of the arrow is right below the aiming eye. Barebow archers believe they can shoot more instinctively by sighting right down the arrow shaft (figure 6.3b; this barebow archer varies the position of his draw hand on the bowstring to accommodate various shooting distances). Recall that barebow archers do not use kisser buttons or peep sights.

Figure 6.3   SIDE-OF-FACE ANCHOR

Setup and Draw

1. Set deep hook.
2. Keep back of hand flat and wrist relaxed.
3. Move draw elbow back.
4. Draw straight to face.

Anchor

1. Feel teeth together.
2. Touch tip of index finger to corner of mouth.
3. Keep draw hand firmly in contact with face.

MISSTEP

You "pluck" the bowstring, flinging the fingers open and moving the string hand out from the face. Or you use a "dead" release, opening the fingers without increasing back tension, and allow the bowstring to move forward before it comes off the fingers.

CORRECTION

Concentrate on aiming and increase back tension so that the release is a surprise rather than anticipated. Keep the string hand relaxed so that the follow-through is a natural recoil of the string arm up and back.

The reminders about the draw and string hand hook discussed for the under-chin anchor apply to the side-of-face anchor as well. The draw should be straight back to the erect head with a deep string hand hook and relaxed hand. Set the draw hand and draw to anchor the same way on every shot.

To release, aim and increase back tension. Move the elbow up and back about 1/2 inch (1.3 cm). Allow the explosion of the release, and maintain the follow-through.

Side-of-Face Anchor Exercise 1   Mimicking With Eyes Closed

Work with a partner. Take only your bow and assume your stance, bow hand hold, and hook. Raise the bow and draw to a side-of-face anchor with your eyes closed. Feel for the proper position, hold for a count of three while maintaining relaxed hands, and then ease the string back. This exercise establishes your feel for the proper anchor position. Repeat the draw and anchor 10 times; your partner should look for consistency on each shot. (Your partner can use the Success Check as a guideline.)

Success Check

- Hook is deep.
- Head is erect.
- String touches nose.
- Tip of index finger is between lips at corner of mouth.
- Draw hand is flat and relaxed.

Score Your Success

10 repetitions with correct form = 5 points

8 or 9 repetitions with correct form = 3 points

6 or 7 repetitions with correct form = 1 point

Your score _____

Side-of-Face Anchor Exercise 2   Attaining New Sight Settings

If you are interested in switching to a side-of-face anchor position, you need to reestablish your sight settings. Start at 15 yards (14 m). Shoot until you attain an accurate sight setting. Move back to 20 yards (18 m), and then move back to 25, 30, 35, and 40 yards (23, 27, 32, and 37 m), shooting until you have an accurate sight setting. If you are using a new anchor, there is likely to be more difference in your setting at a longer distance than at a shorter distance.

TO INCREASE DIFFICULTY

- Add 45- and 50-yard (41 and 46 m) settings.

TO DECREASE DIFFICULTY

- Start at 10 yards (9 m) and stop at 30 yards (27 m).

Success Check

- Touch bowstring to nose.
- Place tip of index finger between lips at corner of mouth.

Score Your Success

Attain new sight settings for 6 to 8 yardages (distances) = 3 points

Attain new sight settings for 5 yardages (distances) = 2 points

Your score _____

Side-of-Face Anchor Exercise 3   Shooting Barebow

This exercise is for those who would like the experience of shooting barebow. Adjust the gap between the bull's-eye and the arrow tip, moving the bow arm as necessary, to shoot your arrows higher or lower. From a distance of 12 to 15 yards (11-14 m), shoot three ends of six arrows barebow and with a side-of-face anchor at a standard target face.

TO INCREASE DIFFICULTY

- Shoot from 20 yards (18 m).

Success Check

- Touch string to nose.
- Touch tip of index finger to corner of mouth.
- Sight down arrow shaft.
- Note gap between bull's-eye and arrow tip to adjust vertically.

Score Your Success

Improve your score over the previous end twice = 5 points

Improve your score over the previous end once = 3 points

Your score _____

Anchoring With a Mechanical Release

The obvious advantage of using a mechanical release is a cleaner release than can be achieved using the fingers. Rather than three fingers holding the string, a loop of rope, a metal pin, or a set of metal jaws (caliper-like) holds the string. The bowstring is less deformed than when held with three fingers and is released with much less interference than rolling off the fingers. The bowstring travels forward from a mechanical release with less oscillation, and therefore, the arrow travels forward more directly (see the Upgrading Equipment section in step 8 for a discussion of the archer's paradox). In archery events, separate classifications are formed for archers using finger releases and archers using mechanical releases because the expectation is that higher scores are possible when using a mechanical release.

Just as with a finger release, anchoring with a mechanical release must be consistent from shot to shot, which consistent contact on the face and jaw provides. With most mechanical releases, archers can anchor with the knuckles of the draw hand behind the jawbone and below the ear.

There are several types of mechanical releases, each with advantages and disadvantages. Each archer must find the release that works best for him or her. Some mechanical releases actually have a trigger (or two!) with some triggered by the index finger, some by the thumb, and some by the little finger. Others release the bowstring when the archer continues to use back tension to move the draw arm slightly. With some releases, the string hand is horizontal at anchor, palm down (figure 6.4), whereas with others, the hand is almost vertical, palm out (figure 6.5a). Archers pull some releases with two, three, or four fingers, and others with all five digits. Some releases have a wrist strap, and others do not.

When selecting a mechanical release, remember that back tension is as important with a mechanical release as it is with a finger release. Release shooters without good back tension tend to anticipate the release and begin to "punch" it, resulting in a jerky release and less-than-accurate results. They often are focused on making the release happen by triggering the release rather than focusing on aiming. For this reason, champion target archers often prefer mechanical releases triggered by back tension over trigger releases. Some archers can shoot a trigger release well, but certainly any archer who falls into the habit of punching a trigger release should consider changing to a back-tension release.

Back-tension releases typically consist of a half-moon cam that triggers the bowstring release when it is rotated under tension. A loop of rope is placed around the bowstring just under the nocked arrow and hooked around a pin on the release. Some archers tie a D loop, also called a string loop, onto the bowstring, one end above the nocking point and the other below it, and actually hook the release onto this D loop rather than directly around the bowstring (figure 6.4). Alternatively, the D loop can substitute for the nocking point with the arrow simply nocked between the two D loop knots.

To shoot with a back-tension release, grasp the release with a deep hook rather than with the ends of the fingers. Just as with a finger release, the string hand and wrist should be relaxed; grasping the release deep in the hand helps you stay relaxed. With the palm out at about a 45-degree angle to vertical, draw the string straight back to your nose; the back of the string hand should be firmly in contact with the side of the face, and the knuckles should be behind the jawbone. Most release shooters use a peep sight, and in addition to having the string touch the nose and corner of the mouth, they center the target in the peep sight to achieve a precise anchor position (figure 6.5a).

The release occurs by increasing back tension, which moves the string hand elbow up and back about 1/2 to 3/4 of

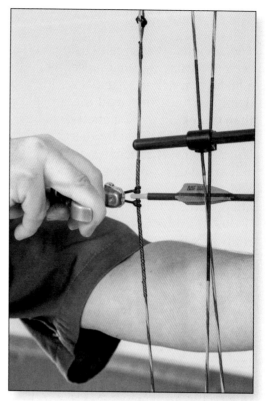

Figure 6.4 Mechanical release looped around the string loop (D loop) rather than around the bowstring.

an inch (1.3-1.9 cm). This rotates the cam and releases the bowstring. Archers often tend to rotate the handle of the release with their hands, but it is preferable to only squeeze the back muscles to rotate the cam.

Some back-tension releases are made with a pin or other device to keep you from accidentally triggering the release prematurely. You set up with the elbow slightly forward of perfect alignment with the target. You then rotate the handle of the release to activate it, increase back tension to move the elbow up and back, and consequently trigger the release with the elbow in perfect alignment. Obviously, you can adjust the "travel," or extent of cam movement, before release to achieve the proper positions. Back-tension releases overcome a tendency to punch releases with triggers. The back tension developed through the release allows the hand and release aid to follow through over the rear shoulder (figure 6.5b).

Figure 6.5 **ANCHOR WITH A MECHANICAL RELEASE**

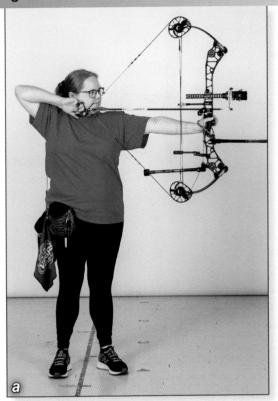

Setup and Draw

1. Attach release to bowstring.
2. Pull slightly to put release under tension.
3. Relax hand and wrist.
4. Move draw elbow back.
5. Draw straight to face.

Anchor

1. Feel teeth together.
2. Touch string to nose.
3. Touch kisser button, if used, to corner of mouth.
4. Place draw hand firmly in contact with jaw.
5. Center target in peep sight.
6. Activate back-tension release or preload trigger release.

Release and Follow-Through

1. Aim.
2. Increase back tension.
3. Allow explosion of release.
4. Maintain follow-through.

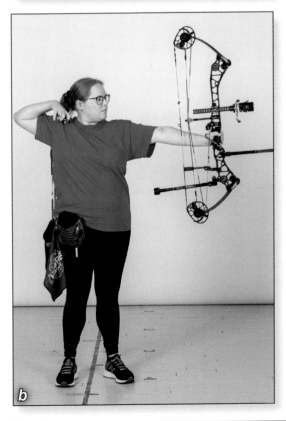

MISSTEP

You punch (jerk) the release.

CORRECTION

Punching comes from anticipating the release rather than maintaining total focus on aiming. Be sure that the release is set with minimal travel (movement to get the release to happen) because a long travel encourages you to anticipate release.

MISSTEP

You pull the bowstring tightly into your face at anchor.

CORRECTION

This misstep causes left-to-right oscillation of the bowstring as it moves forward and therefore causes left-to-right errors. You might have to adjust the rope on the mechanical release, the D loop, or your anchor so the bowstring lightly touches your nose and your draw hand contacts the side of your face or jaw.

Target archers achieve great consistency with back-tension releases because they prevent them from anticipating the release. A back-tension release, though, can be too slow and complicated for a bowhunter. Bowhunters often choose a caliper-type release that clamps directly onto the bowstring and has a trigger. Wrist straps prevent the release from being misplaced or dropped from a tree stand.

If you decide to use a trigger release, you can choose a model that is triggered with the thumb, index finger, or little finger. In all cases, set the release so that the trigger pressure required to release is firm, 3 to 7 pounds (1.4-3 kg), but the travel, or movement of the trigger to release, is very small. Triggers that are very light or have a long travel can lead archers to punch the release or anticipate when the release will occur. The result is arm, hand, or head movements on the release that influence the flight of the arrow and therefore the accuracy of the shot. With firm pressure, you can place your finger on the trigger and actually "preload," or partially deflect, the trigger. Once you aim and are committed to the shot, increasing back tension hinges the hand and moves the finger to bring about the release without anticipation.

Index-finger releases are often grasped with the palm down (figure 6.6). You should select a release that allows the wrist and hand to be straight and relaxed rather than bent. Ideally, the first crease of the index finger should be

Figure 6.6 An index-finger release is often grasped with the palm down.

on the trigger, so you must adjust the length of the release according to the size of your hand.

If you decide to change your anchor, use a mechanical release, or change from one release aid to another and perhaps change your anchor position as well, you will need to determine new sight settings. Anything that changes the position of the rear end of the arrow changes its orientation and trajectory in flight. As with finger shooting, consistency is important when shooting with a release. The mechanical release allows for very accurate shooting, so the scoring in the competitive classifications that allow a release is quite high. Shot-to-shot variations of any type or extent are costly to success!

Anchoring With a Mechanical Release Exercise 1
Mimicking With Eyes Closed

Work with a partner. Take only your bow, assume your stance and bow hand hold, and hook your release aid onto the bowstring. Raise the bow and draw to anchor with your eyes closed (figure 6.7). Feel for the proper position, hold for a count of three while maintaining relaxed hands, and then ease the string back. This exercise establishes your feel for the proper anchor position. Repeat the draw and anchor 10 times, and have your partner look for consistency on every shot. (Your partner can use the Success Check as a guideline.)

Figure 6.7 Mimicking an anchor position for a mechanical release with eyes closed.

Success Check
- Deep hook is used on release aid.
- Head is erect.
- String touches nose.
- Draw hand is flat and relaxed.

Score Your Success
10 repetitions with correct form = 5 points

8 or 9 repetitions with correct form = 3 points

6 or 7 repetitions with correct form = 1 point

Your score _____

Anchoring With a Mechanical Release Exercise 2
Adjusting Your Peep Sight

Most archers who shoot with a mechanical release also use a peep sight. Perhaps you have been shooting with a peep sight, but its position was set for an under-chin anchor with a finger release. It is likely that you will have to adjust the position of your peep sight for your anchor position with a mechanical release. Draw to anchor with your mechanical release and see if you can center the target in your peep sight. If not, untie the peep sight and install it again (see step 5). Then, draw to anchor up to five times, centering the target in your peep sight.

Success Check

- Set anchor position.
- Center target and sight aperture in peep sight.

Score Your Success

Five draws while successfully aiming through the peep sight = 3 points

Three or four draws while successfully aiming through the peep sight = 2 points

Your score _____

Anchoring With a Mechanical Release Exercise 3
Attaining New Sight Settings

If you have decided to shoot with a mechanical release, you need to reestablish your sight settings. Start at 15 yards (14 m). Shoot until you attain an accurate sight setting. Move back to 20 yards (18 m), and then move back to 25, 30, 35, and 40 yards (23, 27, 32, and 37 m), shooting until you have an accurate sight setting. If you are using a new anchor, there is likely to be more difference in your setting at a longer distance than at a shorter distance.

TO INCREASE DIFFICULTY

- Add 45- and 50-yard (41 and 46 m) settings.

TO DECREASE DIFFICULTY

- Start at 10 yards (9 m) and stop at 30 yards (27 m).

Success Check

- Hook release onto bowstring or D loop.
- Grasp release with deep hook.
- Keep hand and wrist relaxed.
- Touch string to nose.
- Touch back of draw hand to face.
- Center target in peep sight.

Score Your Success

Attain new sight settings for 6 to 8 yardages (distances) = 3 points

Attain new sight settings for 5 yardages (distances) = 2 points

Your score _____

SUCCESS SUMMARY

Anchoring is an important aspect of archery technique. A precise anchor helps you establish both horizontal and vertical consistency from shot to shot, whereas a variable anchor position leads to variable success! In anchoring, you'll want to establish as many touch points as practical for your body shape and size and the type of archery you are shooting.

No matter what anchor position you use and no matter whether you release with the fingers or with a mechanical release aid, certain features of the shot are the same. You will want to draw with the back muscles and maintain good back tension throughout the shot. Your attention should be on aiming; you need to trust that the release will come at the proper time. Anticipating the release typically gets you into trouble because you'll gradually and often subtly start moving during or even before the release.

For each of the exercises presented in this step, you can earn points to chart your progress. Enter your score for each exercise and add them up to rate your success. If you earned 25 points or more, move to the next step. If you did not, repeat the exercises for the anchor position you anticipate using from now on. If you chose not to use a mechanical release and earned 17 points, move to the next step.

Kisser Button Exercise

1. Installing a Kisser Button	_____ out of 3

Under-Chin Anchor Exercises

1. Mimicking With Eyes Closed	_____ out of 5
2. Sight-Setting Check	_____ out of 3

Side-of-Face Anchor Exercises

1. Mimicking With Eyes Closed	_____ out of 5
2. Attaining New Sight Settings	_____ out of 3
3. Shooting Barebow	_____ out of 5

Anchoring With a Mechanical Release Exercises

1. Mimicking With Eyes Closed	_____ out of 5
2. Adjusting Your Peep Sight	_____ out of 3
3. Attaining New Sight Settings	_____ out of 3
Total	_____ **out of 35**

You now have all the pieces of the shooting puzzle. You can continue to practice and to improve your scoring. Like all athletes, though, you need a way to monitor your performance and identify the errors that gradually come into every athlete's performance. Moreover, you need a guide for correcting errors to once again achieve good form and get back on the road to high scoring. In step 7, you will learn to detect and correct errors.

Analyzing Performance

Some of the most famous people in sports have been coaches: Andy Reid in football, Patty Gasso in softball, and Jim Boeheim in basketball, for example. Such coaches are known for helping their athletes reach their full potential. Like any other athlete, archers also benefit from coaching. An archery coach can note flaws in shooting technique and suggest corrections. Unfortunately, archery coaches are not as plentiful as football, baseball, and basketball coaches. For this reason, perhaps more than other athletes, archers benefit from detecting and correcting their own errors.

Archers rely on two sources of information for correcting performance mistakes: They analyze where their arrows land in relation to the bull's-eye where their shots are aimed. That is, they analyze the outcome of their performance. They also check their technique—their actual positions and movements—by evaluating the feel of their shots or watching videos of their techniques. Successful archers, no matter what type of archery they shoot, learn how to check their own shooting and make adjustments to their techniques. The technology available today even makes this evaluation fun!

Any archer would probably seize the opportunity to work with a good coach. Even archers lucky enough to have a coach, though, spend many hours shooting without coaches when practicing, competing, or hunting. The sooner an error can be corrected, the better. Remember that most types of archery involve repetitive shooting. Archers who can quickly adjust their techniques to overcome mistakes will score more consistently than those who cannot.

ANALYZING ARROW PATTERNS

You can use two basic methods to monitor errors that may develop in your shooting. The first is to observe the result of your performance. In archery, this method involves an analysis of the pattern your arrows form on the target face. Form errors can cause consistent directional errors. For example, if several arrows in each of your ends land to the right of your other arrows, that pattern may indicate one of several shooting flaws. If you make repeated bowsight corrections and your arrows still land to the right of the bull's-eye, you can consider a number of shooting flaws that lead to right arrows as the cause.

Arrows land in the bull's-eye if they are both vertically and horizontally accurate. Repeated errors in technique result in a consistent directional error easily shown by the pattern of the arrows on the target face. If you make the same error frequently but not on every shot, perhaps once in each end with one arrow landing away from the rest, you will be reminded of the error and will need to continue monitoring that aspect of your shot execution. Consistent directional errors also can be related to equipment. In step 8, you will learn how to adjust your equipment to eliminate directional errors caused by equipment setup.

To help describe shot locations, the target face is often compared to a clock face as you view it from the shooting line. Arrows landing to the right of the bull's-eye, for example, are described as three o'clock errors. Arrows landing right and slightly high are called two o'clock errors, and so on. Obviously, you should analyze only well-aimed shots. If you aim a shot at six o'clock and it lands at six o'clock, there is no need to look for errors in technique!

Horizontal Patterns

Performance errors that affect horizontal accuracy generally include horizontal movements of the bow or bow arm, misalignment of the bowstring and bowsight, misalignment in addressing the target, and releases that give the bowstring too much horizontal movement or oscillation (figure 7.1). Horizontal bow movements can occur as a result of the following:

- Canting (tilting) your bow
- Moving the bow to the right or left when you release the bowstring
- Allowing your bow arm wrist to break upon release
- Holding the bow handle to the side

Many archers are so anxious to see their arrows hit the target that they move the bow sideways upon release. To avoid making this mistake, make sure you use your back muscles to draw, keep your arms in alignment with the target, center your bow arm behind the center of the bow handle, and follow through in T-form. Misalignments of the bowstring and bowsight often occur when the archer varies the anchor position, changes the eye that aligns the bowstring and bowsight from shot to shot, or varies the pattern of alignment between the bowstring and the bowsight from shot to shot.

Because the arrow is snapped onto the bowstring, changing the position of the bowstring in relation to the aiming aperture changes the orientation of the arrow to the bull's-eye from shot to shot. To avoid these misalignments, use a consistent anchor, use at least the tip of the nose as a touch point for the bowstring, and establish a consistent bowstring and bowsight visual pattern from shot to shot. The preferred bowstring and bowsight pattern is to see the string just to the right of the aiming aperture. A peep sight automatically gives you a consistent pattern, but it is prohibited in some competition classifications.

Misalignments in addressing the target usually affect the accuracy of the shot because muscles on one side of the body are working harder than those on the other side. The tensed muscles tend to cause horizontal movements upon release, especially as you tire. When addressing the target, establish a solid base of support with your stance without using a very open or closed position and keep your body aligned to the target by drawing the bowstring close to the bow arm with the back muscles. Also, avoid bows with a draw weight so heavy that you need additional movements to get to full draw.

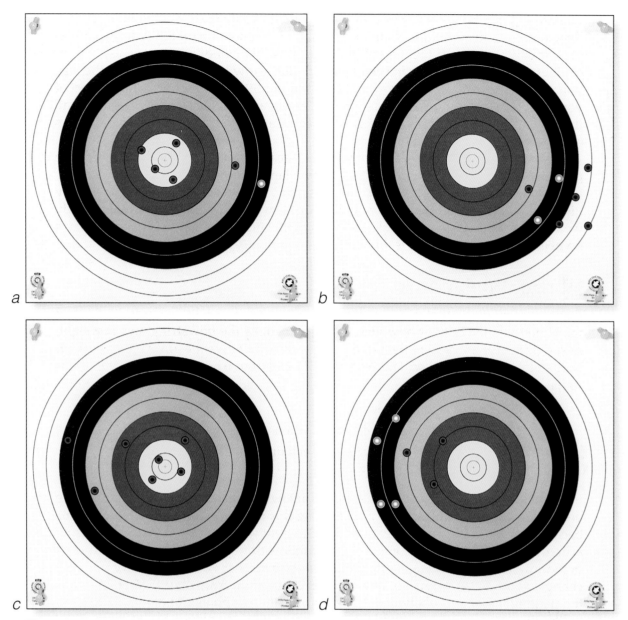

Figure 7.1 Horizontal arrow patterns: *(a)* Some arrows land in and near the bull's-eye, whereas others land at three o'clock; *(b)* arrows group at three o'clock; *(c)* some arrows land in and near the bull's-eye, whereas others land at nine o'clock; *(d)* arrows group at nine o'clock.

Releases that give the bowstring unnecessary horizontal movement affect accuracy because they send the tail of the arrow farther to the side than necessary. Remember that the arrow remains in contact with the bowstring for most of its path forward. The release most likely to cause horizontal errors is plucking the string, which means that the hand flies away from the face rather than recoiling over the rear shoulder. Arrow flight also is affected if you nock the arrow backward so that the index feather strikes the arrow rest or bow window or if the bowstring catches on clothing or jewelry as it moves forward.

Vertical Patterns

Performance errors that affect vertical accuracy (figure 7.2) include the following:

- Moving your bow arm up or down upon release
- Varying your anchor position vertically
- Varying the pressure of the fingers on the bowstring
- Holding the bow too high or too low on the handle
- Deviating from T-form
- Varying your effective draw length

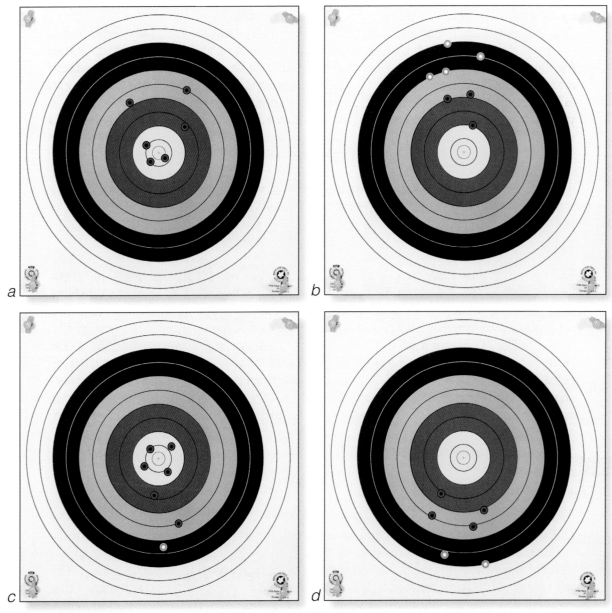

Figure 7.2 Vertical arrow patterns: *(a)* Some arrows land in and near the bull's-eye, whereas others land at twelve o'clock; *(b)* arrows group at twelve o'clock; *(c)* some arrows land in and near the bull's-eye, whereas others land at six o'clock; *(d)* arrows group at six o'clock.

Dropping or raising the bow arm on release can affect the tail end of the arrow as it clears the bow. Always follow through by continuing to push the bow arm to the bull's-eye until the arrow hits the target.

Varying the anchor position vertically orients the arrow differently from shot to shot. Beginning archers often anchor with the mouth open and vary how wide the mouth is open with each shot. Avoid this error by keeping your teeth together on every shot. Varying the pressure of the three fingers on the bowstring also changes the orientation of the arrow. Releases that cause vertical errors are those in which the wrist rotates up or down so that the pressure of the upper or lower finger lessens just before release.

Holding the bow at the same location on the handle on every shot minimizes vertical errors. Holding the handle too high or too low is likely to cause you to move the bow when you release the bowstring. For example, you could heel the bow with the base of the palm and tilt the bow backward as a result.

Deviating from T-form can also contribute to vertical errors, especially if you hunch the front shoulder, slide the hips forward, tilt the head forward or backward, or lean forward or backward. These form errors contribute to vertical bow arm movement and variation in the effective draw length. Even small variations in draw length can affect vertical accuracy by changing the thrust imparted to the arrow. For example, if your arrows land at six o'clock, you may be moving your draw hand slightly forward at release (creeping), bending the bow arm, tilting the head forward, or punching (moving forward) when triggering a mechanical release.

Maintaining T-form and using the back muscles to draw prevent these deviations. Increasing back tension during the aim and then releasing the bowstring by relaxing the fingers produces the most consistent draw and release.

Mixed Patterns

Several situations could result in arrow patterns of mixed vertical and horizontal errors, such as ten o'clock or four o'clock errors. An archer may make multiple errors, some causing vertical errors and some causing horizontal errors. Such a pattern also results from moving the bow arm diagonally rather than just vertically or horizontally.

If your arrows form a mixed pattern, make sure you maintain a loose grip on the bow and continue to push the bow arm straight to the bull's-eye throughout the aim, release, and follow-through. If your arrows still form a mixed pattern, look for errors that affect both horizontal and vertical accuracy. For example, if your arrows land at four or five o'clock, look for errors that cause a right horizontal error and a low vertical error.

MISSTEP

Some of your arrows group around the bull's-eye, and some land at nine o'clock.

CORRECTION

Develop a relaxed bow hand (see the exercises in step 4). When the bow hand grip is tight, you tend to flex the fingers upon release, an action that turns the bow handle. With a relaxed bow hand grip, the bow is free to jump slightly forward upon release and not affect the arrow either horizontally or vertically. Using a bow sling can help prevent you from feeling as though you have to hold the bow so that it will not fall.

MISSTEP

Your arrows spread from twelve o'clock to six o'clock.

CORRECTION

Check your anchor position to be sure it is consistent. Check your head position to be sure you draw to your face rather than push your head forward to meet the string. Changes in your anchor can change your draw length and impart varying thrust to the arrow from shot to shot.

Arrow Pattern Exercise 1   *Analyzing Arrow Pattern*

Shoot several ends from 20 yards (18 m). Before pulling your arrows, plot each arrow's location with an X in figure 7.3. When you finish, look for your most common directional errors. Using the clock face terminology, record where your errant arrows landed. Then identify several potential causes of your errors. Shoot several more ends, and try to avoid the errors you identified. Plot these ends on additional targets to see whether you have eliminated or reduced directional error.

a   *b*

Figure 7.3   Plot arrow locations for each end shot.

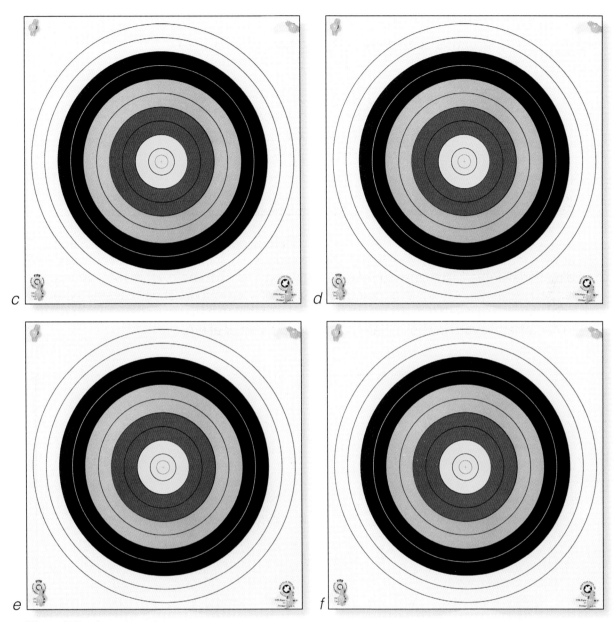

Figure 7.3 *(continued)*

Success Check

- Maintain T-form.
- Establish consistent bow hand and anchor positions.
- Follow through to target.

Score Your Success

Identify at least two causes each for two directional errors = 3 points

Identify at least two causes for one directional error = 2 points

Identify one cause for one directional error = 1 point

Your score _____

Arrow Pattern Exercise 2
Analyzing Arrow Pattern From a Distance

Directional errors often become more noticeable as you shoot from longer distances. Once directed off center, the arrow continues over a longer distance on a line that results in its landing farther from the bull's-eye.

Shoot several ends from 30 yards (27 m). Before pulling your arrows, plot each arrow's location with an X in figure 7.4. When you finish shooting and plotting, look for your most common directional errors. Using the clock face terminology, record where your errant arrows landed. Then identify several potential causes of your errors. Shoot several more ends, and try to avoid the errors you identified. Plot these ends on additional targets to see whether you have eliminated or reduced directional error.

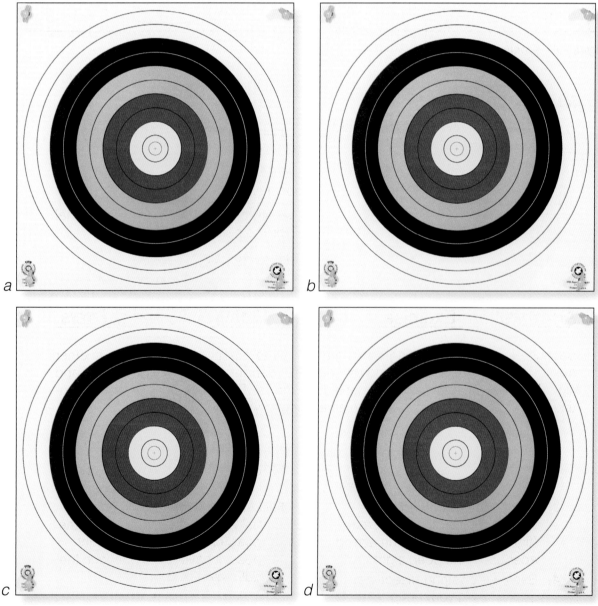

Figure 7.4 Plot arrow locations for each end shot.

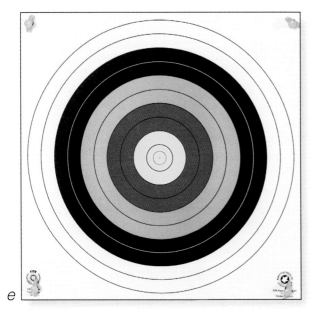 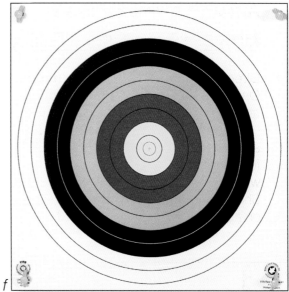

Figure 7.4 *(continued)*

Success Check

- Align stance and shoulders toward target.
- Maintain T-form by drawing with back muscles.
- Stand erect.

Identify at least two causes each for two directional errors = 3 points

Identify at least two causes for one directional error = 2 points

Identify one cause for one directional error = 1 point

Your score _____

Arrow Pattern Exercise 3   Checking Aiming and Sighting Errors

Because aiming and sighting errors are difficult to detect by observation, another method is required. The following list could be your mental checklist for aiming and sighting. Shoot an arrow, and then look down the list. Did you forget any items? Continue shooting until you can execute an entire end without forgetting a step.

1. Visually acquire your aiming spot.
2. Close your dominant eye if it's not on the same side as your string hand.
3. Line up the bowstring just to the right of the aiming aperture (figure 7.5), or center the aiming aperture in the peep sight.
4. See the bowstring bisect the bow limbs in your peripheral vision (or check the bubble in the level).
5. Exhale before aiming and releasing.
6. Let the bowsight settle on the bull's-eye before you release the bowstring. Note that the sight doesn't have to stop dead in the bull's-eye.

(continued)

111

Arrow Pattern Exercise 3   *(continued)*

 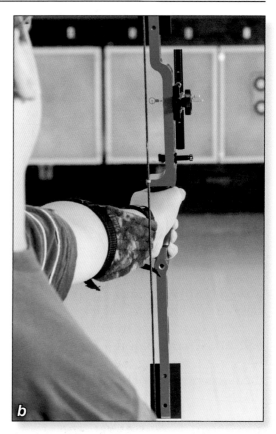

Figure 7.5   Aiming errors: *(a)* bowstring too far to the right of the aiming aperture; *(b)* bowstring too far to the left of the aiming aperture.

Success Check

- Establish consistent string and sight pattern.
- Allow sight to settle on bull's-eye before release.

Score Your Success

Complete your entire mental aiming and sighting checklist within six arrows = 3 points

Complete your entire mental aiming and sighting checklist in seven or more arrows = 1 point

Your score _____

ANALYZING TECHNIQUE

The second method for checking performance is to observe your technique. Observe your stance, draw, anchor, hold, release, and follow-through for alignment, consistency, and proper execution. You can identify technique errors in your shooting by examining videos or pictures of yourself or asking a knowledgeable friend to observe. Watch carefully for T-form in back and front views. Watch for alignment along a line straight to the target in views from behind, looking downrange. You also may be able to feel yourself making a technique error, although archers often do not realize how they are positioning their bodies and limbs.

Errors That Affect Horizontal Accuracy

Many technique errors that cause horizontal errors are detected by positioning a phone with video capabilities on a tripod uprange below the intended flight of the arrow (figure 7.6*a*) or an observer behind the archer, viewing downrange (figure 7.6*b*). From this angle, check for positions or movements that cause horizontal variations in arrow flight (without an arrow nocked!):

- The body leans right or left, perhaps following through in that direction upon release.
- The shoulders are angled downrange (not in proper T-form).
- The bow tilts right or left.

Sometimes a rear view from a location above the archer is helpful in detecting these flaws in technique (figure 7.6*b*). Extend your tripod, or have your observer stand carefully on a ladder.

A few aspects of form that affect horizontal accuracy can be observed in close-ups of the bow hand (figure 7.6*c*) and of the face and draw hand. Watch for slight variations in establishing the anchor position, such as touching the bowstring to the tip of the nose on one shot but the side of the nose on another.

Figure 7.6 HORIZONTAL ACCURACY

Downrange View
1. Stand erect.
2. Keep bow vertical.
3. Keep string hand and wrist relaxed.
4. Use back muscles.

(continued)

Figure 7.6   *(continued)*

Overhead View
1. Align shoulders toward target.
2. Increase back tension.

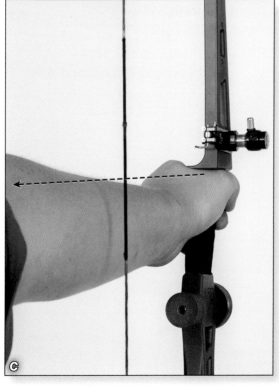

Close-Up of Bow Hand
1. Align bow hand behind bow handle.
2. Relax bow hand.

Errors That Affect Vertical Accuracy

Technique errors that cause vertical errors are most often detected by an observer or video recording with a phone on a tripod positioned along the shooting line and facing the front of the body (figure 7.7*a*). An ideal setting would have vertical and horizontal references in the background so that deviations from T-form can be easily identified. From this perspective, check for these positions or movements that cause vertical variations in arrow flight:

- The shoulder line is uneven.
- The body leans toward or away from the target.
- The hips slide forward and the upper body tilts back.
- The bow arm moves up or down upon release.
- The anchor position varies from shot to shot.
- The bow hand grip varies from shot to shot.
- Finger pressure varies from shot to shot.

Zoom in on the string or bow hand to see whether its position varies from shot to shot (figure 7.7*b*). A person also can stand behind you as you're shooting to observe your form by looking at your back (figure 7.7*c*).

Figure 7.7 VERTICAL ACCURACY

Front View
1. Keep bow arm up.
2. Keep finger pressure on bow-string even.
3. Use consistent anchor.

Figure 7.7   *(continued)*

Close-Up of Bow Hand

1. Use consistent bow hand grip.

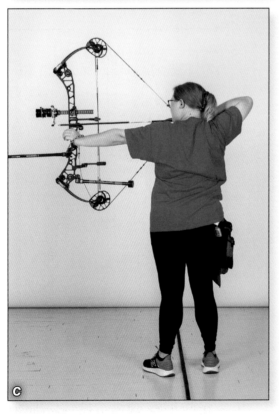

Back View

1. Stand upright.
2. Keep draw length consistent from shot to shot.

MISSTEP

You come out of T-form during the draw, aim, or follow-through.

CORRECTION

Use a bow with a draw weight that you can control without losing T-form. Many flaws in T-form are the result of archers shooting bows that are too heavy in draw weight. Because of the heavy draw weight, they cannot draw with just the back muscles, so they recruit other muscle groups. Be sure to maintain alignment of the limbs and trunk instead of moving the arm, shoulder, and trunk joints or pushing the bow arm while pulling with the string hand (the push–pull draw). Also, avoid an extremely open or closed stance.

MISSTEP

Your alignment varies from shot to shot.

CORRECTION

Use a consistent anchor position. Align the string and bowsight consistently, or use a peep sight if rules allow it.

Technique Analysis Exercise 1

Checking Errors in Vertical Alignment

Place a phone on a tripod about chest high and 10 feet (3 m) along the shooting line from your shooting position so that a video recording provides the view shown in figure 7.8. If possible, suspend a sheet or canvas with vertical and horizontal lines from a coatrack behind you. Record at least 10 shots. Watch the video after each shot and look for errors in body alignment that would affect the arrow vertically, such as those shown in figure 7.9. Compare your alignment with the vertical and horizontal lines on the sheet. Try to correct any errors in alignment by your 10th shot. Record additional shots if necessary to achieve good alignment.

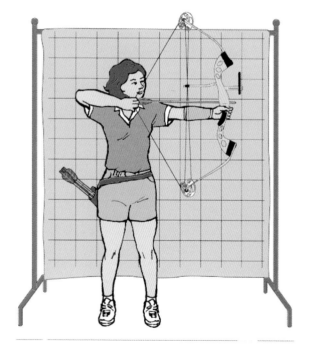

Figure 7.8 Having vertical and horizontal lines behind you will help you identify and correct errors in technique.

(continued)

Technique Analysis Exercise 1   *(continued)*

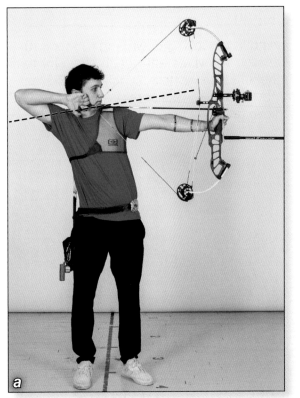 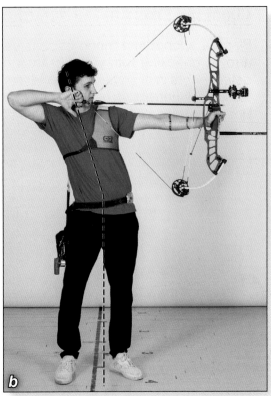

Figure 7.9   Vertical alignment errors: *(a)* front shoulder hunched; *(b)* hips sliding, upper body tilted.

 TO INCREASE DIFFICULTY

• Video the last 10 shots of a 60-shot practice session. Remember that form tends to break down as you tire, yet the last arrow counts just as much as the first in competition.

Success Check

• Keep shoulders level.
• Stand erect.
• Keep bow arm up.

Score Your Success

Correct alignment within 10 recorded shots = 5 points

Correct alignment within 15 recorded shots = 3 points

Correct alignment within 20 recorded shots = 1 point

Your score _____

Technique Analysis Exercise 2
Checking Errors in Horizontal Alignment

Place a phone on a tripod or observer behind you, looking downrange. Shoot 10 arrows, checking with your observer or watching the video after each shot. Try to detect errors in alignment that would affect the arrow horizontally, such as an uneven stance or incorrect T-form (figure 7.10). Attempt to correct those errors within 10 shots. Record additional shots if necessary to achieve good alignment.

Figure 7.10 Horizontal alignment errors: *(a)* upper body bent or twisted (not in good T-form); *(b)* stance misaligned; *(c)* shoulders not aligned to target.

TO INCREASE DIFFICULTY

- Video the last 10 shots of a 60-shot practice session.

Success Check

- Align stance and shoulders toward target.
- Maintain T-form by drawing with back muscles.
- Stand erect.

Score Your Success

Correct alignment within 10 recorded shots = 5 points

Correct alignment within 15 recorded shots = 3 points

Correct alignment within 20 recorded shots = 1 point

Your score _____

Technique Analysis Exercise 3   *Checking Anchor Variations*

Video record five shots from the same position as in technique analysis exercise 1, except zoom in or move the tripod to record a close-up view of your anchor position and release. Watch the video after each shot to detect incorrect anchor positions or variations in your anchor position. Look especially for the flaws shown in figure 7.11. If you find errors in your anchor position, review step 6 and develop a mental checklist to remind yourself to position your anchor consistently. If necessary, record additional shots to see whether you become more consistent.

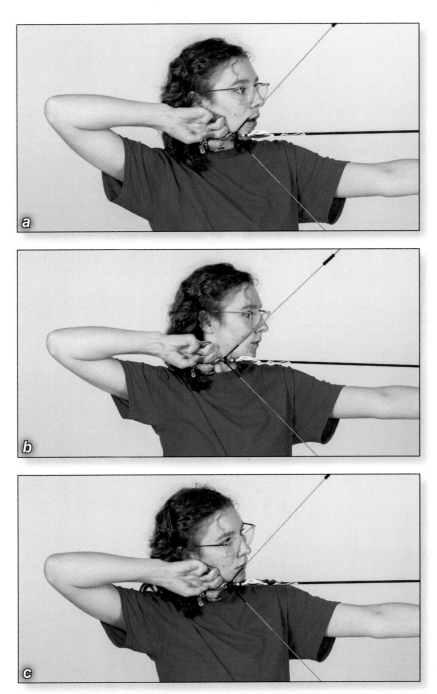

Figure 7.11   Anchor position errors: *(a)* mouth open, anchor lowered; *(b)* string drawn past nose; *(c)* head rotated or tilted.

TO INCREASE DIFFICULTY

- Record your anchor position for 30 shots.

Success Check

- Touch string to nose.

Technique Analysis Exercise 4   Checking Errors in Release

Use your video from technique analysis exercise 3, but examine your release. Compare your technique with the ideal of relaxing the string fingers (or triggering your mechanical release) and the hand following through over the rear shoulder. Errors might involve plucking the string, creeping, or dropping the elbow of the string arm (figure 7.12). Additional errors might include a dead release or punching a mechanical release. Record additional shots to improve your release as needed.

Figure 7.12   Release errors: *(a)* plucking the string rather than relaxing the fingers; *(b)* the string hand creeping forward before the release; *(c)* dropping the elbow of the string arm.

(continued)

Technique Analysis Exercise 4 *(continued)*

TO INCREASE DIFFICULTY

• Record your release for 30 shots.

Success Check

• Increase back tension.
• Relax fingers.

Score Your Success

Correct your release errors within 5 recorded shots = 3 points

Correct your release errors within 10 recorded shots = 2 points

Correct your release errors within 15 recorded shots = 1 point

Your score _____

Technique Analysis Exercise 5 Checking Errors in Bow Hand

Video record five shots from the same position as in technique analysis exercise 1, except zoom in or move the tripod to record your bow hand. You could also work with a partner. Watch the video or consult with your partner after each shot. The bow should jump forward slightly upon release, and the fingers should remain relaxed. If you find that you grab the bow, heel it (figure 7.13*c*), or turn it upon release, review step 4 to work on a relaxed bow hand. Also, watch the time period before release to ensure that your wrist position does not change during the draw and aim. Record additional shots to monitor your improvement.

TO INCREASE DIFFICULTY

• Record the last 10 shots of a 60-shot practice session.

Success Check

• Align bow arm and hand behind handle.
• Relax fingers.

Score Your Success

Correct errors in bow hand within 5 recorded shots = 3 points

Correct errors in bow hand within 10 recorded shots = 2 points

Correct errors in bow hand within 15 recorded shots = 1 point

Your score _____

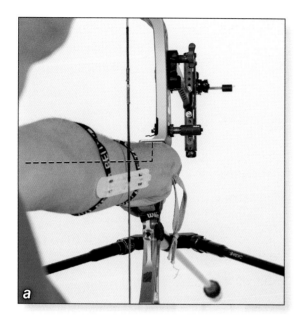
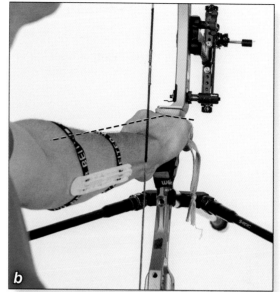
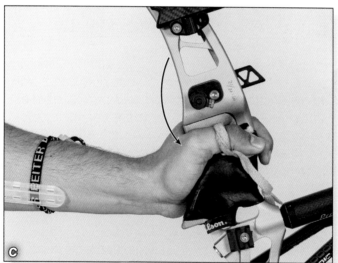

Figure 7.13 Bow hand errors: *(a)* wrist hyperextended; *(b)* wrist flexed; *(c)* heeling the bow.

Technique Analysis Exercise 6   Checking Errors in Draw

Video record five shots from the same position as in technique analysis exercise 1, and then watch the video or work with a partner after each shot. Analyze your draw. Identify errors such as those pictured in figure 7.14. Ideally, your bow arm is extended throughout the draw, and your draw comes all the way to your anchor position. After you identify any draw errors, record additional shots and analyze them to achieve a consistent draw.

(continued)

Technique Analysis Exercise 6   *(continued)*

 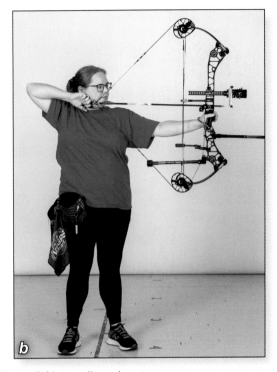

Figure 7.14   Draw errors: *(a)* not going to full draw; *(b)* bow elbow bent.

TO INCREASE DIFFICULTY

* Record the last 10 shots of a 60-shot practice session.

Success Check

* Extend bow arm to target.
* Touch string to nose.

Score Your Success

Correct draw errors within 5 recorded shots = 3 points

Correct draw errors within 10 recorded shots = 2 points

Correct draw errors within 15 recorded shots = 1 point

Your score _____

Technique Analysis Exercise 7

Checking Errors in Follow-Through

Video record 15 shots from the same position as in technique analysis exercise 1, and then watch the video or work with a partner after each shot. Analyze your follow-through. Identify errors such as those pictured in figure 7.15. Ideally, your bow arm should be extended throughout the draw and follow-through. When you release the bowstring, your head and bow arm should maintain their positions, and you should maintain T-form. After you identify any errors in follow-through, record additional shots and analyze them as necessary to eliminate your errors.

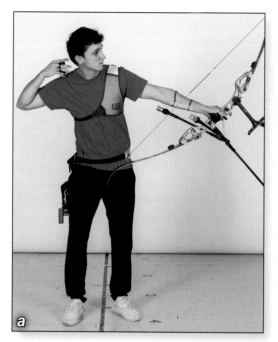
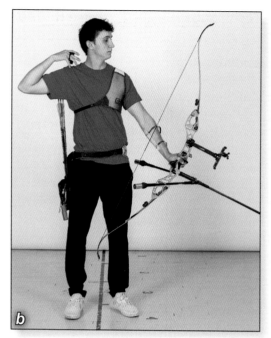
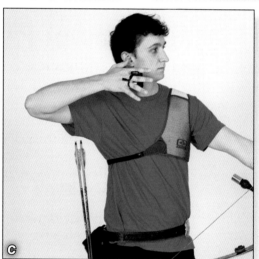

Figure 7.15 Follow-through errors: *(a)* peeking at the arrow after release; *(b)* dropping the bow arm after release; *(c)* plucking the string.

TO INCREASE DIFFICULTY

- Record the last 10 shots of a 60-shot practice session.

Success Check

- Maintain head position upon release.
- Bow arm extends to target even after release.

Score Your Success

Correct errors in follow-through within 5 recorded shots = 3 points

Correct errors in follow-through within 10 recorded shots = 2 points

Correct errors in follow-through within 15 recorded shots = 1 point

Your score _____

How Sport Scientists Analyze Performance

This step demonstrates easy ways to analyze your performance. With just a phone and tripod, archers can analyze their T-form, anchor, release, and follow-through. This equipment is more than sufficient for novice archers. Sport scientists, in contrast, often want to study elite archers with sophisticated research equipment. They focus on minute details to identify the factors that make a small difference in scoring, such as the extent of body sway or eye movements, which could mean finishing in or out of the medals in international competition. This information also can identify the important factors in an archery shot for novice archers.

In previous steps, we identified some of the tools used by sport scientists to study archery performance. We discussed force platforms used to measure an archer's weight distribution, weight shifts, and extent of sway during a shot. We learned that sport scientists use accelerometers to record limb and trunk movement and electrodes placed near the eye to record eye movements. To learn the sequence and timing of muscle contractions associated with accurate shots, electrodes are also placed over muscles, especially those in the arms and hands, to mark when muscles contract or relax.

OVERCOMING TARGET PANIC

Target panic is the anticipation of the release of the bowstring, which disrupts a smooth release and follow-through. If archers anticipate release, they begin to move the head, arms, or hands before the follow-through. With time, the movement can begin closer and closer to the time of release. Eventually, the movement might occur at or even before the release of the bowstring and influence the flight of the arrow and the accuracy of the shot.

Target panic varies in severity and frequency, but most archers who shoot long enough eventually have one or more of its symptoms:

- Flinching is any sudden movement immediately before or during the release, often of the bow arm, that affects the clearance of the arrow as it leaves the bow.
- Punching refers to jerking a mechanical release to release the bowstring.
- Plucking the bowstring or creeping forward toward the target when using a finger release is a sign of target panic.
- Snap shooting means releasing immediately when the sight aperture crosses the bull's-eye and before the sight has settled on the bull's-eye. This tendency might progress to the point that release occurs even before the sight aperture gets to the bull's-eye.
- Freezing is the inability to move the sight aperture from a spot off the bull's-eye to the bull's-eye (or, in hunting, to the kill zone). Freezing can also refer to the inability to release even when the aperture is settled on the bull's-eye or the inability to move the arrow through the clicker, a device that promotes an increase in back tension (see step 8).

Remember, you can have more than one symptom of target panic. As the symptoms progress, you might struggle to shoot well. Shooting then becomes a frustration, and it is tempting to stop shooting altogether. More than any other reason, target panic causes many archers to leave the sport.

One cause of target panic is trying to control every aspect of the shot (especially trying to make the release happen at a particular time) when you should be devoting attention to aiming. It is a classic case of not being able to do two things at once and do them well. Through repetitive practice, athletes progress from conscious control of every aspect of a skill to an automatic stage at which well-practiced movements are carried out subconsciously. For example, you do not have to think about alternately swinging your legs and planting your feet when you walk. Archers ideally devote conscious attention to aiming and relegate the execution of the release to the subconscious. When archers let their conscious attention switch back to making the release "happen"—and happen at a specific time—over time they begin anticipating the release, and then target panic can develop.

Your goal as a new archer should be to consciously control your stance, draw, and anchor. Once you are anchored and in the position you want to be in, commit to executing the shot (figure 7.16). Begin to increase your back tension; then switch your attention to aiming. Focus on the center of the target and trust your body to take the sight aperture there. It takes three to four seconds to develop sufficient back tension to release, so continue to focus on the center of the target and let your release occur as a natural consequence of increasing back tension.

Figure 7.16 **SUBCONSCIOUS RELEASE**

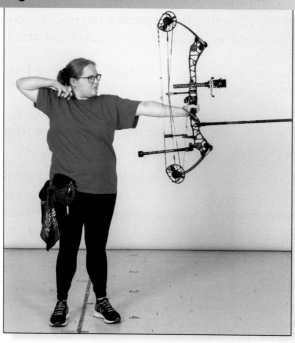

1. Assume stance and nock arrow.
2. Place the release or fingers on string.
3. Set bow hand.
4. Draw to anchor.
5. Check position; if OK, commit to shot.
6. Begin increasing back tension.
7. Aim.
8. Allow release explosion to occur.
9. Maintain position to the follow-through.

MISSTEP

On the release, you move (flinch, creep, pluck, punch). You freeze the sight aperture off the bull's-eye, or you release when the aperture first approaches the bull's-eye without settling.

CORRECTION

Practice shots with your conscious attention on aiming only. Try rotational aiming as described in target panic exercise 1. If you cannot overcome target panic this way, reprogram your shot (see target panic exercises 2 and 3).

Pellerite (2001) suggests that archers with target panic reprogram a subconscious release through two practice phases designed to rebuild the shot sequence. The first phase involves practicing on a blank bale or target butt at a short distance (5 yd, or 4.6 m)—that is, with no target of any kind. This type of practice also can be done with a bow simulator. During this time, you must suspend participation in all tournaments or leagues in which scoring occurs. There should be no shooting at a scoring target! Target panic exercise 2 is based on this phase of reprogramming.

The second phase of the Pellerite program is equally important. It serves as a bridge back to shooting at a target. It begins with shooting at a very short distance to a large target and progresses very gradually back to a longer distance and a smaller target. Target panic exercise 3 is based on this phase. It is important to refrain from using shortcuts; go back to the previous yardage (distance) for three days if any symptom of target panic returns.

If you notice the symptoms of target panic, the best course of action is to begin the target panic exercises that follow. The sooner, the better! Symptoms tend to worsen, so the sooner you can address them, the sooner you can get back to enjoyable scoring.

Target Panic Exercise 1   Rotational Aiming

Place a handful of dot stickers randomly on a target face. Being careful to execute your shot sequence, draw and aim at one of the stickers from 5 to 10 yards (4.6-9 m) away. Hold for four to six seconds, and then let down. Rest; then draw again and aim at another sticker. Continue until you have aimed at each of the stickers. The more you repeat this exercise, the better; it is especially helpful when practiced at the first symptoms of target panic. If you have target panic, you would benefit from doing this exercise 30 to 60 times a day for three weeks.

Success Check

- Draw, anchor, and check position.
- Focus on target.
- Aim.

Score Your Success

Aim at each sticker three times ("ends") = 3 points

Aim at each sticker twice = 2 points

Aim at each sticker once = 1 point

Your score _____

Target Panic Exercise 2   **Blank Bale Program**

This exercise is based on the first phase of Pellerite's reprogramming. Take your equipment to shoot at a bale or target butt with no target face from a distance of 5 yards (4.6 m). Shoot 30 to 60 shots per day for a minimum of 21 days. Shoot with your eyes open. Be sure to execute your shot sequence correctly (i.e., make good shots even though you are not scoring).

Success Check

- Check position; if OK, commit to shot.
- Increase back tension.

Score Your Success

Complete the blank bale program = 5 points

Your score _____

Target Panic Exercise 3   **Bridge Program**

This exercise is based on the second phase of Pellerite's reprogramming. Place a 9-inch (23 cm) diameter paper plate on the target butt. From a distance of 5 yards (4.6 m), shoot 30 to 60 shots per day for at least three days. Don't worry about hitting the middle of the plate. Shoot one arrow at a time, pulling that arrow after the shot. Next, move back 2-1/2 yards (2 m) and decrease the size of the paper plate's diameter by 1 inch (2.5 cm). Shoot another 30 to 60 shots per day for at least three days. Continue this pattern until you reach 20 yards (18 m). If at any time a symptom of target panic returns, move back to the previous yardage (distance) and larger plate and repeat the three days of practice.

Success Check

- Commit to shot.
- Increase back tension.
- Aim and let release occur.

Score Your Success

Complete the bridge program = 5 points

Your score _____

SUCCESS SUMMARY

Errors in technique affect horizontal accuracy, vertical accuracy, or both. You can avoid horizontal deviations in your shots (also called three o'clock and nine o'clock errors) by maintaining bow and string alignment. Watch for these causes of horizontal errors:

- Canting the bow
- Moving the bow sideways on release
- Breaking your bow wrist on release
- Holding the bow to the side of the center of the handle
- Misaligning the bowstring with the sight aperture
- Taking a stance that is not aligned to the target

You can avoid vertical deviations in your shots (also called twelve o'clock and six o'clock errors) by keeping T-form, keeping your draw length consistent, and following through. Possible causes of twelve o'clock vertical errors are raising the bow arm upon release, opening the mouth and therefore lowering the anchor, and overdrawing. Possible causes of six o'clock errors include dropping the bow arm, creeping, and not coming to a full draw. Diagonal errors, such as eight o'clock and four o'clock errors, can indicate that you are making multiple technique errors that are affecting both horizontal and vertical accuracy.

Repeat the exercises in this step periodically. Detecting and correcting your errors early can minimize the chance that they will become bad habits. Enter your score for each exercise to monitor your progress. Add up your scores to rate your success. If you have 33 or more points, go on to the next step. If you did not do the target panic exercises, go to the next step if you have 24 or more points. If not, repeat some of the exercises to earn additional points.

Arrow Pattern Exercises

1. Analyzing Arrow Pattern _____ out of 3
2. Analyzing Arrow Pattern From a Distance _____ out of 3
3. Checking Aiming and Sighting Errors _____ out of 3

Technique Analysis Exercises

1. Checking Errors in Vertical Alignment _____ out of 5
2. Checking Errors in Horizontal Alignment _____ out of 5
3. Checking Anchor Variations _____ out of 3
4. Checking Errors in Release _____ out of 3
5. Checking Errors in Bow Hand _____ out of 3
6. Checking Errors in Draw _____ out of 3
7. Checking Errors in Follow-Through _____ out of 3

Target Panic Exercises

1. Rotational Aiming _____ out of 3
2. Blank Bale Program _____ out of 5
3. Bridge Program _____ out of 5

Total _____ **out of 47**

With the completion of this step, you have covered the basic techniques of shooting. If you have been practicing and becoming a more proficient shooter, it may be time to maximize the contribution of your equipment setup to your scoring. One way to do this is to upgrade your equipment. Better equipment is generally more consistent and more forgiving of errors in technique. Another way that equipment can help you score better is through proper adjustment to provide smoother arrow flight. Smoother flight also is more forgiving of errors in technique. In step 8, you will learn what you should look for in upgrading your equipment and then how to adjust it so that it makes the best contribution possible to your score. You also will consider what you need to do to keep your equipment in good working order.

Upgrading, Tuning, and Maintaining Equipment

What percentage of accurate shooting is due to the archer, and what percentage is due to equipment? This question would keep any two archers in debate for a long time, especially if they tried to attach exact numerical percentages to each. In general, though, if every archer had a good set of matched arrows, beginning archers' technique would have more impact on accuracy than their equipment would; skilled archers would benefit relatively more from equipment that is adjusted for their technique; and expert archers would have such good technique that they could shoot accurately with almost any contemporary archery setup. Archers at all levels depend on their equipment, but particularly at this point in your climb up the steps to success, you can benefit from good equipment adjusted for your technique.

In this step, we consider three aspects of archery equipment. First, we review upgrades you can make to your equipment. Perhaps you have been refining your archery technique with basic equipment but now realize you would like to pursue archery activities more seriously. You need to know what equipment to upgrade and how to be a critical consumer of archery accessories. Second, we cover the process of adjusting, or tuning, your archery equipment so it operates efficiently, given your unique body structure, shooting style, and technique. Finally, we cover the maintenance you should perform to keep your equipment in good working order.

UPGRADING EQUIPMENT

You know the saying, "You get what you pay for." Why is this true in archery? Equipment that's made of good materials and has the latest technological advances performs more consistently than cheaper equipment. Like shooting form, archery equipment must be consistent. At the same time, it is important to be a critical consumer and recognize when and if an equipment purchase benefits shooting performance. Someone will always want to sell you the latest magic bow that can't miss its mark or the latest accessory that instantly makes you a champion. Remember that form is the biggest factor in the beginning and intermediate phases of learning to shoot.

Arrows

Good arrows are so important to accurate shooting that it is often said that if you give a skilled archer a choice between high-quality arrows and a basic bow or basic arrows and a high-quality bow, the archer would choose high-quality arrows and a basic bow. Good arrows are the foundation of an equipment setup that maximizes scoring, so a matched set of quality arrows should probably be your first significant upgrade in equipment. The best arrows are those that are consistent in the degree to which they bend when stressed. This bendability is called spine.

To appreciate why spine is so important, you must understand how an arrow clears the bow when you release the bowstring. First, consider what happens to the bowstring when a finger shooter releases it. Even with the cleanest release, the bowstring rolls off the archer's fingertips and finger tab, sending it slightly in toward the archer as it moves forward. It then rebounds away from the archer and next moves slightly toward the archer as it reaches brace, or string, height—the distance between the bow (measured at the pivot point) and the string when the bow is strung. The string, being attached to the limbs, reaches its limit of forward movement and reverses direction, moving slightly away and then oscillating at brace height (figure 8.1).

The arrow is attached to the bowstring at release, so the nock end of the arrow moves toward the archer with the bowstring. At the same time, the full forward force of the bow's stored energy is transferred through the string to the arrow. The point end of the arrow, resting against the bow, pushes against the bow. The bow resists this push. The arrow's center is free to bend between the two pressure points. It first bends slightly to the right of a direct line to the target for a right-handed archer (figure 8.2). As the arrow continues forward, the center of the shaft bends to the left in an equal and opposite reaction to the first bend. The shaft is bending around the bow handle at this point. Just as

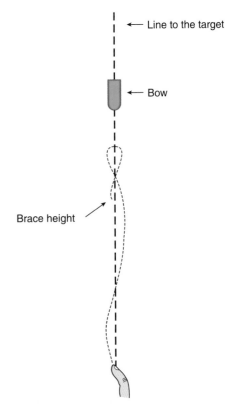

Figure 8.1 String path after release.

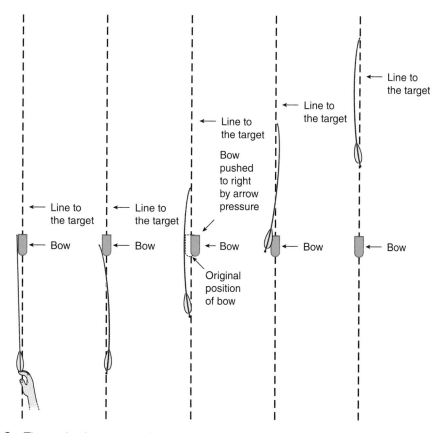

Figure 8.2 The archer's paradox: how an arrow clears the bow.

the fletching approaches the bow handle, the shaft bends to the right once more and moves the fletching away from the arrow rest and bow handle. In effect, the arrow bends around the bow without touching it. This action is referred to as the archer's paradox. The arrow continues toward the target, alternately bending right and left in decreasing amounts until it straightens out about 10 yards (9 m) in front of the bow and flies on line to the target.

In light of how they clear the bow, arrows must have two qualities. First, the spine must be just right for your draw length and bow weight so that the arrow fletching clears the bow handle without contact. Second, every arrow you shoot must have the same spine. Arrows do not group unless their spines are identical, no matter how good your form is.

When an archer shoots with a mechanical release, the deflection of the string to the side is negligible, so the arrow bends vertically rather than horizontally. The alternate vertical bending or cycling of the arrow still necessitates matching arrow shafts to equipment. The arrow's fletching must still clear the arrow rest and handle riser without contact. Therefore, release shooters also need consistent arrows that are matched to their equipment setups.

CHOOSING ARROW SHAFTS

Historically, arrows were made of wood. It wasn't until the 1950s that archers widely adopted fiberglass shafts. Fiberglass shafts allow for various degrees of spine, and archers are better able to select a spine that matches their setup. Easton made the first aluminum arrows in 1946, and by the 1970s, serious archers routinely chose aluminum arrows. Aluminum offers more possibilities to match the arrow spine to an individual archer's setup, plus a range of nocks and arrow tips can be used on aluminum shafts. Today, wood and fiberglass arrows typically are used only in youth programs, although aluminum arrows also are used in youth programs and for beginning archers.

For serious archers, aluminum, carbon, or aluminum–carbon hybrids are today's arrows of choice. You can be very selective with these materials in matching the arrow spine to draw length, bow weight, point weight, and for compounds, cam type. If you would like to compete, you should upgrade to arrows designed for your type of competition. The exception, of course, would be if you are a traditional archer and want to use wood arrows.

Aluminum arrows are often the choice for many target archers and hunters. They provide a good balance between cost and performance. Aluminum shafts are available in several alloys. The more expensive varieties are the strongest and do not bend on impact as easily as others do. Aluminum arrows generally are durable and easy to maintain, and they can withstand more impact from other arrows than carbon arrows can. If bent, aluminum arrows can be straightened. For indoor shooting at short distances and when many arrows are shot at one bull's-eye, aluminum shafts are a good choice. Nocks, fletching, and tips are easily changed on aluminum shafts.

Some target archers select all-carbon arrows. They are stronger than aluminum arrows and can be made in smaller diameters, so they are fast and forgiving. Carbon is strong and stiff, so all-carbon arrows do not bend as much as aluminum ones do. However, they must be consistently inspected for damage because they can shatter when they fail, creating sharp splinters. They *must* be discarded when damaged. Also, the epoxies used to mount nocks and tips or inserts and fletching make a change in setup more difficult.

Many types of aluminum–carbon hybrid arrows are available. These can have a carbon core and aluminum outer casing or an aluminum core with a carbon casing of various thicknesses. Archers shooting in outdoor target events with long distances, such as Olympic-style events, often use hybrids. These arrows are made of strong carbon fiber bonded to aluminum core tubes. A popular shaft is barreled; the middle is a little less than 1/4 inch (0.6 cm) in diameter, and the ends are just over 1/8 inch (0.3 cm) in diameter. The result is a lighter (less than 3/4 oz, or 21 g), stiffer arrow that is faster (140-145 mph, or 225-233 km/h) than an aluminum arrow and less susceptible to crosswind effects. Because the shaft is light, smaller fletching can be used to stabilize it, helping to minimize contact with the arrow rest or handle riser.

In some situations, archers put a priority on the diameter of an arrow shaft. Many 3-D target shooters and release shooters who shoot at multispot targets (one arrow in each end per minitarget) prefer large-diameter arrows. Such arrows are more likely to cut the lines on a target and score at higher values. Fat shafts are available in carbon, making them relatively light despite their diameter. Because multiple arrows are usually not shot at the same target, damage to the carbon is minimized. As mentioned previously, target shooters faced with the challenge of shooting outdoors at long distances usually prefer thin shafts to minimize the effect of wind on arrows in flight.

There is a wide range in the cost of arrows. More expensive arrows are made with a manufacturing process that makes the type or model of each arrow identical to others of that type or model, whether they are made on the same day or a year later. If you are still perfecting your technique, aluminum arrows are a good choice. When you advance to high-level competition, the more expensive carbon or carbon hybrid arrows provide the type of performance you need.

Hunters have the same range of choices in arrow shafts as target archers do, and hunters use all of the shaft materials described earlier. As the number of setups for hunting bows has increased, the number of possibilities for arrows has also increased. Hunting brings additional factors into the choice of arrow. Hunting arrows must accommodate the weight of broadheads, which do a good job of penetrating game. There are many trade-offs. For example, a smaller and lighter arrow is faster and likely to be more accurate, whereas a heavier arrow penetrates game better. We discuss the advantages and disadvantages of hunting arrow setups in step 11.

High-quality arrows usually provide many choices of nock styles (figure 8.3) and tip styles. Today, many arrows, especially carbon and hybrid arrows, use nock inserts. An advantage of inserts over the tapered or swaged ends of aluminum shafts is the precise alignment of a nock that can be obtained with an insert. The insert also minimizes damage from the rear impact of another arrow to the arrow shaft. Wooden and fiberglass arrows do not allow for this wide range of choices.

Tips are sometimes mounted directly into the shaft and sometimes mounted on an insert (figure 8.4). Arrow manufacturers recommend a range of tip weights for given arrow shafts. The archer then decides on a weight within that range. Some tips are break-off styles that allow archers to easily change the tip weight. If you shoot light poundage, long distances, or both, you should start with a lighter tip weight. Tungsten tips are denser than stainless steel tips. Tungsten tips also shift the weight of the arrow forward, which is advantageous in windy conditions.

Remember that all your arrows need to be the same weight, and they should be identical in weight distribution. Some archers adjust the percentage of an arrow's total weight that is in the front half of the arrow. This weight distribution shapes an arrow's trajectory. At shorter distances and indoors, this adjustment is not significant, so only archers shooting very long distances tend to experiment with front-of-center adjustments. Tip weight is the chief means of adjusting this distribution. Again, wooden and fiberglass shafts do not allow for various tip styles.

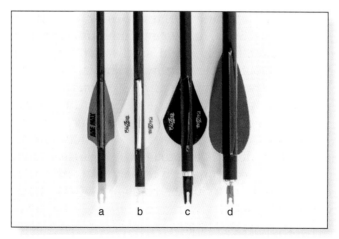

Figure 8.3 Various nock and fletching styles. Note that nocks can be attached directly to the swaged end of an aluminum arrow, inserted directly into the shaft, or attached to an insert or bushing.

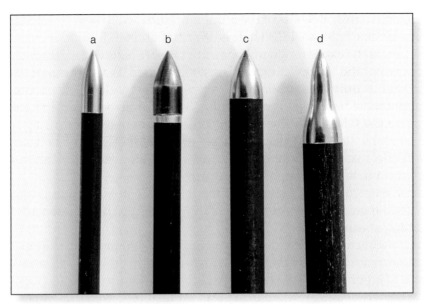

Figure 8.4 Various arrow tip styles. Note that *(b)* is a screw-in tip, and you see the lip of the insert between the shaft and the tip.

Arrow shafts are typically shipped at a long length and need to be cut to the appropriate length. It is better to have a pro shop do this with the proper cutting tools than to try it yourself. Some shops include cutting in the purchase price of a dozen arrows.

SELECTING ARROW SIZE

In addition to having arrows that are uniform in spine and weight, you need arrows matched to your draw length and to your bow's draw weight, which also reflects your draw length. Compound bow archers also need to consider their bow's speed rating. To select the best arrow size for you and your equipment, you need to first know how arrows are sized and marked for that size. Then, you need to know how to read an arrow spine chart or how to enter your specifications into an online arrow selector.

The size of an arrow shaft is printed on the side of the shaft. Arrows are tubes that vary in material, diameter, shape, and wall thickness. Both diameter and wall thickness determine spine. Table 8.1 is a guide to reading target arrow shaft sizes. As you can see, aluminum arrow shafts are labeled with a four-digit number. The first two numbers indicate the outside shaft diameter, measured in 64ths of an inch. The second

Table 8.1 Arrow Shaft Sizes

Type of arrow	Shaft marking	Key
Aluminum	4-digit number	• First two digits: shaft diameter in nearest 64ths of an inch • Second two digits: wall thickness in thousandths of an inch
Carbon and aluminum–carbon	3- or 4-digit number	• Deflection in thousandths of an inch (spine) of a 28 in. (71 cm) shaft

two numbers give the thickness of the aluminum tube wall, measured in thousandths of an inch. For example, an 1813 shaft is 18/64 of an inch in diameter and 13/1,000 of an inch in wall thickness. Generally, a stiffer arrow is recommended as bow draw weight increases, and a heavier arrow is recommended as arrow length increases.

Carbon and aluminum–carbon arrows are usually marked with a three- or four-digit number that represents spine deflection. For example, a carbon arrow marked 500 deflects, or bends, 0.500 inch when placed on supports 28 inches (71 cm) apart with a 2-pound (1 kg) force applied to its midpoint. Generally, the lower the number, the more appropriate the shaft is for a heavier draw weight. An alternative marking convention is to print the range of appropriate draw weights, so a 4565 arrow is acceptable for bows between 45 and 65 pounds (20 and 30 kg). To be sure you understand what the size marking on an arrow means, go to the arrow shaft manufacturer's website to read about the specifications.

Arrow manufacturers provide arrow spine charts listing one or more shaft sizes and types for a given bow draw weight, arrow length, bow speed rating, and point weight. You can obtain one of these charts from the manufacturer or from an archery pro shop. They are usually available on the manufacturer's website. Most manufacturers now provide arrow selectors online so you can enter your personal information (e.g., arrow length, bow weight, bow speed rating, point weight) to obtain a list of recommended shaft sizes. Keep in mind that such tables or selectors provide only a guideline. Sometimes the unique qualities of bow and archer result in an arrow selection other than the recommended one, but unless you have a specific reason for varying, stick with the sizes recommended.

Even though you can use an arrow selector online, learning how to read an arrow spine chart helps you understand the principles behind the changes in arrow shaft as factors such as arrow length and draw weight change. Let's consider how you select your arrow size from an arrow spine chart.

First you need to know the length of arrow you require. To determine arrow length, add 1/2 to 3/4 inch (1.3-1.9 cm) to your draw length, or draw an extra-long arrow and have someone mark 1 inch (2.5 cm) in front of the farthest point forward of where the arrow contacts the arrow rest. If you are using a clicker, keep in mind that your arrow length must allow for the use of the clicker. The clicker must strike the handle riser to make a sound, so arrows must be cut so that the clicker is on the arrow tip at full draw. Some handle risers can be fitted with extensions for the clicker to allow a slightly longer arrow. Bowhunters sometimes need extra arrow length to accommodate a broadhead (see step 11).

Some bows, especially compounds, feature C-shaped handle risers that curve away from the archer. This places the arrow rest closer to the archer than with a straight handle riser, allowing the archer to use a shorter and therefore lighter arrow. Before this feature was incorporated into bow designs, some archers mounted attachments called overdraws to their bows. These overdraws included arrow rests on an extension toward the archer. Hence, they also achieved the goal of allowing a shorter arrow. Archers using bows of the C-shaped design or overdraw attachments should determine arrow length by drawing a long arrow and marking 1 inch (2.5 cm) in front of the rest rather than adding to draw length, especially if the preference is to shoot a short and light arrow.

Table 8.2   Condensed Aluminum Arrow Spine Chart

Compound bow peak draw weight (lb)*	27 in. arrow length		28 in. arrow length		29 in. arrow length		Recurve bow draw weight (lb)
35-40	T4		T5		T6		36-40
40-45	T5		T6		T7		40-44
45-50	T6		T7		T8		44-48

T4		T5		T6		T7		T8	
Size	Shaft type	Size	Shaft type	Size	Shaft type	Size	Shaft type	Size	Shaft type
650	A/C	600	A/C	550	A/C	500	A/C	450	A/C
660	C	660	C	600	C	550	C	500	C
1913	75	1914	X7	2013	75	2212	75	2212	X7
1914	X7	1916	75	2014	X7	2114	X7, 75	2213	X7, 75

Sample columns selected from the Easton arrow selection chart, 2020, www.eastonarchery.com. *Note*: X7 and 75 refer to aluminum alloys; C is carbon; A/C is aluminum–carbon.

*Assumes use of release aid and bow speed rating of 301 to 320 feet per second (FPS).

Table 8.2 is a small portion of an Easton target arrow selection chart. The columns of the chart are arrow lengths, and the rows are peak draw weights. Here, we are just looking at the recommendations for a few arrow lengths and for a recurve bow or compound bow with a speed rating of 301 to 320 feet per second (FPS). A complete chart would include a larger range of arrow lengths, compound bows with other speed ratings, and various point weights.

Depending on which bow you use, you can locate the row corresponding to your draw weight and then read across to arrow length. In the box at the intersection of draw weight and arrow length is a reference to a group of arrow spine sizes. For example, if you are shooting a recurve bow with a draw weight of 38 pounds (17 kg) and your arrows need to be 27 inches (69 cm) long, you would read along the first row to the 27-inch arrow column. This tells you to choose one of the shaft sizes in group T4. Below the first chart, you can see that group T4 includes shaft sizes 1913 and 1914 in aluminum, 650 in aluminum–carbon, and 660 in carbon.

It is typical to have a choice of several spine sizes and aluminum alloys, carbon, and aluminum–carbon shafts. The price of the arrows depends in part on the type of shaft you choose. Recall that you can obtain a complete chart from the arrow manufacturer, the manufacturer's website, or an archery pro shop.

You can see from the arrow spine chart that, generally, a stiffer arrow is recommended as bow draw weight increases and a heavier arrow is recommended as arrow length increases. There is a risk of bow breakage if arrows are too light for a bow, so you should also check charts for the minimum recommended arrow weight for your type of bow and poundage.

SELECTING ARROW ACCESSORIES

Once you have selected your arrow shaft, you then must decide what type of nock, tip, and fletching to use. All modern nocks should be snap-on nocks. A snap-on nock lightly holds the arrow on the bowstring and minimizes the chances of a dry-fire (releasing the string with the arrow having slipped off). However, the nock should not be too tight, especially with light-poundage bows. Test nocks by holding your bow horizontally and snapping an arrow onto the string so that it hangs down. Tap the string an inch or two (2.5-5 cm) from the arrow. The arrow should fall off. If it does not, change the nock size or the thickness of the center serving on your bowstring.

Most carbon and hybrid arrow shafts require an insert or bushing to which the nock is attached; the nocks are not bonded directly to the shaft. Aluminum arrows often have a tapered or swaged end to which the nock is directly cemented. When you become skilled enough to shoot tight groups of arrows, you will likely break nocks by hitting arrows already in the target. You want an arrow setup that makes it easy to replace nocks. Later in this step, we consider how to replace a broken nock.

You also can vary the weight of the arrow tip you use. Most archers experiment to find the best tip weight. A heavier tip results in a heavier arrow weight, but heavier tips are usually more effective than lighter tips in crosswind conditions. A heavier tip also makes an arrow stiffer in the spine. Archers sometimes adjust arrow tip weight as part of the tuning process that we consider later.

You must decide whether to shoot arrows fletched with feathers or plastic vanes as well as what size of fletching to use (figure 8.3). These decisions often hinge on whether you anticipate shooting indoors or outdoors. Many archers fletch their arrows with feathers for indoor shooting and vanes for outdoor shooting to take advantage of the strengths of each type of fletching.

Feathers are lighter and can better compensate for shooting flaws such as a poor release than plastic vanes can. Slight contact between feathers and the arrow rest or bow window does not usually affect arrow flight as significantly as the same contact by plastic vanes because feathers "lie down," or give, with contact. On the other hand, feathers are affected by rain and wind. Vanes are thinner and smoother than feathers and do not slow down an arrow as rapidly as feathers do. Being uniformly produced, they typically yield better arrow groupings at longer distances because the vanes are better matched over a set of arrows.

Archers using mechanical release aids typically use vanes for both indoor and outdoor shooting. Because the arrow does not bend very much with the mechanical release of the string, the forgiveness of feathers can be sacrificed for the consistency of vanes. Also, small vanes are sufficient for stabilizing the arrow in release shooting, and it is easier to obtain good arrow clearance of the bow and arrow rest with small vanes.

Generally, the larger and heavier the arrow, the larger the fletching needed to stabilize the arrow in flight. Arrows with broadheads require larger fletching than arrows with target tips require. Archers generally use the smallest fletching that can stabilize their arrows quickly. Because large fletching increases arrow weight, you do not want to use it unnecessarily.

Many archers like to mount their fletching on the arrow shaft at a small angle rather than aligning it precisely along the shaft's centerline. The oncoming wind striking the fletching causes the arrow in flight to spin around its long axis, providing stability. This spinning also slows down the arrow—the greater the spin, the slower the arrow flies. If you decide to angle the fletching and you are shooting feathers, be sure to offset the feathers so that the oncoming air contacts the rough side of the feathers. Others mount their fletching straight on the shaft, preferring speed over the spinning effect. Later, we will cover how to fletch your own arrows.

UPGRADING ARROWS

1. Determine draw length.
2. Determine arrow length.
3. Determine draw weight.
4. With a compound bow, determine cam type and bow speed rating.
5. Select arrow size from an arrow spine chart.
6. Choose tip weight.
7. Choose fletching.

MISSTEP

The arrows you are shooting have mixed types and sizes of fletching.

CORRECTION

Feathers and vanes differ in weight, as do feathers or vanes of different sizes. No matter how good your technique is, you will not achieve good arrow grouping with arrows of differing weights. Buy arrow shafts of the same weight and fletch them with the same size and type of fletching to keep the arrow weight consistent within a set of arrows.

Arrow Selection Exercise 1   Reading an Arrow Spine Chart

Practice reading the arrow spine chart in table 8.2. For each combination of draw weight and arrow length, indicate the arrow size you should choose for the aluminum alloy indicated. Answers appear at the end of this step.

1. Recurve bow with a draw weight of 46 pounds, 28-inch arrow

   Aluminum spine sizes _____

   Carbon and aluminum–carbon spine sizes _____

2. Compound bow with a release aid, peak bow weight of 50 pounds, 29-inch arrow

   Aluminum spine sizes _____

   Carbon and aluminum–carbon spine sizes _____

3. Compound bow with a release aid, peak bow weight of 39 pounds, 27-inch arrow

   Aluminum spine sizes _____

   Carbon and aluminum–carbon spine sizes _____

Success Check

- Find arrow length and read down.
- Find bow weight and read across.

Score Your Success

Identify all six sets of arrows correctly = 5 points

Identify four or five sets of arrows correctly = 3 points

Identify two or three sets of arrows correctly = 1 point

Your score _____

Bows

If you are serious about participating in some form of archery, you should have your own bow, matched to you for draw weight and for bow or draw length. Also, the bow can be tuned specifically for you. A good general rule is to buy the best bow you can afford that is commensurate with your interest in the sport.

The first obvious decision is whether to buy a recurve or compound bow. Your choice should be related to the archery activity in which you are interested, but remember that not all hunters use compounds and not all target archers use recurves. Important considerations are the advantages and disadvantages of any type of bow you might buy and any restrictions on equipment at the events you might participate in. Be sure to research these restrictions before you buy a bow. If possible, shoot the bow you are considering, or one similar to it, before buying.

RECURVE BOWS

There is a distinct advantage to buying a recurve bow that is center shot. A center-shot bow has a bow window cut into the handle, which allows the drawn arrow to sit at a point close to or at the centerline of the limbs. A bow without a window puts the arrow in a position in which it is pointed significantly to the side. Even allowing for the effect of the archer's paradox with the arrow bending around the bow, an archer with a bow without a window must aim so that the arrow flies off center. A center-shot bow overcomes this problem. An arrow of appropriate spine can compensate for the slight offset from center caused by the archer's paradox.

Center-shot bows must be wooden bows that are laminated (usually with layers of fiberglass on the face and back of the bow) or bows with metal handle risers. A simple wooden bow would not be strong enough if a bow window were cut into the handle. Competition bows today have metal handle risers, often made of magnesium or aluminum alloys to be strong enough to withstand the forces to which they are subjected in shooting even when cut exactly center shot (see figure 12 in The Sport of Archery).

Many handle risers today use a cutout design (see figure 10.11a). This feature minimizes the effect of wind because the wind can flow through rather than push the riser broadside when held at full draw. Cutouts also allow the riser to be lighter in weight yet able to absorb the shock and vibration that accompany the release.

Recurve bows with metal handle risers have detachable limbs made of a variety of materials. Most have a wooden or foam core and layers of fiberglass or carbon, or both, on each side. Higher-quality limbs can be multilaminated. The quality of bow limbs is very important for an archer using a recurve bow because the limbs determine the speed of the shot and the stability and smoothness of the bow. If you decide to upgrade to a quality recurve bow, it is likely that the more you spend on limbs, the better quality you will get. Yet there is no need to spend more than your performance level warrants. Until your shooting is very good and your scores are very high, the most expensive set of limbs will not improve your score over a moderately priced set.

One thing a good recurve bow affords you is the opportunity to fit the bow closely to your size and strength. For example, a riser might be available in two lengths, such as 23 inches (58 cm) and 25 inches (64 cm). Limbs then might be available in three lengths. So, a 68-inch (173 cm) bow might have a shorter riser with long limbs or a longer riser with medium-length limbs. You can then get a combination of poundage and cast that is ideal for you. Bows with detachable limbs allow you to replace the limbs without having to purchase an entirely new bow should you decide to upgrade your limbs or should the older limbs become damaged. Recurve bows can be taken apart for easy transportation too; for this reason, they are frequently called take-down bows.

Most archers using a finger release, whether they have a recurve or a compound bow, eventually add a device called a clicker to their bow (figure 8.5). Typically, a clicker is a piece of spring steel about 1/4 inch (0.6 cm) wide and 3 inches (7.6 cm) long. It is mounted in the sight window of the handle riser. The upper end is anchored, and the lower end is free and extends to a point in front of the arrow rest. When you nock the arrow, the arrow is placed under the clicker—that is, between the clicker and the handle riser. The position of the clicker is adjusted so that when you reach full draw, the clicker just begins to slide down the arrow tip. When you are satisfied that the shot is set up, aim and increase back tension. As back

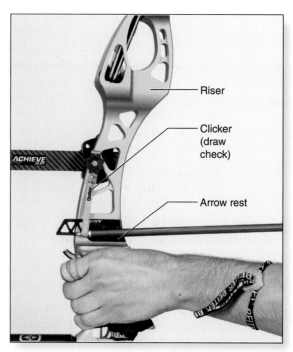

Figure 8.5 The clicker.

What Sport Science Says About Clickers

Most Olympic-style archers use a clicker. Sport scientists are interested in the ways that clicker use contributes to accurate shooting among these elite archers. Spratford and Campbell (2017) studied 39 elite archers prior to their participation in a World Cup event. They recorded the draw force and arrow length for each archer and measured postural stability, as discussed in step 4, and clicker reaction time. The researchers also used four high-speed cameras to calculate arrow flight time and score. After analyzing their data, the researchers concluded that the accuracy of a shot was predicted by faster clicker reaction time (the time from the sound of the clicker to bowstring release), higher bow draw force, and lower maximum body sway speed after shot release. The average clicker reaction time for this group of elite archers was 0.163 seconds.

The variation of clicker reaction time among the 39 archers was very small, so Spratford and Campbell (2017) suggested that trying to reduce clicker reaction time was of limited value to elite archers. In contrast, archers can work to improve upper-body strength to use a higher draw force and control their follow-through. A later study by Simsek and colleagues (2019) recorded clicker reaction time for archers with different levels of expertise. They found that elite archers had a faster clicker reaction time than beginning archers. These results tell us that the goal for all archers using a clicker should be to react immediately to its sound.

tension increases, the draw hand moves the bowstring and the arrow back so that eventually the arrow slides out from under the clicker. The clicker slaps the handle riser and makes a noise, hence its name. You release only on the sound of the clicker. Archers who would like to use a clicker but have longer arrows can extend a plate out from the bow and angle the clicker to strike this plate instead of the bow itself.

The clicker facilitates the use of back tension, plus it discourages anticipation of the release because the archer is never quite sure when back tension will have increased enough to slide the arrow from under the clicker. For finger shooters, these are important advantages in setting up consistent and well-executed shots. Most Olympic-style shooters use clickers. Finger shooters in bowhunter classifications might not be allowed to use clickers.

Another advantage to using a clicker is an identical draw length on every shot. Draw length doesn't vary, so the thrust imparted to the arrow doesn't vary even slightly on any shot. In fact, it is not clear whether the clicker was invented as a draw check or as a cure for snap shooting. For long shooting distances, standardizing draw length from shot to shot is important for accurate shooting. Clicker shooters find it advantageous to make sure the draw elbow is high, slightly above nose level, to facilitate using the back muscles in drawing through the clicker.

COMPOUND BOWS

Compound bows also are made with metal risers and composite limbs, but their cams and cable system provide their unique performance feature, a holding weight that is lighter than the bow's draw weight. Since compound bows entered the archery market, they have undergone numerous changes in design. Early compounds were just a little shorter than recurves and featured round eccentric (off-center axle) pulleys at each end. The most recent evolution has resulted in compound bows that are short (axle to axle), have short brace heights, and use two cams as part of the levering system of cables and pulleys.

Metal handle risers can be straight, reflex, or deflex (figure 8.6). The reflex handle places the grip behind the limb's fulcrum points, where the limbs attach to the handle riser, resulting in a short brace height. The advantage of this design is that the nock of the arrow stays on the string until it is approximately 7 inches (18 cm) from the handle, imparting more energy to the arrow and increasing arrow speed. The deflex handle has a grip farther from the bowstring than the other designs have, resulting in a long brace height. Arrow speed is therefore slower, but the bow is more stable to aim, more forgiving of shooter errors, and consequently more accurate. Early compound bows tended to use deflex handle shapes, but there has been a definite trend toward the reflex design, especially in bows designed for hunting. So, a commonly seen compound bow today is short in overall length with a relatively long reflex handle riser and short limbs that can sometimes be almost parallel to each other. This design promotes speed of arrow flight but makes the bow less forgiving of a shooter's mistakes, although the parallel limbs minimize recoil and vibration at string release. Because this design typically results in a very sharp string angle at full draw, most archers using this bow design also use a mechanical release, whether for target shooting or hunting.

Compound bows with reflex handles are often equipped with a string stopper or backstop (figure 8.6b). This device is typically mounted below the grip and extends toward the shooter in line with the stabilizer. It is designed to stop the string's forward motion so the arrow leaves the bowstring sooner. This minimizes any slapping of the string against the bow or its parts and makes the bow somewhat more forgiving of shooter errors.

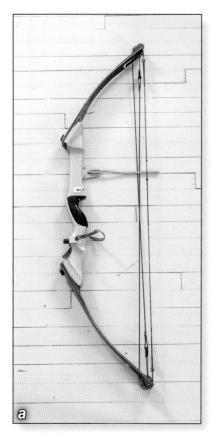  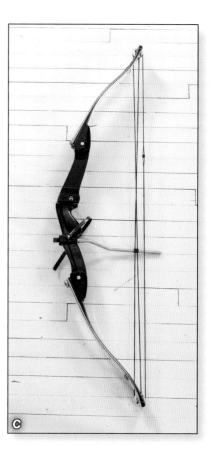

Figure 8.6 Compound bow handles: *(a)* straight; *(b)* reflex; *(c)* deflex.

A common feature in compounds today is a handle riser design with an opening in the center of the riser, allowing an arrow rest to be mounted in the center and the arrow to be shot from the center of the riser (see figure 8.6*a*). Recall that earlier we described the archer's paradox, wherein an arrow curves around the bow on release from an arrow rest mounted on the side of the handle riser. This center-shot design in today's compound bows eliminates the need to tune the equipment to accommodate the archer's paradox.

The combination of stiff limbs and the cable and cam system determines how energy is stored in a compound bow's limbs when it is drawn. Recall that the force required to move a wheel is a function of both the amount of force applied and the radius of the wheel, or the distance from the axle to the rim. An eccentric axle on a round pulley allows the radius to vary at points along the rim. Early compounds used simple eccentric wheels positioned so that an archer would have to apply more force to the string at mid-draw (corresponding to a wheel position with a shorter radius) than at full draw (corresponding to a wheel position with a longer radius). The force required during the draw as a function of the pulley's type and shape can be plotted as a force-draw curve (figure 8.7). An archer who can apply a greater force for a short distance at mid-draw and be spared applying that greater force at full draw while anchoring, sighting, and aiming can store more force in the limbs of a compound bow than in the limbs of a recurve bow. That is, the archer can shoot a compound with a much heavier peak draw weight than a recurve with its increasing draw weight through the draw to anchor. The holding weight of the early compound was usually 50 percent

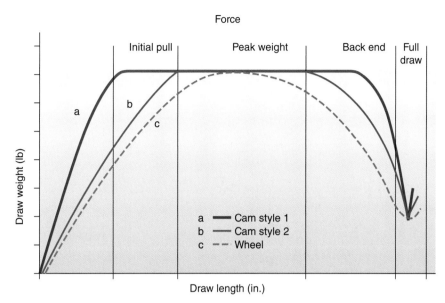

Figure 8.7 A force-draw curve for compound bows. Curves *a* and *b* are two styles of cams; the bow is at or near peak weight for a greater portion of the draw and decreases abruptly near full draw. Curve *c* is a round eccentric (axle off center) wheel; draw weight increases gradually to a peak, decreases gradually, and provides a valley of approximately 1 inch (2.5 cm) or so with minimal holding weight at full draw when matched to an archer's draw length.

or less of its draw weight. Today's compounds typically have holding weights of 65 to 95 percent of the draw weight.

Most compounds today use cams instead of round pulleys (figure 8.8). Cams are egg shaped rather than round so they can accentuate the leverage effect as the radius length is varied. There is much variation in the design of cams for modern compounds. Cam-shaped wheels result in the bow being at or near its peak weight over a greater distance in the draw stroke so that more energy is stored in the bow limbs. This energy propels the arrow at higher speeds. Eccentric wheels can be cam shaped on one or both sides; the two-sided, or full, cams yield the highest speeds.

Both target compounds and bowhunting compounds use cams. They both have reflex-shaped handle risers, but the more extreme degrees of reflex are typical of hunting bows. Naturally, the greater the degree of reflex, the shorter the brace height of the compound bow. The limbs on hunting bows tend to be closer to parallel than the limbs on target compounds. These design features are largely based on speed-accuracy trade-offs, with an edge in speed being desirable for hunting and an edge in accuracy being desirable for target shooting. Target shooters must keep in mind that even though the let-off available in today's compound bows is dramatic, they must still pull through the draw weight of the bow. While a bow hunter might only draw a few times a day, a target archer must shoot dozens of arrows in a day. Just as with recurve bows, hunters generally choose a heavier draw weight than a target archer. As you can see from the force-draw curve in figure 8.7, cams tend to have a point of maximum let-off rather than a valley. If you try to draw a bow with this force-draw curve past the point of maximum let-off, the force needed to continue rises sharply. Archers describe this as "drawing to the stops" or to the wall. Some archers use

Figure 8.8 Various cam styles.

drawing to the stops as a draw check. This method lends itself more to shooting with a mechanical release than a finger release.

With today's compounds having such light holding weights, there is less force to pull the fingers, hand, and arm joints into alignment. Archers tend to fall into shooting flaws such as bending the wrist of the bow arm or holding the string with the arm rather than the back muscles, both of which make collapsing at release more likely. Many archers adjust their compounds so that they have more holding weight than is possible with their bow model. For example, instead of a 95 percent let-off, they will shoot with an 80 percent let-off.

Since their advent in the archery market, compound bows have had the disadvantage of requiring a fit to an individual archer that is more restrictive than that of recurve bows. Yet early manufacturers tried to build adjustments into the eccentric pulleys. Slots in the eccentric pulleys for the cables allowed draw length adjustments of 3 inches (7.6 cm). Today's compounds generally have even larger ranges of possible draw lengths. Many have 4 to 6 inches (10-15 cm) of adjustment, with a few allowing up to 15 inches (38 cm) of adjustment. Adjustments of the bolt attaching the limb to the handle riser can change the limb angle slightly and therefore the draw weight. Compounds with cams can adjust anywhere from 10 to 30 pounds (4.5-13.6 kg) in peak weight. The limited draw length ranges of early compound bows made them less appropriate for young and growing archers. They required youth to frequently replace outgrown equipment. Today, compound bows with light draw weight, no let-off, and a long maximum draw length are available for youth. The bow functions much like a recurve, but changes in draw length are accommodated as the archer grows.

When purchasing compound bow equipment, buy bowstrings and cables made of the highest-quality materials, such as high-modulus polyethylene, that you can afford. Quality material is strong and stretches very little. It contributes to an efficient transfer of the bow's energy to the arrow. Most release shooters attach a small loop of string, called a D loop, to the bowstring, bracketing the nocking point. They attach the release to the D loop rather than to the bowstring itself.

Many compound bow design innovations resulted from prioritizing speed of arrow flight over smoothness, consistency, comfort of the shot, and forgiveness of minor shooting flaws. Hunters tended to embrace these innovations, whereas target archers stayed with existing designs. Remember, too, that because target archers usually shoot far more arrows than hunters do, they absolutely need bows that are consistent and forgiving; for this reason, they are less tolerant of vibration with every shot. Bow designers have addressed some of the disadvantages of very fast compounds with further innovations. For example, the near-parallel limbs on short bows dampen vibration better than angled limbs do. Still, archers who target shoot with compound bows tend to choose handle risers that are straight or less reflexed than those on most hunting bows and that are longer axle to axle. Because longer bows are more difficult to torque than shorter bows are, they forgive any tendency of a target archer to torque the bow at release. Target archers want speed of arrow flight, but they cannot sacrifice the forgiveness of small shooting errors, and therefore accuracy, for that speed. As noted earlier, the type of archery you are participating in influences your choice of bow. Serious archers sometimes buy different types of bows for different archery activities.

Arrow Rests

For relatively little cost, you can add to the accuracy of your shooting by upgrading your arrow rest, particularly if you have been shooting off the bow shelf itself. Your first decision is whether to upgrade to a shoot-around rest or a shoot-through rest. Finger shooters most often use shoot-around rests because they compensate for the string (and therefore, tail-of-the-arrow) deflection on release by the fingers. Archers shooting recurve bows typically use a finger release, so recurve bows are most often seen with a shoot-around rest. Release shooters most often use shoot-through rests; because they don't have to worry about horizontal deflection, they want the arrow to take the most direct path to the target. Some handle risers now provide two mounting holes for arrow rests, accommodating a range of arrow lengths.

If you decide on a shoot-around rest, the ideal combination is a plastic or metal arm on which the arrow rests and a plunger button (see figure 12 in The Sport of Archery). When a finger shooter releases the string, the tip end of the arrow pushes against the bow because the nock end, which is attached to the bowstring, has deflected to the side. The cushion plunger gives as the arrow pushes. When tuning your equipment, you can adjust the tension on the plunger for the amount of give (figure 8.9). You can also adjust how far out from the handle the plunger protrudes, which changes

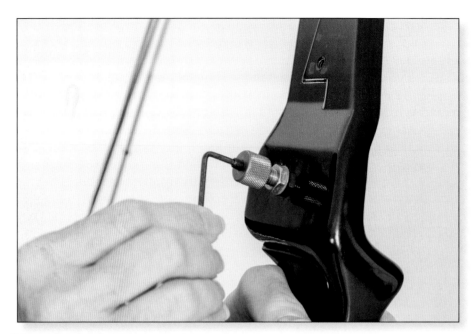

Figure 8.9 Adjusting the plunger tension.

the orientation of the arrow. Many serious archers shoot with a plastic, stick-on rest, but you might want to upgrade to a rest with a collapsible arm that is spring-loaded or magnetized. If the fletching does contact the arm, the arm will collapse instead of remaining rigid, minimizing the effect of the contact. It then springs back into position for your next shot. Some handle risers allow an arrow rest to be bolted to the riser and even adjusted for position relative to the cushion plunger button.

An alternative shoot-around rest is a spring, the end of which forms the arm the arrow sits on. You can adjust the amount of give by choosing a heavier or lighter spring. Spring rests are now rarely used. Archers prefer the adjustability of a cushion plunger with an arrow rest.

Shoot-through rests come in a variety of styles. In some styles, the arrow sits on two arms that are rather close together or on a flat arm with a V notch for the arrow. The index, or cock, feather or vane, which is usually a different color than the other two, then is placed straight up (figures 8.10 and 8.15). An alternative is to have the two arms wide apart and to orient the arrow so that the index vane is straight down. Remember, nocks have to be mounted for the desired orientation. The arms have to be stiff enough to support the weight of the arrow but flexible enough to give when the arrow pushes against them at release. This type of rest is commonly seen with handle risers that provide a center window.

A type of shoot-through rest that is more often seen on hunting equipment is a whisker biscuit, or containment-style rest. A nearly complete plastic circle has nylon bristles mounted toward the center of the circle with a small hole in the center of the bristles. An arrow is slipped through the small opening in the plastic circle and is supported and held, centered in place, by the brush bristles. An arrow rarely falls off one of these rests.

Drop-away rests are an innovation in shoot-through rests. The arms are designed to collapse downward as the arrow clears the bow to ensure that there is no contact with the vanes. Some models are triggered by the cables moving forward upon release

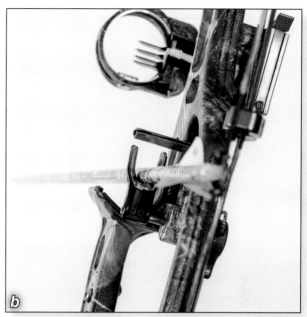

Figure 8.10 A shoot-through rest on a hunting bow. Note that when the arrow is nocked *(b)* the index feather points up.

Figure 8.11 A drop-away rest. The rest drops down when the cables contact the plunger on the arrow rest assembly so that there is no contact with the arrow fletching as the arrow clears the bow handle.

(figure 8.11), while others are triggered by limb movement. These rests can be expensive, but they allow for a clean exit of the arrow from the bow. Many bowhunting setups today include drop-away rests.

If you have used this opportunity to upgrade your equipment or have decided to continue shooting with the equipment you have, will now learn how to adjust your equipment so that it yields the best possible performance.

TUNING EQUIPMENT

Archers want the equipment setup that gives them the very best possible result considering their technique and performance on a given day. An equipment setup is most helpful when it is forgiving (that is, when it compensates for a mistake to produce the best possible result at the target). An arrow that is poorly shot with properly tuned equipment might result in 7 points out of a possible 10, for example, instead of 2 points if it were shot with poorly tuned equipment. In archery, the process of adjusting equipment to the particular size, build, strength, and technique of an archer is called tuning. You will learn how to tune archery equipment according to various techniques over several stages of tuning precision. The arrow rest you have chosen should be installed on your bow at this point.

State-of-the-art archery equipment is complex and can be adjusted in many ways. Although it is always possible to get help when tuning equipment, you should understand how and why specific equipment adjustments affect shooting. This knowledge will keep you from spending unnecessary money or time on something touted to be the latest "can't miss, everyone must have it" gizmo that actually does not change results one bit.

You are most likely to achieve your tightest arrow groups with smooth arrow flight. The more cleanly your bow launches your arrows, the fewer arrows porpoise (wobble up and down, as in figure 8.12*a*) or fishtail (wobble side to side, as in figure 8.12*b*) in flight. Smooth-flying arrows travel faster, minimizing the time during which

a

b

Figure 8.12 *(a)* An arrow porpoising in flight. *(b)* An arrow fishtailing in flight.

any mistake on your part can affect the arrow. Ideally, tuning achieves good clearance for the arrow as it leaves the bow and minimizes all porpoising and fishtailing of arrows in flight.

The combination of settings that achieves this goal is unique to you and your equipment. By tuning your equipment yourself, you can be assured that your equipment maximizes your performance, and you can make timely adjustments as needed. Expert archers can shoot bull's-eyes with matched arrows that fishtail or porpoise simply because they shoot each arrow exactly the same way. This has been demonstrated by shooting machines that launch arrows from out-of-tune equipment! Most of us, though, are not machines and not expert archers, so we benefit from tuning our equipment to minimize the effects of any mistakes.

You might hear archers talk about tuning their *bows*, but in fact, tuning involves adjustments to the *bow, arrow rest, and arrows*. Tuning is accomplished in a specific order of steps; you adjust some things first and then move on to finer adjustments (fine-tuning or microtuning). There are sometimes differences in the tuning process for recurve versus compound bows and for finger shooters versus mechanical-release shooters. We begin with the initial necessary adjustments to the bow itself, both recurve and compound bows.

Making Initial Bow Adjustments

You must make several determinations as the first steps in tuning your equipment. These include the bow's draw weight, the bow's string height, and the bow's tiller (the perpendicular distance between the string and each limb, measured where the limb attaches to the handle riser); your draw length, the size of the arrow shaft, fletching type and size, and tip weight; and the stabilizer setup. Changes in any of these factors could make it necessary to retune the bow. Some of these factors are more pertinent for recurve bows than for compound bows, and others are more pertinent for compound bows than for recurve bows.

RECURVE BOWS

First, determine your bow's draw weight and your arrow length to choose an arrow size. You need to determine your draw length to determine your arrow length. If you have not checked your draw length recently, recheck it before purchasing arrows and tuning your bow to them (see step 1, fitting exercise 2). Your form is probably more consistent now than it was when you began. A common error archers make is setting up their equipment for a draw length that is too long for them. This can gradually lead to form flaws, such as leaning back.

Most bow shops have scales that give the draw weight of a bow at any draw length (figure 8.13). Bows are labeled for draw weight at a standard draw length, but you should make sure the label is correct and the appropriate adjustment is made for draw lengths longer or shorter than the standard.

Figure 8.13 **DETERMINING DRAW WEIGHT**

1. Install accessories.
2. Recheck draw length.
3. Determine draw weight at draw length.

4. Set tiller.
5. Set brace height.

You should also set the tiller on a bow with removable limbs according to the manufacturer's specifications (see figure 8.14 in the Compound Bows section). The tiller is the perpendicular distance between the string (with the bow strung) and each limb at the point the limb attaches to the handle riser. You can measure it with a bow square or metal tape. Use an Allen wrench to turn the limb bolt clockwise to lengthen the tiller or counterclockwise to shorten it.

The string, or brace, height of a recurve bow (the distance between the bow's pivot point and the string) must be set before tuning. The bowstring's length fixes the string height. For straight-limb bows, you should use a string length that results in a string height of 6 to 8 inches (15-20 cm). For recurve bows, the string height should be slightly over 8 inches (20 cm; table 8.3). Manufacturers typically specify a string height for their quality recurve bows. You can adjust the string height from this starting point. If the manufacturer gives a range of brace heights, experiment with the shorter heights first.

The sound of the bow upon release is often a good indicator of the ideal string height for that bow and archer. The string height that results in the quietest action is

Table 8.3 Recommended Brace Heights and Ranges for Recurve Bows

Recurve bow length (in.)	Suggested starting height (in.)	Height range (in.)
64	8-1/4 to 8-1/2	7-3/4 to 9
66	8-3/8 to 8-5/8	8 to 9-1/4
68	8-1/2 to 8-3/4	8-1/4 to 9-1/2
70	8-5/8 to 8-7/8	8-1/2 to 9-3/4

the ideal one. You can make slight changes in string height by twisting or untwisting the bowstring. Obviously, twisting the bowstring shortens its length and increases the string height. The twists should always be in the same direction as the center serving. Never remove all the twists from a bowstring. It should have 6 to 10 twists to keep it round and without flat spots that plane in the air upon release and slow its speed. On the other hand, the increased friction of too many twists increases the likelihood of string breakage. If you cannot adjust the string height enough by twisting or untwisting the bowstring, purchase a shorter or longer bowstring as needed.

Before tuning, install any accessories you plan to use, such as stabilizers, a bowsight, a clicker (draw check), and a kisser button. Changes in accessories, especially those that can affect arrow clearance or the weight of the bowstring, can affect the tuning.

COMPOUND BOWS

You must follow several steps before tuning a compound bow. Some are similar to those involved in setting up a recurve bow; others are unique. With the various types of compound bows on the market today and those sure to be introduced in the near future, it is best to check the manufacturer's specific instructions for tuning a particular compound. Following is a typical procedure from which you can learn the principles of tuning.

First, have your compound bow set for your draw length. This procedure should have been done at the pro shop when you purchased your bow. Just as with recurve bows, this is a good time to double-check your draw length because your form is probably more consistent now than when you began shooting. Using a bow with too long a draw length for you can lead to form flaws. You want to anchor at the draw length at which the weight lets off. If you need to adjust the draw length of your compound bow, it is best to take it to a pro shop or distributor that has a bow press made to accommodate your brand of bow. A technician can make the adjustment.

Next, adjust and tighten the cable guard if your bow is equipped with an adjustable guard. The cable guard holds the cables away from the nocked arrow so that the bowstring and arrow can pass freely upon release. Set the cable guard to route the cables just out of the way but no farther than necessary. On some compound bows, changes in the position of the cable guard slightly affect the draw length, which is why you need to make this adjustment before tuning your bow.

Compound bows have a range of draw weights. Before setting the desired draw weight, you must adjust the tiller (figure 8.14). This is done just as with a recurve. Set the tiller to the manufacturer's recommendation. Most compound bows are meant to shoot with the same top and bottom tillers. With compound bows, exact tiller measurements are not as important as setting them and checking them periodically to be sure they remain the same, top and bottom.

Figure 8.14 COMPOUND BOW ADJUSTMENTS

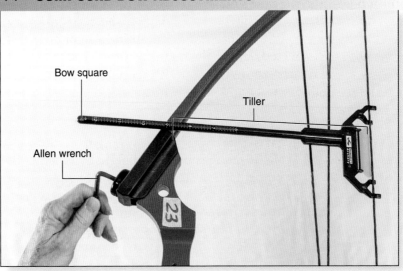

1. Install accessories.
2. Recheck draw length.
3. Set draw length.
4. Set cable guard.

5. Set tiller.
6. Set draw weight.
7. Set brace height.
8. Set wheel and cam rollover.

MISSTEP

Your bow's draw weight or draw length is not set for you.

CORRECTION

If you are shooting a compound bow, determine your draw length and set the bow for that draw length. For either type of bow, choose a draw weight and set it so you are shooting the most weight you can handle and maintain good form for an entire shooting round. Ill-fitted bows encourage form flaws.

After you set the tiller on your compound bow, you can measure the draw weight with a scale and adjust the poundage by turning the limb bolts with an Allen wrench. The draw weight should be the weight you can shoot with good form over the course of a shooting round. A clockwise turn increases the poundage. Be sure to adjust the top and bottom bolts by an equal number of turns to maintain the tiller ratio.

Manufacturers also specify the brace heights for compound bows. You can adjust this height by using the same methods used for recurve bows. Remember that changing the brace height of a compound bow affects its draw weight and draw length.

As with a recurve bow, you should install all accessories on your compound bow before tuning it. These include stabilizers, a D loop on your bowstring (used with mechanical releases), a string stop, a bowsight, a draw check, a kisser button, a peep sight, any cable keepers that hold the cables close to one another, and limb bands.

Finally, if you are shooting a two-wheel or cam compound bow, you should check to see that the wheels and cams are synchronized. Assuming your normal stance, come to full draw and have someone check to see whether the bowstring or cable comes off the wheels at the same point on each wheel, within 1/16 of an inch (0.16 cm). If the wheels are not synchronized, follow the manufacturer's procedures for adjusting them. Once they are synchronized, you can mark the wheels so you can check from time to time that their alignment remains the same.

Preliminary Adjustment Exercise 1   Settings

Your bow must be prepared for tuning just as it is for shooting. Consider the bow you are now using. Record your draw length and weight and your preliminary bow settings.

Draw length: _____

Draw weight: _____

Brace height: _____

Tiller measurements:

Top: _____

Bottom: _____

Accessories installed: _____

Success Check

- Measure carefully.
- Record accurately.

Score Your Success

Begin a log of your settings = 3 points

Your score _____

Setting Bow Alignment

The next step in the tuning process is adjusting the horizontal and vertical orientations of the nocked arrow for proper arrow alignment. Later in the fine-tuning process, you will make fine corrections for alignment and adjust the tension of the cushion plunger, if you are using one. At this point, you will make larger adjustments for how the arrow is oriented when nocked.

Select your arrow rest and install it before tuning your bow. If you are using a finger release, it is best to use an arrow rest in combination with a cushion plunger because the plunger allows for both movement of the pressure point in and out and independent adjustment of the spring tension. With a cushion plunger, adjust the arrow rest support arm so that the center of the arrow shaft is at the center of the cushion plunger button when the shaft rests on the support arm. If you decide to use a spring rest, you will not be able to adjust as finely as with a cushion plunger, but adjustments are still possible in the tuning process.

Archers using a mechanical release often prefer a shoot-through rest. This rest commonly consists of a V, or two arms, on which the arrow rests (figure 8.15). Be sure that the type you are using provides good vane clearance (figure 8.16). Drop-away rests are made to depress when the bowstring is released and the arrow flexes to push down on the rest, thus promoting clearance of the arrow's fletching without contact. The amount of tension on the arm should be just enough to keep the arm from sagging at full draw. If it is too stiff, the arm might pop back up too soon after the arrow's initial push, contacting the fletched end of the arrow before it clears the bow.

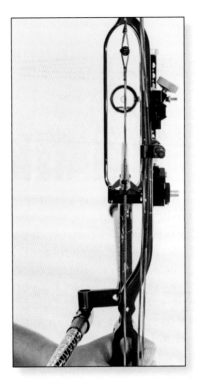

Figure 8.15 A shoot-through rest that is a true center-shot bow with a single piece of metal with a V notch in which the arrow rests.

Figure 8.16 Shoot-through rests must provide good vane clearance: *(a)* good vane clearance; *(b)* poor vane clearance.

HORIZONTAL ADJUSTMENT

Your first step in preliminary alignment is to horizontally align the nocked arrow as it sits in the bow. When an arrow bends, it oscillates around two points, or nodes (figure 8.17). Ideally, the two nodes are aligned with the target when the arrow starts forward upon release. This preliminary adjustment estimates the best horizontal position for the arrow.

When you sight down the arrow to align it, you must have the bowstring centered on the bow limbs. On a recurve bow, the bowstring is aligned with the center of the bow limbs, so it is relatively easy to center the sight of the bowstring on the limbs. But on a compound bow, the bowstring is offset to the outside because of the cams. If you are tuning a compound bow, place a piece of masking tape across the top and bottom limbs near the handle riser. Mark the actual center of the limb and then place

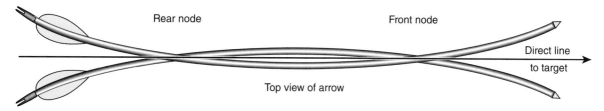

Figure 8.17 On release of the bowstring, the arrow bends, oscillating around two points called nodes.

a second mark 3/16 of an inch (0.5 cm) to the left of it (for a right-handed bow). Use this second mark to center the bowstring.

The most desirable starting position for an arrow depends on the type of equipment and release you are using. If you are shooting a finger release with a recurve bow and have a cushion plunger, you can screw the plunger in or out so that it protrudes from the handle riser a lesser or greater amount. Nock an arrow and hold the bow away from you. Align the bowstring with the center of the bow limbs. Adjust the cushion plunger in or out until you see the tip of the arrow just outside the bowstring, pointing away from the handle riser, about 1/16 to 1/8 of an inch (0.16-0.3 cm; figure 8.18*a*).

If you are shooting a finger release with a compound bow and have a cushion plunger, you can follow the same procedure, but be sure to align the bowstring with the second mark you made on the masking tape (figure 8.18*b*).

If you are using a mechanical release with a compound bow, nock an arrow and hold the bow away from you. Align the bowstring with the second mark you made on the masking tape. Adjust the launcher assembly left or right so that the arrow tip is directly in line with the bowstring (figure 8.18*c*).

Figure 8.18 HORIZONTAL PRELIMINARY ALIGNMENTS

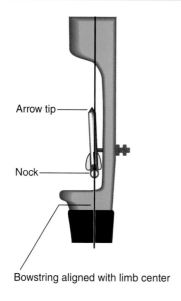

a Bowstring aligned with limb center

Recurve Bow, Finger Release

1. Arrow tip is 1/16 to 1/8 inch (0.16-0.3 cm) outside bowstring.
2. Bowstring is aligned with limb center.

(continued)

Figure 8.18 *(continued)*

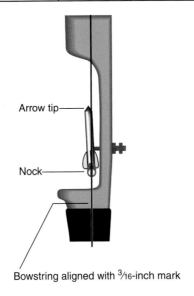

b   Bowstring aligned with ³⁄₁₆-inch mark

Compound Bow, Finger Release

1. Arrow tip is 1/8 inch (0.3 cm) outside bowstring.
2. Bowstring is aligned with 3/16-inch (0.5 cm) mark.

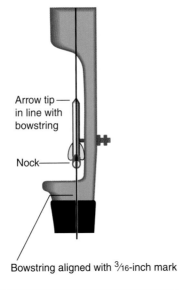

c   Bowstring aligned with ³⁄₁₆-inch mark

Compound Bow, Mechanical Release

1. Arrow tip is directly aligned.
2. Bowstring is aligned with 3/16-inch (0.5 cm) mark.

Why are the settings different for finger and mechanical releases? When you release the bowstring from your fingers, the bowstring with the rear of the arrow attached deflects slightly left if you are a right-handed archer. The front of the arrow pushes against the cushion plunger, which gives in, so that the arrow's nodes are aligned with the target as the arrow starts forward. With a mechanical release, the arrow bends vertically but not horizontally upon release, so you want the arrow's nodes aligned as it sits in the bow. Remember, these alignments are starting points. You will make further adjustments in the fine-tuning process.

VERTICAL ADJUSTMENT

The next phase in preliminary alignment is to position the nock locator on the bowstring so that the nock locator is approximately 1/2 inch (1.3 cm) above the line forming a perfect 90-degree angle with the string (figure 8.19) for a finger release and 1/4 inch (0.6 cm) above the line for a mechanical release. Ideally, you should use a clamp-on nock locator. It should be clamped on firmly but not tightly at this time. In fine-tuning, you can thread the locator up or down to make a fine adjustment and then tightly clamp it down. Be careful not to clamp down the nock locator too tightly and cut the bowstring's strands, especially if your bowstring is made of a delicate material such as Kevlar.

Figure 8.19   VERTICAL PRELIMINARY ALIGNMENT

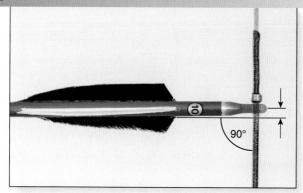

1. Locator is 1/2 inch (1.3 cm) above line at a 90-degree angle with the string for finger release.
2. Locator is 1/4 inch (0.6 cm) above line at a 90-degree angle with the string for mechanical release.

Preliminary Adjustment Exercise 2   Clearance Test

Even though you will next fine-tune your equipment, it is interesting to note whether your arrows are clearing the bow without the fletching contacting the handle riser or rest. Put some powder on the fletching of one of your arrows. Shoot your arrow, and then examine your bow and rest for any evidence that the fletching touched them.

Success Check

- If your fletching is making contact, proceed to fine-tuning and repeat the clearance test after fine-tuning.

Score Your Success

Conduct a clearance test = 2 points

Your score _____

Fine-Tuning Arrow Orientation

There are two phases of fine-tuning arrow orientation: one for the horizontal orientation of the arrow and one for the vertical orientation of the arrow. The fine-tuning methods vary slightly depending on whether you use a finger release or a mechanical release aid. Remember, when tuning, to ignore bad shots. Make decisions only on well-executed shots. You will be able to fine-tune only if your technique is good enough to produce arrow groups. If it is not, work on your form and return to fine-tuning at a later time.

HORIZONTAL FINE-TUNING

If you use a finger release with either a recurve or a compound bow, turn an indoor target face over and place one or two strips of black tape vertically down the center of the target. Strips should be about 1 inch (2.5 cm) wide. Shoot an arrow from 15 or 20 yards (14 or 18 m), aiming at the black line at the top of the target. Shoot five additional arrows, aiming at the black line but spacing the arrows vertically. Take note of the width of the group. Now move your rest (plunger button or spring rest) a small amount in or out and shoot another end of six arrows. If the width of the group is narrower, continue moving the plunger in that direction and shoot more ends, noting the width of the group until the group gets wider. Note the plunger position that provided the narrowest group; then go back to your starting position and move the rest in the opposite direction. Follow the same procedure to try to find a better setting, one that gives an even narrower group. Put your plunger in the position that produces the narrowest group.

If you use a mechanical release, fine-tune your horizontal alignment by using the walk-back method. Put a new target face at the top of the target butt and set your sight for 20 yards (18 m). Shoot three arrows from 30 yards (27 m) with your 20-yard (18 m) setting. Now shoot three more arrows from 35 yards (32 m). Continue walking back in 5-yard (4.6 m) increments until your arrows are landing at the bottom of the target butt. If your groups land farther left as you move back, move your rest (launcher arm assembly) slightly to the right if you shoot right-handed and repeat the walk-back. Continue until the arrows line up directly below the bull's-eye. If your groups land farther right, move your rest slightly to the left. Again, continue until your arrows fall in a straight line. Be careful not to cant your bow or torque your bow handle when tuning. Both of these flaws produce a diagonal line of arrows as the shooting distance increases.

FINE-TUNING STEPS

1. Shoot at preliminary setting.
2. Adjust in one direction to find best setting.
3. Return to preliminary setting and adjust in opposite direction to determine whether a better setting can be found.

VERTICAL FINE-TUNING

To fine-tune your nock locator setting, prepare a target with a black line, as when doing horizontal fine-tuning. This time, place the target on the target butt with the line running horizontally. Shoot six arrows from 15 or 20 yards (14 or 18 m) and note the vertical spread of the arrow group. Do not worry about left or right movement; just spread your shots across the target. Your only concern is the vertical spread. Move your nock locator slightly up or down and shoot again. Keep going in this manner as long as the vertical spread decreases. Stop when your group increases in vertical spread. Note the point at which you shot the narrowest group; then go back to your starting point and go in the other direction. Look for the setting that produces the narrowest spread.

Fine-Tuning Exercise 1   **Horizontal**

Choose one of the methods to fine-tune your horizontal setting, depending on whether you shoot with a finger or mechanical release. If you shoot with a finger release, note the width at your preliminary setting. Move the plunger out and note the width of the first, second, and third groups of arrows you shoot. Move the plunger in and note the width of the first, second, and third groups of arrows you shoot.

If you shoot with a mechanical release, mark your groups on figure 8.20. Note the distance the button or launcher rest is from the handle riser for the narrowest group.

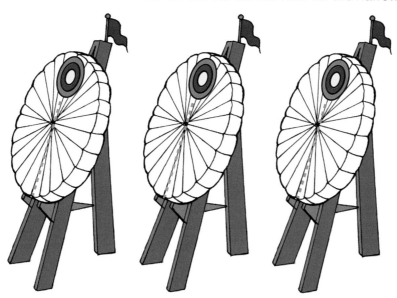

Figure 8.20   Mark your arrow groups. Use the setting that produces arrow groups along the dotted line straight down the target butt rather than the setting that produces a diagonal line of arrow groups.

Success Check

- Note whether group is wider or narrower.
- Use position yielding narrowest group.

Score Your Success

Determine horizontal setting from fine-tuning = 3 points

Your score _____

Fine-Tuning Exercise 2   **Vertical**

Adjust your nock locator setting, and record the vertical spread of your groups as you proceed. Note that your nock locator will always be above the point your arrow forms a perfect right angle with the bow string.

Move the nock locator up. Note the vertical spread of your arrows for the first, second, and third groups you shoot.

Move the nock locator down. Note the vertical spread of your arrows for the first, second, and third groups you shoot.

Note the distance of the nock locator above the perfect right-angle intersection for the narrowest vertical group.

(continued)

Fine-Tuning Exercise 2   *(continued)*

Success Check

- Note vertical spread.
- Use setting producing narrowest group.

Determine nock locator position by fine-tuning = 3 points

Your score _____

Testing Fine-Tuning

Several methods are available for testing fine-tuning; this section addresses the bare-shaft and paper-tuning methods. You will have an opportunity to experiment with both and determine which you prefer. These methods are described for right-handed shooters. If you shoot left-handed, transpose the directions for left and right.

BARE-SHAFT METHOD

For bare-shaft testing, you need three fletched arrows and three identical arrows without fletching. Some archers like to add a little tape to the rear of the shafts of their unfletched arrows so that they weigh the same as their fletched arrows.

The first step is to test for porpoising of the arrow in flight (figure 8.21a), which means that the nock end of the arrow appears to move up and down in flight. Shoot three fletched arrows to a target from 10 to 15 yards (9-14 m). Then shoot three unfletched arrows that are identically aimed. If the unfletched shafts hit higher on the target than the fletched shafts, move the nock locator slightly up on the bowstring. If the unfletched shafts hit lower than the fletched shafts, move the nock locator slightly down. After an adjustment, repeat this process until the fletched and unfletched shafts hit at the same height on the target. You must correct porpoising before moving to the next step.

The second phase in bare-shaft tuning is a check for fishtailing (figure 8.21b), which means that the nock end of the arrow appears to move from side to side in flight. Repeat the procedure used in testing for porpoising. If the unfletched shafts land to the left of the fletched shafts, your arrow reaction is too stiff. If the unfletched shafts land to the right of the fletched shafts, your arrow reaction is too weak. Consult table 8.4 for corrections.

After each adjustment, repeat the process until you can bring the unfletched shafts within at least 4 inches (10 cm) of the fletched shafts at a distance of 15 yards (14 m). If you cannot make further adjustments to bring the unfletched shafts within 4 inches (10 cm), you may have to change the size of your arrow shaft to achieve good arrow flight. Some right-handed release shooters prefer to have their bare shafts strike low and left of their fletched arrows, believing that an arrow that clears the bow slightly nock high and left is more forgiving.

The final check in bare-shaft tuning is a check for proper clearance of the arrow through the arrow rest and bow window (figure 8.21c). This step is important if you are using lightweight arrows such as carbon shafts. Sprinkle powder on the arrow rest and bow window, or spray both the fletched end of the arrow and the arrow rest assembly with dry-spray deodorant. Shoot an arrow and examine the bow. You will be able to identify places where the arrow fletching strikes the arrow rest or bow window. Arrows that strike the arrow rest or bow usually move side to side in flight, similar to fishtailing but with quicker, smaller movements. This action is called minnowing. Consult table 8.4 for ways to correct minnowing.

Figure 8.21 **BARE-SHAFT TUNING**

Porpoising

1. Shoot three fletched arrows.
2. Shoot three bare arrow shafts.
3. If bare shafts strike high, move nock locator up.
4. If bare shafts plane up, move nock locator up.
5. If bare shafts strike low, move nock locator down.
6. If bare shafts plane down, move nock locator down.
7. When bare shafts are within 4 inches (10 cm) of fletched shafts, proceed to next stage.

Fishtailing

1. Shoot three fletched arrows.
2. Shoot three bare arrow shafts.
3. If bare shafts land left, arrow reaction is too stiff.
4. If bare shafts land right, arrow reaction is too weak.
5. When bare shafts are within 4 inches (10 cm) of fletched shafts, proceed to next stage.

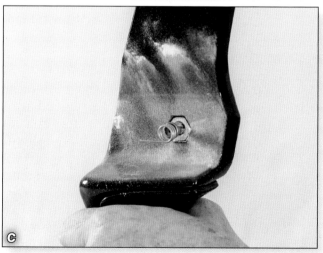

Clearance

1. Sprinkle arrow rest and bow window with powder.
2. Shoot arrow.
3. Inspect bow for contact.
4. Inspect arrow for contact.
5. If contact is visible, make corrections for minnowing (table 8.4).

Table 8.4 Adjustment for Tuning Results

Finding	Adjustment
Arrow reaction is too stiff.	• Decrease the spring tension on the cushion plunger. • Use a weaker (lighter) spring rest. • Slightly increase the draw weight of your bow if it is adjustable. • Use a heavier arrow point. • Use a lighter bowstring. • Use a weaker arrow shaft. • With a compound bow, move the cushion plunger in. • For release shooters, move the arrow rest left; check for arrow clearance of the cables and cable guard.
Arrow reaction is too weak.	• Increase the spring tension of the cushion plunger. • Use a stiffer (heavier) spring rest. • Decrease the bow's draw weight if it is adjustable. • Use a lighter arrow point. • If you do not have a cushion plunger, move the pressure point out. • With a compound bow, move the cushion plunger or pressure point out. • Use a stiffer arrow shaft. • For release shooters, move the arrow rest to the right.
Arrow contacts rest on bow window and minnows in flight.	• Rotate the arrow nock very slightly. • Trim the arrow rest support arm so that it does not protrude beyond the arrow shaft. • Use lower-profile fletching. • Move the cushion plunger or pressure point farther out and retune your bow for fishtailing. • Make sure the bowstring is not catching on something, such as a shirt pocket or sleeve.
Arrow minnows even after corrections have been made.	• Change your arrow shaft size. • Change the weight of your bowstring; decrease strands if the arrow reaction is stiff. • Change your bowstring's center serving; a heavier serving causes stiffer arrow reaction. • Change your arrow tip weight and include the insert if you use one; try a heavier point plus insert weight if your arrow reaction is too stiff. • Adjust your bow's brace height.

Some archers use only one bare shaft when they tune. If you decide to do so, be sure to base your adjustments on bare-shaft shots that are well aimed and well executed. You will spend considerably more time tuning your bow if you make unnecessary or incorrect adjustments after a poorly executed shot with a bare shaft.

PAPER-TUNING METHOD

Paper-tuning has been very successful with compound bows, especially for archers using a mechanical release. To do a paper test, you need a large picture frame that can be hung 2 yards (1.8 m) in front of a target butt at shoulder height. Tape paper onto the frame; then shoot arrows through the paper and use the pattern of the tear to help you make tuning adjustments. Finger shooters should shoot from a distance of 8 to 10 yards (7-9 m), and release shooters should shoot from 4 to 5 yards (3.7-4.6 m) from the frame for paper-tuning.

Before paper-tuning, check for proper clearance of the fletching as it passes the arrow rest and handle riser. As described in the section on bare-shaft tuning, sprinkle powder or apply dry-spray deodorant on the arrow fletching or the arrow rest and the bow window of the handle riser (figure 8.21c). Shoot an arrow and then look for evidence that the fletching contacted the arrow rest or handle riser. Slight contact can sometimes be corrected by rotating the arrow nock. Severe contact can result from a nock that fits too tightly on the string or from an arrow that is too stiff. Torquing the bowstring with the draw fingers can also cause this problem. Experiment with nock size and hand position. If these changes do not correct the problem, you may need to change arrow sizes.

When you first shoot arrows through the paper and examine the tear pattern, you might see that your tears are angular. This indicates a combination of factors affecting both vertical and horizontal arrow flight. Archers differ on which problem to correct first, horizontal or vertical, but clearly you should fix one direction before moving to the other.

As with the bare-shaft tuning method, the first adjustment is for porpoising. Shoot several fletched arrows through the paper. The ideal tear pattern is a perfect hole or a hole that shows that the arrow went through slightly nock high or slightly nock high and left if you are a right-handed archer (figure 8.22a). If the hole indicates that the arrow went through the paper with the nock 3/4 inch (1.9 cm) or more high, move the nock locator down. If the arrow goes through the paper nock down, move the nock locator up. It is perfectly acceptable for the arrow to be slightly nock high, as much as 1/2 inch (1.3 cm), at this point in arrow flight because this means that the arrow is probably not hitting the rest as it passes the handle riser. A tear up to 1 inch (2.5 cm) high may be acceptable for carbon or aluminum–carbon arrows. If you cannot correct a higher tear by moving your nocking point, you might still have clearance problems. If you use a mechanical release, your arrow shaft could be too weak, so you could try a stiffer shaft, a more flexible or lighter-tension shoot-through arrow rest, or a lighter peak draw weight on your bow.

The next adjustment is for fishtailing. If you are right-handed and your shots tear holes with the nock left (figure 8.22b), the arrow reaction is too weak. If you shoot arrows that tear holes with the nock right, the arrow reaction is too stiff. Consult table 8.4 for corrections.

Figure 8.22   PAPER-TUNING

Porpoising

1. Shoot several fletched arrows through paper.
2. Examine for ideal tear pattern.
3. If tear shows nock is too high or low, move nock locator.
4. Recheck; if you can't correct it, recheck clearance.

Fishtailing

1. Shoot several fletched arrows through paper.
2. If tear shows nock is left, correct for weak arrow reaction.
3. If nock is right, correct for stiff arrow reaction.

As with the other methods of tuning, make adjustments in small increments and shoot several arrows through the paper afterward to check the effect of your adjustment. The ideal pattern is a perfect hole or a hole slightly nock high and left for a right-handed shooter and nock high and right for a left-handed shooter. If you shoot a compound bow and cannot correct high or low tears by fine-tuning, check the synchronization of your bow's cams. Once satisfied with your tuning at this distance, you can move back about 3 yards (2.7 m) more to ensure that your tuning is correct and not merely a reflection of early arrow orientation that changes downrange.

Testing Exercise 1   Porpoising Test

Use one of the testing methods described in this step to test for porpoising. Sketch either the paper tear if you paper-tuned or the impact pattern if you used the bare-shaft method. Describe any adjustments you made on the basis of your test.

Success Check

- Rely on well-executed shots.

Score Your Success

Successfully test for porpoising and make indicated adjustments = 3 points

Your score _____

Testing Exercise 2   Fishtailing Test

Assume that you have corrected for porpoising. Use one of the testing methods to test for fishtailing. Sketch either the tear pattern if you paper-tuned or the impact pattern if you used the bare-shaft method. Describe any adjustments you made on the basis of your test.

Success Check

- Rely on well-executed shots.

Score Your Success

Successfully test for fishtailing and make indicated adjustments = 3 points

Your score _____

Microtuning

The ultimate test to use to check your tuning is to shoot arrows to see that they group well. Occasionally, archers find that the tuning setup that produces the best groups is not the one that produces the most smoothly flying arrows, and vice versa. Shoot ends of 8 to 10 arrows from the longest distance you plan to shoot in competition. If your arrows do not group, you might want to make further, but very fine, adjustments.

If your groups spread vertically, you can make a 1/32-inch (0.8 mm) adjustment in your nocking point. If an adjustment increases the size of your groups, return to the starting point and move in the other direction. If your groups improve and then open up with further adjustments, you probably went too far. Go back to your best setting.

If your groups spread horizontally and you use a compound bow, make 1/32-inch (0.8 mm) in-and-out adjustments of the cushion plunger. Finger shooters should make 1/8-turn adjustments in the cushion plunger tension. Move up 20 yards (18 m) and make your left-to-right impact adjustments again. Continue to move up 20 yards (18 m) at a time until you reach a shooting distance of 20 yards (18 m).

A kisser button or peep sight may need minor adjustments in its position after tuning. The need for these adjustments is a result of changes in the position of the nocking point in the fine-tuning process and the resulting changes in the position of the hand or release aid on the string.

As you can see, tuning requires time and patience. You must be willing to experiment and find out what effect an adjustment has on arrow flight. Try to make one adjustment at a time, shooting after each change. You will be rewarded in the end by knowing that your equipment is contributing the utmost to your shooting accuracy.

Microtuning Exercise 1   Obtaining New Sight Settings

Once you have tuned your bow to your satisfaction, obtain a set of sight settings for the distances you commonly shoot. Many of the adjustments you made in tuning might have influenced your sight settings. Record your sight settings in table 8.5.

Table 8.5   New Sight Settings

Yardage	New sight setting
15	
20	
25	
30	
35	
40	
45	
50	
55	
60	

Success Check

- Rely on well-executed shots.

Score Your Success

Obtain new sight settings = 10 points

Your score _____

MAINTAINING EQUIPMENT

Over months of shooting, you will need to keep your bow in good working order, maintain your arrows, and sometimes replace parts and accessories. You can save money by doing the simpler maintenance yourself and leaving the maintenance requiring special tools and expertise to the staff of a pro shop. For example, you can often purchase a dozen nocks for the price that a pro shop charges to replace one nock.

You also learn more about your equipment when you maintain it yourself. You can see how changing a setup affects shooting. Then you can begin to customize your equipment to match your shooting style. Once you are comfortable with adjusting and maintaining your equipment, you will find that these tasks are an especially rewarding part of archery.

Maintaining Arrows

If your form is consistent enough to shoot groups, arrows will group if they are exactly matched. You can replace nocks, replace tips, replace fletching, and care for your shafts yourself, but be sure to do it with precision. This section covers some of the maintenance you can do yourself, but you should also check for any specific procedures the arrow manufacturer recommends. Pay particular attention to recommendations about the amount of heat you can apply to arrow shafts and about the types of adhesives and solvents you can use with specific shafts and components.

NOCKS

Archers who shoot tight arrow groups often break the plastic nocks on the ends of their arrows. It is worthwhile to purchase replacement nocks in bulk quantities and replace your own nocks. Straight nocks are important to shooting accuracy. A nock misaligned by a few thousandths of an inch can send an arrow 6 inches (15 cm) off its mark at 40 yards (37 m). The procedure for replacing a nock depends in part on the type of shaft and nocking system used.

Conventional Nocks   Aluminum shafts are typically tapered (swaged) at the nock end. Nocks are simply glued onto the taper. Nocks vary in size according to the size of the arrow shaft. Table 8.6 lists the appropriate size to purchase for your arrows.

To replace a nock, carefully heat the old nock over a candle. (Do not place the arrow in an open flame.) When the nock begins to melt, remove it with pliers. Wipe the nock area with lacquer thinner or methyl ethyl ketone (MEK) to clean the area of old glue residue. Avoid touching the area because your fingers will deposit oil on the shaft. It is preferable not to cut off broken nocks or sand the taper because this could change the shape of the taper and the new nock's alignment.

Archery suppliers sell fletching cement appropriate for bonding nocks and fletching to aluminum shafts. Place a drop of such fletching cement on the taper. Rotate the shaft as you spread the cement evenly around the arrow with your finger. Place the new nock on the arrow, and turn the nock several times counterclockwise to further spread the cement. Rotate the nock clockwise with a slight downward pressure, and align it at a right angle to the index feather (figure 8.23, *a* and *b*). Wipe off any excess cement oozing from under the nock.

Table 8.6   Replacement Nock and Insert Sizes

ALUMINUM SHAFTS, CONVENTIONAL NOCKS		UNIVERSAL NOCK INSTALLATION (UNI) SYSTEM	
Shaft size	Recommended nock size (in.)	Shaft size	Recommended insert
1413-1518 1614-1816 1818-2016 2018-2219 2317-2419	7/32 1/4 9/32 5/16 11/32	Smaller than 2012 2012 and larger	Standard UNI insert Super UNI insert

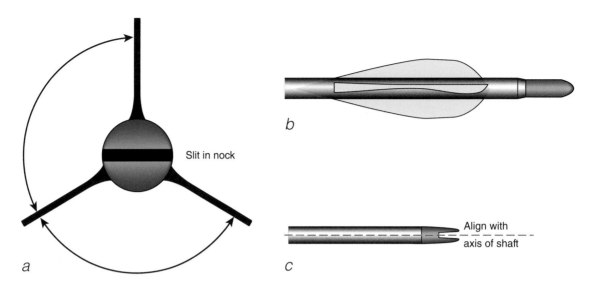

Figure 8.23 Arrow nock: *(a)* cross-section; *(b)* mounted on shaft; *(c)* aligned with axis of shaft.

Place the arrow on a table with the index feather up. If the nock is on properly, you should not see either side of the nock when you look directly down on it from above. Adjust the nock if necessary before the cement sets. This is the standard nock position. Some archers, though, rotate their nocks slightly to achieve feather or vane clearance of the bow if they do not get the effect they desire with the standard position. Note that earlier we saw how archers using shoot-through rests oriented the arrow with the index vane either straight up or straight down for certain arrow rests. If you are using this type of rest, be sure to adjust your nock accordingly.

Another test of nock straightness (figure 8.23c) is to roll the shaft on a smooth table with the fletching hanging off the table. Watch the nock to make sure its rotation doesn't have a wobbly appearance. You can also test nock straightness by resting the shaft on the fingernails of your thumb and middle finger with the arrow point on the palm of your other hand and blowing against the fletching. The arrow will spin, so you can watch for any wobbling of the nock. Adjust the nock if necessary before the cement sets. Stand the arrow up to allow the cement to dry.

Bushing Systems Aluminum shafts can also use a bushing system, often known as the universal nock installation (UNI) system (see figure 8.3c). This system features a tapered insert (bushing) that is glued into the arrow shaft. A plastic nock is then inserted flush against the bushing for good alignment. An advantage of this system is that the plastic nock can be easily replaced if it breaks. To remove a broken nock, use pliers to twist and pull it off. If the nock is broken flush with the bushing, you can use a multinock tool with an extractor, or you can thread a small screw into the plastic and pull the unit out with pliers.

There are two sizes of UNI inserts, super and standard (see table 8.6), so be sure to purchase nocks to match your bushing. The nocks may come in various string groove sizes too, to fit various bowstring thicknesses.

A UNI insert, or bushing, is installed into aluminum shafts with a hot-melt adhesive stick available from archery suppliers, the same adhesive used for arrow tips. Clean the inside of the shaft with a cotton swab and 91 percent isopropyl alcohol, and then let it dry. The bushing should be twisted on a sharpened pencil to hold it. Heat the glue stick over a small gas flame, and apply a small ring of adhesive inside the shaft. Heat the bushing just enough to melt a coating of adhesive from the adhesive stick around the bushing shank. Lightly reheat the bushing and insert it into the shaft. Wipe off excess glue and allow the adhesive to set before removing the pencil. Several types of quick-setting glues are available for this purpose, too.

Some carbon and aluminum–carbon hybrid shafts accept the UNI system bushing. The plastic nocks used on these shafts and bushings can actually be installed without adhesive. They can be pushed into the bushing by hand with a nock tool. Some archers prefer to use an adhesive, but only a light, removable glue or rubber cement should be used. Be sure to align the nock precisely as described earlier.

Overnocks   Carbon shafts sometimes use overnocks, which fit over the outside of the shaft. They can be twisted onto the shaft without an adhesive or with a small amount of rubber cement. Broken nocks can be removed with pliers. Wipe the shaft with 91 percent isopropyl alcohol before installing the new nock. Outserts can also be installed over the shaft and a nock inserted into them. Outserts are permanently bonded to the shaft, though.

ARROW TIPS AND INSERTS

It is not difficult to replace tips and inserts, but you should be careful not to overheat shafts and to use only recommended adhesives. Check the arrow shaft manufacturer's website for recommended solvents and adhesives.

Aluminum Shafts   To remove an old point or insert, heat the shaft over a small gas flame just enough to melt the old adhesive. Pull the tip or insert out with pliers. Leave the tip screwed into the insert so you can grip it with the pliers. To replace the tip or insert, clean the inside of the shaft with 91 percent isopropyl alcohol. Heat the end of the shaft just enough to melt a ring of hot-melt adhesive inside the shaft. Grip the point or insert with pliers. Heat

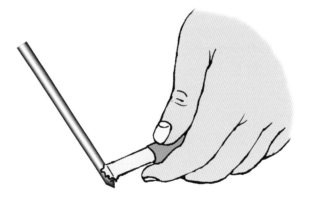

Figure 8.24   Melt a layer of cement on the entire point shaft.

the end of the shaft slightly and insert the tip or insert about 1/4 inch (0.6 cm). Heat the exposed part of the tip or insert the shank so that you can rotate it over the hot-melt adhesive stick to apply a thin layer of adhesive (figure 8.24). While the adhesive is fluid, push the tip or insert into the shaft until it seats against the shaft. Wipe off excess adhesive before it dries.

Aluminum–Carbon Shafts   To install tips and inserts in aluminum–carbon shafts, follow the same procedures as with aluminum shafts, but be cautious when using heat with these shafts. When possible, heat the tip rather than the shaft.

Carbon Shafts Arrow tips and inserts are installed in all-carbon shafts with epoxy such as a flexible, two-part, 24-hour epoxy. Fast-drying epoxies are sometimes brittle. Use a cotton-tipped applicator to wipe the tip, its shank, and the inside of the shaft with 91 percent isopropyl alcohol. Let them dry, and then place a small ring of epoxy into the end of the shaft and around the point or insert shank. Rotate the shaft while slowly inserting the point or insert, and continue several more rotations once the tip or insert is seated so that the inside of the shaft is thoroughly coated with epoxy. Wipe off any excess epoxy, and stand the shaft perfectly vertical for the cure time. Once installed with epoxy, arrow tips and inserts cannot be removed from a carbon shaft.

FLETCHING

With time and use, the fletching on your shafts can wear. Certainly, contact with the arrow rest or bow window can cause feathers to fray. Both feathers and vanes can be damaged when struck by other arrows. You can have your existing fletching removed and replaced at a pro shop. You might enjoy fletching your own shafts, although you need to have a fletching jig (figure 8.25). Fletching arrows yourself may only be worthwhile if you do it frequently or do it for others in your family. A fletching jig holds the arrow shaft to ensure that the fletching is precisely positioned and that a set of arrows can be fletched so that all arrows match. The fletching process varies with the type of shaft.

Aluminum Shafts To remove old vanes or feathers, scrape them and any excess glue off the shaft with a dull knife. Clean the shaft with MEK, acetone, or lacquer thinner, and then wipe the shaft with 91 percent isopropyl alcohol. Keep solvents away from your nocks and cresting. You can refletch the arrow shaft when it dries. If you are fletching with vanes, you can also wipe the base of each vane with MEK or lacquer thinner. Avoid handling the base of a feather or cleaned vane. Oils from your fingers could prevent a good bond. Be sure to use a fletching cement intended for this purpose.

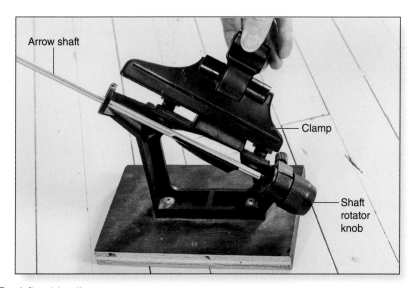

Figure 8.25 A fletching jig.

Insert the vane or feather into the clamp of your fletching jig. The rear of the vane or feather should be 1 to 1-1/4 inch (2.5-3.2 cm) from the bottom of the nock groove.

Place your arrow into the jig. The jig provides an obvious mark for one position where the odd-colored feather should be attached. Apply a thin line of cement along the length of the feather or vane, and then insert the feather or vane into the clamp and the clamp into the jig so that the entire length of the fletching makes contact with the arrow shaft. Let the cement dry for the length of time recommended; then open the clamp and remove it so that you can rotate the jig to the next position. Repeat the process with the next feather or vane. When finished, apply a drop of cement at each front end of each feather or vane to minimize the chances that it will be ripped off if the arrow completely penetrates a target.

Many archers mount plastic vanes straight—that is, parallel to the long axis of the arrow. Feathers, on the other hand, are always mounted at a slight angle, and some archers prefer to do this with plastic vanes as well.

Feathers come from either the right or left wing of a turkey. The underside of the feather is rougher than the top side. The underside is the side of the fletching you want to expose to the oncoming air as the arrow flies. You can tell if you have right- or left-wing feathers by holding them on a shaft and looking down the shaft from the nock end. See how the catch lip of the feather matches figure 8.26.

If you have left-wing arrows, you should offset them slightly so that the oncoming air meets the underside of the feather. This will cause the arrow to spin, providing a stable flight.

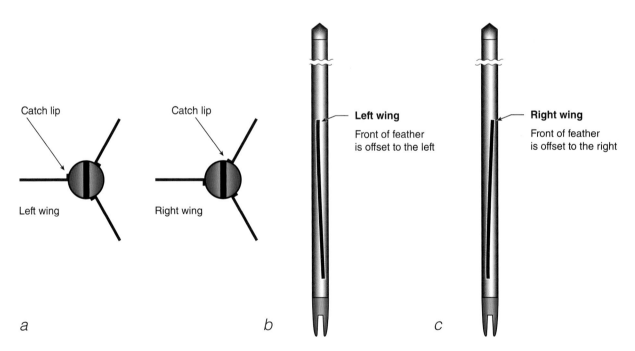

Figure 8.26 *(a)* Viewing from the nock end, note the location of the catch lip to determine whether your feathers are from a left or right wing. *(b)* Left-wing feathers are mounted with the front of the feather to the left; *(c)* right-wing feathers are mounted with the front of the feather to the right.

It makes no difference whether you use left- or right-wing feathers, but you should use the same type for all of the fletching on an arrow and probably on your entire set of arrows. Fletching jigs can be set to mount feathers at this slight offset. Remember that you do not need a large angle and that the entire length of the feather must be in contact with the arrow shaft.

You can choose from a wide range of fletching options. Vanes are cheaper and weatherproof, but advocates of feathers believe that they are faster, lighter, and more forgiving. Fletch colors are a personal preference, except that it is a tradition to use a different color for the cock, or index, feather than for the hen feathers, the other two feathers, to minimize the chances that arrows are nocked backward. Most archers make it a habit to fletch the cock feather first. It makes little difference whether feathers are round or shield shaped. As a starting point, lightweight arrows can be stabilized with three 4-inch (10 cm) feathers, and arrows with broadheads attached can be stabilized with three 5-inch (13 cm) feathers.

Archers who use vanes probably select a size somewhat smaller than the feathers they might otherwise use. Archers who shoot long distances, such as in Olympic-style shoots, often use spin-wing vanes, which are very light, curled Mylar vanes (figure 8.27). They provide minimum drag and high spin rates for this style of shooting. Spin-wing vanes are attached with double-sided tape rather than adhesive. Once you gain more experience, you can experiment with combinations to find the one that provides good arrow clearance and arrow grouping.

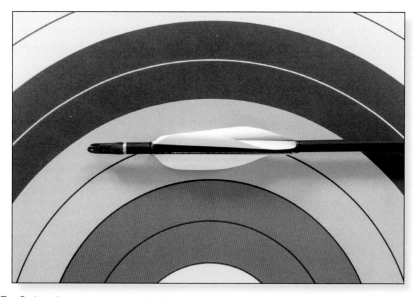

Figure 8.27 Spin-wing vanes are curled.

Aluminum–Carbon and Carbon Shafts Generally, the process of fletching aluminum–carbon and carbon shafts is similar to that for aluminum shafts, but you must pay particular attention to the materials used for cleaning shafts and to the adhesives. Use only those recommended for these shafts and for this purpose. For example, superglues provide a good bond with carbon, but it might be impossible to remove fletching attached with a superglue without ruining the carbon shaft.

To remove old fletching attached with an instant adhesive, peel it off with a dull knife. Be careful not to scrape so deeply as to damage the carbon fibers. You should be able to pull off old fletching attached with standard fletching cement. Wipe the fletching area with lacquer thinner; be sure to keep it away from the nock and any size markings or logos. Use 91 percent isopropyl alcohol for a final wipe, and let the shaft air-dry. Do not touch the area to be fletched after cleaning. Try to fletch within eight hours of cleaning the fletching area; if you can't, you should repeat the cleaning process. Many archers who use carbon shafts put a wrap on the arrow shaft and attach the fletching to the wrap. When fletching must be replaced, the wrap and fletching together can be removed. This prevents having to scrape and perhaps damage the carbon fibers.

If you are fletching plastic vanes, wipe the base of each vane with MEK or lacquer thinner unless the manufacturer says this is unnecessary. Avoid touching the base with your fingers after cleaning. Be sure to use an adhesive made for the carbon surface of the shaft, and follow the same fletching process as described for aluminum shafts.

ALUMINUM ARROWS

Straight arrows are as important to shooting accuracy as straight nocks. You can straighten aluminum shafts on any of several commercial straighteners if they are not too severely bent. Most pro shops make a straightener available to their customers.

Arrow straighteners have two adjustable blocks, each of which has two ball-bearing wheels. The arrow rests in the trough created by the two wheels (figure 8.28). For slight bends, leave the blocks at the ends of the straightener. For sharp bends or bends near the end of the shaft, move the blocks closer together. Raise the plunger and place the arrow underneath it and in the trough of each block. Starting at the point end, rotate the arrow with your index finger, being sure to position your finger on the arrow directly over the wheels in either one of the blocks. Repeat, moving the arrow through the straightener until you reach the fletched end.

If at any point the needle on the straightener's dial swings more than two lines, the arrow should be straightened. Find the place on the arrow shaft that yields the most needle deflection by rotating the arrow until the needle swings the greatest amount in the clockwise direction. The peak of the bend is now uppermost. Press down on the straightening lever. Rotate the arrow to see whether the bend has been removed. If it hasn't, repeat the process. When the needle deflection remains within the two lines on the dial, the arrow is straight.

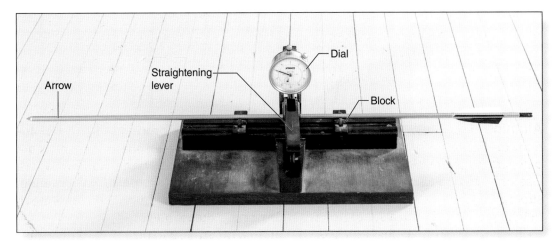

Figure 8.28 An arrow straightener.

Arrow straightness is important, so you should check your arrows frequently. To check your arrows when you are away from a straightener or are on the range after scoring, put the fingernails of your thumb and middle finger together. Rest the arrow shaft on your fingernails below the fletching with the arrow point resting in your other palm. Blow on the fletching. If the shaft jumps on your fingernails rather than spinning smoothly, the shaft might have a bend.

CARBON ARROWS

When carbon shafts enter a target mat, the heat generated from friction slows the arrow and can cause particles from the target mat to bond to the carbon surface. This can make it difficult to remove the arrow from the target. You can avoid this by periodically putting a coat of hard paste wax on the point end of the shaft or even rubbing a bar of soap on the point end. You also can wipe the point end of the shaft with a rag coated in silicone wax. When pulling arrows, use an arrow puller or rubber sheet such as a jar opener.

Check carbon shafts for cracks and damage before shooting and after every shot. Carbon shafts are more susceptible to cracking than other arrow shafts when they hit hard objects. To check for damage, hold the arrow at each end. Bend it an inch or two (2.5-5 cm) away from you and listen for cracking noises. Repeat four to six times as you rotate the shaft until you have gone around the entire arrow. If you hear or feel cracking, the arrow is damaged. You should also twist the shaft in both directions as you hold each end. If it twists easily or relaxes, it is damaged. Do not shoot a damaged arrow. It could splinter on release and injure you or someone around you. Discard this damaged arrow so that no one can shoot it.

Maintaining a Bow

Most bows will shoot well for years if properly maintained. One key to maintaining a bow is remembering that laminated bows and limbs have layers of materials that are bonded together. Extreme heat, such as that in a closed car on a hot, sunny day, can affect the adhesives used in manufacturing a bow. Prolonged exposure to moisture can affect them as well. Never lay a bow in damp grass. If you shoot a bow in the rain, wipe it dry when you finish shooting. You can help protect the bow by waxing it frequently with a special bow wax, as you do a bowstring, or other wax (figure 8.29). Solid fiberglass bows can withstand heat and moisture better than laminated bows can, but you should still avoid extremes.

Store bows in a case that lies flat or is hung vertically. In these positions, neither limb takes more pressure than

Figure 8.29 Waxing your bowstring minimizes fraying and protects it from moisture.

the other. Standing a bow in a corner eventually weakens the lower limb. Recurve and straight-limb bows should be unstrung for any month that they will not be shot. Storing them in a relaxed position helps maintain their strength. Stringing and unstringing a bow with a bowstringer is better than doing it by hand because bowstringers put equal tension on both limbs and do not twist the limbs (figure 8.30).

Bowstringers made of cord are easy to use, easy to transport, and inexpensive. To string your bow, slide one loop of the bowstring down the upper limb of your bow, and seat the loop of the other end of the bowstring on the lower limb tip. The leather pockets at the end of a bowstringer's long cord are placed on the limb tips. One leather pocket is usually bigger than the other. The bigger pocket slides over the limb tip where the bowstring loop is already positioned. Hold the bow handle in your dominant hand with the string hanging below the bow; then step on the middle of the bowstringer's cord. As you pull up on the bow handle, the bow bends toward its strung shape. As you bend the bow, use your other hand to slide the bowstring loop up the bow limb until it is seated in the limb tip's groove. You can then remove the bowstringer's leather pockets from each limb tip. Inspect both ends of the bowstring to be sure they are properly seated in the limb tip grooves before you shoot.

Compound bows should remain strung. Their limbs are not under as much tension as those of a strung recurve or straight-limb bow because the cam does much of the work. If you are going to store your compound bow for a long time, however, you should unscrew the limb bolts to reduce the poundage.

You may also need to lubricate your compound bow periodically. Usually, the bow manufacturer gives specific instructions on what parts need lubrication (some may be sealed or self-lubricating), how to do this, and what lubricant to use. Most pro shops also provide this service. You also need to have the cables on a compound bow replaced periodically. Archers shooting four or more times per week often replace their cables about every 18 months.

Bowstrings deserve your attention. Breaking a string can cost you points in competition because the arrow might not score well or at all. Waxing your bowstrings

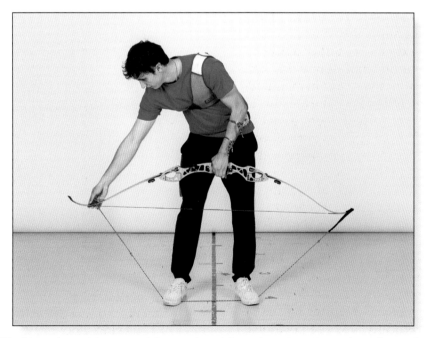

Figure 8.30 Use a bowstringer to string and unstring a bow to put equal tension on both limbs.

frequently with a bowstring wax minimizes fraying and wards off moisture (see figure 8.29). Waxed strings are also less likely to tangle when not in use. Compound bow archers should wax the string and synthetic cables on a regular basis. To wax a string, rub the wax on the string once or twice, and then run your fingers up and down the string for a few minutes to distribute the wax evenly.

You don't have to wax the serving on a bowstring. You should, however, replace the serving if it is loose. If the serving begins to fray during a tournament or shooting session, you can tie it off temporarily and replace it later.

Tournament archers always carry one or more backup strings with them. Because new strings stretch slightly when they are first put on a bow, the well-prepared archer breaks in backup strings by shooting them for a practice session or two. Tournament archers often keep a log of the number of shots they have taken with a string so they can replace it before it is likely to break.

You must replace arrow rests periodically because they become worn or broken. To ensure good equipment performance, make sure the new rest is in the right place. If your bow is equipped with a cushion plunger, adjust the height of the new rest so that the center of your arrow shaft contacts the center of the cushion plunger. Adjust your arrow rest in the forward or backward direction so that the arrow contacts the rest below the cushion plunger.

If your bow does not have a cushion plunger, install an arrow rest that has a pressure point made of a flexible material such as plastic. Place the arrow rest so that the pressure point is directly above the pivot point of the bow. Deviating from this point either forward or backward usually magnifies the effect of poor bow hand position and the torque caused by the bow hand.

Maintaining Exercise 1   Replacing a Nock

Obtain an aluminum arrow without a nock and a nock of the appropriate size for that arrow shaft size (table 8.6). Obtain a tube of fletching cement, and install the nock as directed. Allow the adhesive to dry; then test the straightness of your nock. Place the shaft on a table with the fletched end extending off the table. Roll the arrow back and forth on the table and examine the nock. If it does not have a wobbly appearance, it is ready to be used. If the nock does appear to wobble, the nock is crooked. Remove the nock and reinstall it.

Success Check

• Align nock with axis of shaft.

Score Your Success

Properly install nock on the first try = 3 points

Properly install nock on the second try = 2 points

Your score _____

ANSWER KEY

ARROW SELECTION EXERCISE 1. READING AN ARROW SPINE CHART

1. Aluminum spine sizes 2212, 2114; Carbon and aluminum–carbon 500, 550
2. Aluminum spine sizes 2212, 2213; Carbon and aluminum–carbon 450, 500
3. Aluminum spine sizes 1913, 1914; Carbon and aluminum–carbon 650, 660

SUCCESS SUMMARY

In archery, success depends on equipment as well as form. You must have confidence that your equipment will produce the best score possible, given your performance on a given shot on a given day. You want equipment that is durable, consistent, and forgiving. At the same time, because archery involves so much equipment of various types, someone is always willing to sell you the latest innovation. Learn to be a critical consumer. Identify the advantages and disadvantages of new equipment, and decide whether any new equipment is likely to make a difference in your score.

Whatever the level of equipment you can afford, you can make sure it is set up and adjusted to your benefit. Tuning is a sequence of activities that requires time and patience. Tuning your own equipment teaches you how equipment settings interact with technique and affect results. Use this knowledge to make good judgments when choosing accessories such as an arrow rest.

Finally, be sure to keep your equipment in good working order. Proper maintenance also ensures that you get the most from your equipment. Many of the exercises in this step gave you practice in upgrading, tuning, and maintaining your equipment. Record your progress in the exercises and total your score. If you earned at least 25 points, you can move to the next step. If you scored fewer than 25 points, repeat some of the exercises to earn additional points.

Arrow Selection Exercise

1. Reading an Arrow Spine Chart _____ out of 5

Preliminary Adjustment Exercises

1. Settings _____ out of 3
2. Clearance Test _____ out of 2

Fine-Tuning Exercises

1. Horizontal _____ out of 3
2. Vertical _____ out of 3

Testing Exercises

1. Porpoising Test   _____ out of 3
2. Fishtailing Test   _____ out of 3

Microtuning Exercise

1. Obtaining New Sight Settings   _____ out of 10

Maintaining Exercise

1. Replacing a Nock   _____ out of 3

Total   _____ **out of 35**

In the preceding steps, you worked on your technique; in this step, you worked on upgrading and tuning your equipment. If you are getting the most from your equipment and you have been refining your technique, your scores should be improving. Now you might be wondering what distinguishes elite performers from all the other archers. Certainly, dedicated practice is a large part of the difference, but solid mental skills are another important contribution. In fact, among elite performers with similar equipment and form, mental skills could be the major difference between finishing first and finishing last! It is never too early to acquire and practice good mental skills. Aside from helping you improve your scores, strong mental skills increase your enjoyment of archery.

Sharpening Mental Skills

Athletes from many sports talk about performing in the zone. When they do, they are referring to a time or contest in which their performance was superior and success came almost without thought or effort. Their concentration was extremely focused, even to the point that objects appeared larger than normal or actions seemed as if they were in slow motion. Experiencing the zone while shooting archery is truly an incredible experience. The bull's-eye seems so large that it is hard to miss. The bow feels light. Drawing the bow is effortless.

Performance in the zone is rare. Most athletes would be fortunate to experience it once in their careers. Athletes cannot make themselves perform in the zone, but they can prepare themselves mentally as well as physically to perform. With good mental preparation, athletes open the door to superior performance. They create the conditions that almost always result in success and occasionally result in a once-in-a-lifetime performance. In this step, you will learn how to take a positive mental approach to shooting archery.

As you have learned, the movements involved in archery are relatively simple. Most participants can develop good shooting form if they have an interest in doing so. What often distinguishes elite performers from good performers is their mental approach to shooting. You can enhance your performance by learning to focus on the important aspects of shooting and blocking out both unnecessary or distracting thoughts and distracting events or conditions. This step focuses on these mental skills: managing anxiety, focusing attention, and building confidence.

MANAGING ANXIETY

Sport psychologists often describe an optimal level of anxiety for skill performance. This reflects the fact that being overly anxious can detract from peak performance, but so can being totally relaxed, because a lethargic athlete might not be as alert and attentive as required. An intermediate level of anxiety is optimal, although what constitutes an intermediate level can vary. It can be somewhat higher or lower depending on the nature of the task. It also might be slightly higher or lower for different people on the same task.

Research on shooting tells us that the optimal level of anxiety in archery is probably lower than that for most other sports. Archers must be calm and steady, make only a fine movement to release, and maintain the follow-through position. They also must replicate their shot setups as exactly as possible over and over again.

Each person's optimal level of anxiety is unique, but overall, a low level of anxiety is necessary for accurate shooting. It is natural to be nervous when shooting competitively or shooting game, but archers must learn to attain a relatively low level of anxiety.

Shooting is a rather strange mixture of tension and relaxation when compared to most sport skills. You must hold upward of 25 pounds (11 kg) of force while you hold the bow steady. At the same time, the act of releasing is a small movement, and you must maintain a completely relaxed bow hand throughout the shot, release, and follow-through. You must learn to be selective about which parts of the body are under tension and which are relaxed. The points noted in figure 9.1 include cues to help you relax your bow hand and draw hand. You can add these to your personal mental checklist, especially if you tend to grip your bow or wrap your fingers around the bowstring tightly. You also can practice relaxing specific parts of your body so you can more easily relax your bow hand and draw hand on cue.

Figure 9.1 **STAYING RELAXED**

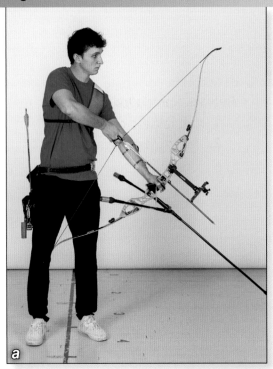

Stance

1. Set sight for shooting distance.
2. Mentally rehearse feeling of perfect shot.
3. Begin mental checklist.

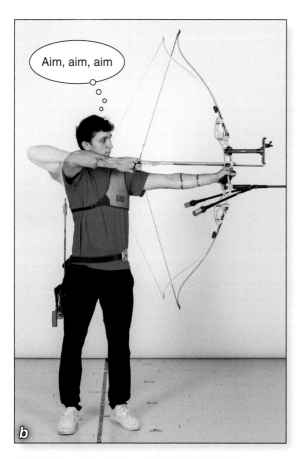

Draw and Aim

1. Continue checklist to draw and anchor.
2. Cue yourself to relax bow hand.
3. Cue yourself to relax draw hand.
4. Shift attention to aiming.

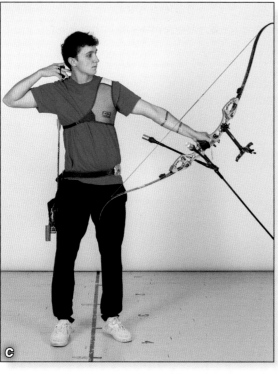

Release and Follow-Through

1. Let release occur.
2. Maintain position until shot hits target.

MISSTEP

You get so nervous shooting that your performance in competition is below that in practice.

CORRECTION

Learn to expect that you will be nervous, but focus on the task at hand. Practice relaxation techniques and associate a cue with your relaxed state. Use the cue when you feel nervous; then focus on the task of shooting.

You might find it more difficult to maintain relaxation under certain situations. Often, when archers really want to shoot well, they tend to tighten their hands so that the bowsight is forced into the bull's-eye. This action is self-defeating because a tight bow hand causes bow torque and a tight draw hand works against a smooth release.

If you shoot archery competitively or hunt, you are likely to experience nervousness. This nervousness comes with competition in most sports; it shows that you care about the outcome. However, you will not be moving about to relieve some of the nervous energy. In archery, you do not run, you do not hit a ball, and you do not throw a ball. Instead, you must relax and hold steady! Accept the fact that you will be nervous but need to give your attention to executing every shot. One archer, commenting on his performance just after he had won a national championship, said that he always got nervous in important competitions, but he simply refused to focus on being nervous and instead focused on executing his shots.

Many archers visualize shooting in the situations that make them nervous. They visualize being at the shooting range with others watching, standing in front of the target, holding their equipment, nocking an arrow, setting up the shot, aiming, releasing, and following through. They mentally practice (cue) relaxing during their shots so the process comes more easily when they are in the actual setting.

Although most people experience the challenge of being nervous and needing to relax, some archers may need to raise their level of alertness. Remember, the optimal level is an intermediate one! Mental imagery often helps archers prepare and center themselves for the tasks at hand if they are lethargic or unfocused as the time to compete approaches.

The more you compete or hunt, the better you should become at identifying your own optimal level of alertness. Learn to recognize when you are too laid back and need to center yourself or gear up for competition. Learn to recognize when you are too anxious and need to relax. Your optimal level might be different from another archer's optimal level; find the state that allows you to perform at your best.

Relaxation Exercise 1   Hand and Arm Relaxation Routine

Practice this exercise in a quiet place where you can sit or lie down. Go through the following steps:

1. Extend right wrist. Hold for 10 seconds; then relax. Repeat.
2. Flex right wrist. Hold for 10 seconds; then relax. Repeat.
3. Repeat extending and flexing with left wrist.
4. Extend and flex right wrist as in steps 1 and 2 but with half as much tension.

5. Extend and flex left wrist as in step 3 but with half as much tension.
6. Extend and flex right wrist with just enough tension that you feel the hold.
7. Extend and flex left wrist with just enough tension that you feel the hold.
8. Bend (flex) at right elbow. Hold for 10 seconds; then relax. Repeat. Repeat with left elbow.

9. Flex right elbow and then left elbow with half as much tension.
10. Flex right elbow and then left elbow with barely enough tension to feel.
11. Clench fist and tighten right arm. Hold for 10 seconds; then relax. Repeat.
12. Clench fist and tighten left arm. Hold for 10 seconds; then relax. Repeat.

TO INCREASE DIFFICULTY

- Add legs and feet.
- Add trunk.

Success Check

- Think about only one body part at a time.

Score Your Success

Complete the entire routine = 3 points

Complete part of the routine = 1 point

Your score _____

Relaxation Exercise 2   Visualization

Practice this exercise in a quiet place where you can sit or lie comfortably. You can play quiet music if you like. Close your eyes. Imagine that you are lying on a warm, sunny beach. Imagine how the sand and sun feel. Then imagine the sound of the ocean. Add more and more details to your mental picture. Or imagine being in any location that you consider relaxing. Associate a label with your image, such as *beach.* The more you practice this visualization, the more likely you will be to be able to relax just by recalling the label!

TO INCREASE DIFFICULTY

- Play relaxing music compatible with your imagined location.

Success Check

- Put your mind in the imagined environment.

Score Your Success

Achieve a totally relaxed state = 3 points

Achieve a slightly relaxed state = 1 point

Your score _____

FOCUSING ATTENTION

The previous steps to success emphasize the need to repeat as exactly as possible every aspect of putting a shot together. This repetition requires concentration. Letting the mind wander to other things and forgetting a critical aspect of shooting form will cause errors. Following your mental checklist through every detail on every shot maximizes the number of good shots you take. Of course, your checklist may need updating from time to time. Yet your ability to concentrate on putting a shot together by moving through the list is related to your success. The secret to archery is learning how to make the perfect shot and then repeating it over and over again.

It is easy to accept that concentration is the key to good shooting. What is difficult is knowing which aspects of putting a shot together need your attention. This information changes as you acquire more skills. You may recall that some of the early steps included details about preparing a shot that were later dropped. With practice, these preparations became second nature. As archers acquire skill, they trim their checklists of items needing conscious attention to a minimum so they can devote more of their attention to aiming.

All athletes find it difficult to let go of a prior shot, swing, throw, or kick that was an error. They are still thinking about the error as they try to execute the next skill, only to make another error. To overcome this natural tendency, an athlete might use the imagery of pushing the thought of the prior mistake out of their mind and turning their attentional focus back to the task at hand. In archery, disciplining yourself to go through the mental checklist is a means to focus on the current shot.

Successful shooters have been studied with the use of tools such as an electroencephalograph (EEG) and heart rate monitors. An EEG measures electrical activity in the brain. Good archery performance is associated with lower levels of brain activity, indicating that movements are carried out automatically. Skilled shooters have little conscious regulation of the release movement. Heart rate during the shot also has been studied. Experienced shooters' heart rates decelerate just before release. This is thought to indicate their focus on something external to themselves—aiming. Successful shooters also report that their total focus is on aiming when they shoot well, allowing the release to happen when the time is right rather than attempting to make it happen. They free themselves of any thoughts or worries about their form, technique, equipment, or even the release of the bowstring (figure 9.2).

Figure 9.2 **FOCUSING ATTENTION**

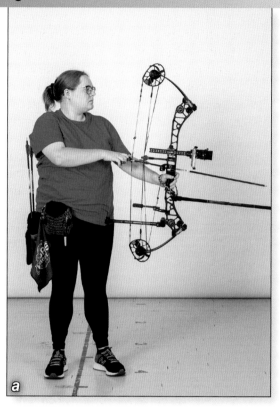

Stance

1. Set sight for shooting distance.
2. Mentally rehearse feeling of a perfect shot.
3. Begin mental checklist.

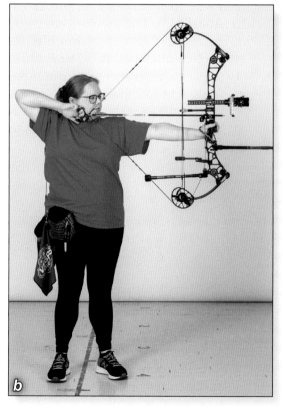

Draw and Aim

1. Continue checklist to draw and anchor.
2. Cue yourself to relax the hands.
3. If setup feels right, shift attention to aiming.
4. Aim at bull's-eye, mentally repeating, *Aim, aim, aim.*

(continued)

Figure 9.2   *(continued)*

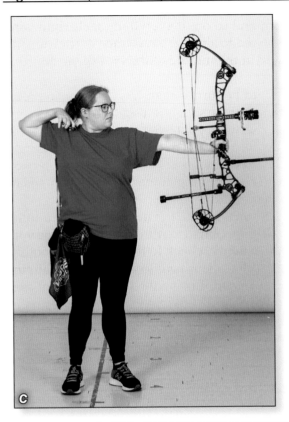

Release and Follow-Through
1. Let release occur.
2. Maintain concentration on bull's-eye.

MISSTEP
You think about other things while you shoot.

CORRECTION
Practice concentrating outside of your archery sessions. While shooting, focus your attention on your mental checklist.

MISSTEP
You think about the prior shot that you executed poorly.

CORRECTION
Push the memory of the prior shot away and refocus on your mental checklist for your current shot.

MISSTEP
You think about form when you should be aiming.

CORRECTION
When you arrive at the aiming step in your mental checklist, shift your attention completely to aiming. It may help to repeat a verbal cue to yourself over and over, such as *Aim, aim, aim*.

Ideally, you should give conscious attention on every shot to the items on your checklist up until the time you are ready to aim. Consider your stance, bow hand position, draw hand position, anchor, leveling, and so on. If everything feels right, aim. All of your concentration must now be devoted to aiming. Your concentration should be so intense that you seem to burn a hole in the middle of the bull's-eye. Nothing should interfere with the aiming process.

The physical aspects of the release should be turned over to your subconscious. You must trust that if there is any indication that the shot is not right, you can assume conscious control and let the shot down. Otherwise, your subconscious will take care of making the release happen at the right time. You do not have to worry about when to make the release happen. The zone described by some athletes probably reflects their intense concentration on their goal, such as aiming at the bull's-eye in archery, and turning over the physical execution of their skills to their subconscious.

Mental imagery can improve your attentional focus. If you tend to let your mind wander to things other than archery, visualize shooting an entire end. Every time your mind wanders to another topic, bring your attention back to the image of shooting. You can do something similar if you tend to think about your form rather than aiming once your shot is set up. Visualize shooting an end. During the visualization of each shot, proceed through your personal mental checklist. When it is time, imagine the bull's-eye and your sight settling on the bull's-eye before the release. If your attention wanders to anything other than aiming, bring it back to focus on the bull's-eye.

Concentration Exercise 1 **Concentration Grid**

You can practice your concentration outside archery practices with a concentration grid (figure 9.3). A concentration grid is a 10-by-10 box grid filled with scrambled two-digit numbers starting with 00. Starting with 11, find the next number in order and put a slash (/) through it. See how many numbers you can put a slash through in one minute.

85	61	55	84	27	51	78	59	52	13
57	29	33	28	60	92	04	97	90	31
86	18	70	32	96	65	39	80	77	49
46	88	00	76	87	71	95	98	81	01
42	62	34	48	82	89	47	35	17	10
94	69	56	44	67	93	11	07	43	72
14	91	02	53	79	05	22	54	74	58
66	20	40	06	68	99	75	26	15	41
45	83	24	50	09	64	08	38	30	36
19	12	63	03	73	21	23	16	37	25

Figure 9.3 Concentration grid.

(continued)

Concentration Exercise 1   *(continued)*

TO INCREASE DIFFICULTY

- Extend time to 90 seconds and double numbers you need to earn points.

Success Check

- Focus on grid.
- Push other thoughts away.

Slash 25 or more numbers in 1 minute = 3 points

Slash 18 to 24 numbers in 1 minute = 2 points

Slash 10 to 17 numbers in 1 minute = 1 point

Your score _____

Concentration Exercise 2   Verbal Cue Exercise

Shoot two ends of six arrows each from any distance you choose. Prepare your shot to the point of aiming. When you are ready to aim, say to yourself, "Aim, aim, aim," until the release occurs.

TO INCREASE DIFFICULTY

- Bring a friend along to watch you shoot.
- Have the friend talk while you are aiming.

Success Check

- Proceed through checklist.
- Refocus if your mind wanders.

Score Your Success

Complete 10 to 12 repetitions with focus on the bull's-eye at release = 3 points

Complete 7 to 9 repetitions with focus on the bull's-eye at release = 2 points

Complete 4 to 6 repetitions with focus on the bull's-eye at release = 1 point

Your score _____

What Sport Science Says About Attention

Sport scientists have studied attention through measurements of visual scanning behavior. Generally, they found that expert performers visually scan the environment to attend to task-relevant information. That is, expert performers selectively extract task-relevant information through visual scanning to make performance decisions. Of course, visual scanning patterns depend on the task. For example, a soccer goalie periodically surveys a large area with many offensive players scattered throughout her field of vision. In contrast, an archer has a much smaller area of importance: the sight aperture and target.

Kim, Chang, and Park (2019) studied the visual scanning behavior of archers, comparing members of the Korean national team with collegiate archers. Eye movements were recorded while the archers watched a video, taken from the archer's perspective, of a shot sequence from approaching the shooting line to aiming. They found that national team archers looked more often at objects such as wind flags and trees at the beginning of the shot sequence compared to collegiate archers. Presumably, this gave the expert group task-relevant information about wind speed and direction. As the shot sequence progressed, both groups narrowed their visual attention. During aiming, archers at both levels had small eye movements and long fixations.

The sport scientists also repeated their eye movement recordings during just the aiming phase of the shot, but with visual or auditory distractors randomly presented. The national team archers demonstrated a more stable and consistent visual scanning pattern when distracted compared to the collegiate archers. They were better able to focus their attention. The ability to maintain attention can be improved by training. This research points to the value of training to improve attentional focus in order to become a more successful archer.

BUILDING CONFIDENCE

For an arrow to hit the center of the bull's-eye, you must believe that it will hit the center of the bull's-eye. You must have confidence that every one of the arrows you shoot has the potential to be a bull's-eye. Remember, success in archery competition comes not from shooting one bull's-eye but from scoring high when all the arrows that have been shot are totaled. Successful archers report having this positive expectation during a peak performance. Bowhunters practice repetitively so that when the opportunity arises, they expect their lone shot to be a successful one.

It is very easy in archery to blame the equipment for your mistakes. The action in archery is so small that it is easy to convince yourself that the equipment is responsible for the outcome, whether good or bad. Archers who lack confidence in their shooting and their ability to execute good shots often blame their failure on their equipment. Continuing to blame the equipment stands in the way of developing confidence in shooting.

As you perfect your form and practice, you will build confidence. You will believe that you control every shot. Think of the saying, "Success breeds success." In archery, success in practice builds confidence and breeds success in competition or in hunting.

What undermines confidence? A common problem with archers is trying to please others with their shooting. Many archers want to live up to someone else's expectations, even on those days when, try as they might, nothing seems to work well. The only person you need to please is yourself. If you make a mistake, don't spend your time trying to explain it away to everyone around you. Accept it, and go on.

When archers make a mistake, they often begin to expect that they'll make that mistake again. They talk about and think about making that mistake. This undermines their confidence. If you find yourself verbalizing a negative statement about your shooting, either aloud or to yourself, turn it into a positive statement. For example, if you find yourself saying, "Oh, no, it's windy, and the last time I shot in the wind I scored terribly," turn this statement around. Say, "The wind will give me a chance to improve over my last score on a windy day." This helps you develop a positive expectation and, over time, confidence in your shooting.

Some archers undermine their confidence when they set unrealistically high goals for themselves. For example, an archer who has been shooting 270 on a 300 round consistently for the past several weeks might go to a tournament wanting to shoot 280. If the 280 happens, great. But is it realistic to expect to shoot above average in the tournament? Of course not! Most likely, this archer is destined to come back from every tournament disappointed and discouraged when she shoots anything but a personal best. If her goal had been to shoot 270 and she achieved that goal, she would be building rather than undermining her confidence.

John Williams, an Olympic gold medalist, recommends setting scoring goals conservatively. Even in practice, if you set what is really the minimum score you would ever want to shoot on a given round, your chances of feeling confident and positive after every practice session are good. Setting the minimum goal makes you work to achieve at least that level. Most often, you will score above it, and in your mind, you will be that many points up rather than points down. When you set a very high–scoring goal and fail to reach it, you create a negative mindset, even if your score was a very good one.

Mentally rehearse shooting a bull's-eye. Sit or lie down in a comfortable position with your eyes closed. You can visualize from an internal perspective or an external one (seeing yourself on television, for example), as you prefer.

MENTALLY REHEARSING A BULL'S-EYE

1. See yourself take your stance and nock an arrow.
2. Imagine yourself standing tall.
3. See yourself taking your bow hand grip and raising the bow.
4. See yourself setting your draw hand hook or your release aid.
5. Feel yourself drawing and setting your anchor.
6. See yourself aligning the bow, string, sight, and target and aiming.
7. Imagine the release.
8. See the arrow hit the bull's-eye.
9. See yourself maintaining your follow-through position.

MISSTEP

You verbalize negative statements about your shooting.

CORRECTION

Stop the statement immediately and formulate a positive statement on the same topic.

MISSTEP

You hold a visual image of a bad shot and keep seeing it over and over.

CORRECTION

Stop imagining the bad shot. Mentally rehearse a perfect shot that lands in the middle of the bull's-eye.

Confidence Exercise 1   Mental Rehearsal

At a regular practice session, shoot three ends as you normally do. After any shot you consider a mistake, mentally rehearse the feel of a good shot, and see the arrow hitting the bull's-eye before you take your next shot.

Success Check

- Proceed through your mental checklist.

Score Your Success

Improve your score 5 points or more over three ends with mentally rehearsed shots = 3 points

Improve your score 1 to 4 points over three ends with mentally rehearsed shots = 1 point

Your score _____

Confidence Exercise 2   Imagery Practice

Sit quietly with your eyes closed. Practice using imagery by trying to see every detail of a close friend. Make the image as vivid as possible, almost as if you were seeing this friend on television. When you can do this exercise well, picture your bow, including every detail possible.

Then picture yourself performing with the bow. See every detail and hear the sounds that accompany shooting. Feel your muscles as they tense or relax. Note that you can picture your performance from the outside as if you were seeing yourself on television or from the inside as it feels to perform.

Success Check

- See more and more detail.
- Stay relaxed.

Score Your Success

8 minutes or more of imagery practice = 3 points

6 minutes up to 8 minutes of imagery practice = 2 points

Less than 6 minutes of imagery practice = 1 point

Your score _____

Confidence Exercise 3   **Thought Stopping**

In this exercise, you turn negative statements about archery performance into positive statements. For each negative statement in table 9.1, write a positive counterstatement. Verbalize these statements. Then write several negative statements you find yourself saying and create positive counterstatements. Say the positive statements aloud several times.

Table 9.1   Turning Negative Statements Into Positive Statements

Negative statement	Reformulated positive statement
It's so windy, I can't keep the arrows on the target.	
I can't shoot well from 40 yards (37 m).	
I'm afraid I'll miss the whole target.	

Success Check

- Think positively.

Score Your Success

Write five positive statements about your archery performance = 3 points

Write one to four positive statements about your archery performance = 1 point

Your score _____

Confidence Exercise 4   **Goal Setting**

Athletes often overlook setting goals for performance on several levels. For example, you can set goals for the very near future or the distant future. Considering your recent archery performance, write goals for the time frames listed in table 9.2. Also, set a target date for achieving your long-term goals.

Table 9.2   Setting Goals

Time frame	Goal	Target date
Next practice		
Short term		
Intermediate		
Long term		

Success Check

- Keep goals realistic.

Establish goals in four time frames = 3 points

Establish goals in three time frames = 2 points

Establish goals in two time frames = 1 point

Your score _____

SUCCESS SUMMARY

Archers can be successful by establishing good form and repeating that good form on every shot. As with many sports, though, often little separates archers in physical skills and equipment. Therefore, a good mental approach is very important.

Strong mental skills help archers achieve success and long-lasting enjoyment of the sport. Good mental skills are no more accidental than good shooting skills. Both must be practiced. The time spent practicing mental skills will return to you in years of archery enjoyment. Your goals and expectations will be realistic, and you will stay relaxed and feel competent when shooting.

For each of the exercises in this step, you can earn points to chart your progress. Enter your scores and add them up to rate your success in applying mental skills. If you earned at least 17 points, move to the next step. If you earned fewer than 17 points, repeat some of the exercises before moving on.

Relaxation Exercises

1. Hand and Arm Relaxation Routine _____ out of 3
2. Visualization _____ out of 3

Concentration Exercises

1. Concentration Grid _____ out of 3
2. Verbal Cue Exercise _____ out of 3

Confidence Exercises

1. Mental Rehearsal _____ out of 3
2. Imagery Practice _____ out of 3
3. Thought Stopping _____ out of 3
4. Goal Setting _____ out of 3

Total _____ **out of 24**

The movements in archery are small and fine. Most people can learn the movements and good technique with adequate instruction and practice. Continued practice can bring them more scoring success. What often distinguishes archers is their mental approach to shooting. Now that you have acquired both physical and mental skills for archery, it may be time to apply those skills in either competitive target shooting or bowhunting. In the next step, you will read about competing in target archery tournaments, and you can decide whether this archery activity is for you.

Competing in Target Archery

Probably no group was more touched than the archery participants in the opening ceremonies of the 1992 Olympics when an archer lit the Olympic torch with a flaming arrow. It demonstrated the challenge and the majesty of accurate shooting with a bow and arrow. That opening ceremony gave them a special memory in addition to a special event in their lives: representing their countries in Olympic competition. Sharing this event with the best archers in the world was probably a long-standing goal for most. Interest in the archery events at the Olympics has increased, partly because of popular movies featuring archery and partly because the competition format was redesigned to use technology to increase spectator interest. Under the format used in the 2012 Olympics, the women's gold medal match was decided by a single, closest-to-the-center shot. Nothing can be more exciting than that! Although few archers can have an Olympic experience, every archer can come together with others to shoot in tournaments and weekly leagues.

Submitting your skills to the test of a tournament provides a landmark for which you can prepare by bringing your mental and physical skills together. The results also motivate you to continue practicing and striving to achieve new goals. This step will familiarize you with tournament shooting and give you an opportunity to shoot a tournament score, either alone or with a group of archers.

While learning a skill such as archery, most people find it helpful to have clear goals. This is particularly true once you have learned the basics and need further practice and refinement to reach a higher level. Shooting for a score is one way to do this; you can set your sights on obtaining an appropriately higher score the next time you compete.

Monitoring your scores over time tells you how you are progressing; scoring is a source of feedback on your progress in archery skills. If you improve on your previous scores, it is likely that your form is good and you are on the right track. A drop in score can signal that you have fallen into a bad habit. You can then review your form for the basics and reestablish your form. Archery is the type of sport in which competition is within more than it is against another archer. Yet scores also provide a means of comparing your skill with that of other archers.

Tournaments are the ultimate test of archery skills. They are a good test of your skill in a more public setting than practice sessions. If you can perform well when your score counts, then you can take pride in your archery achievements. Competing in tournaments also is an excellent way to meet other archers and to talk with them about equipment and shooting. Tournaments are held at many levels: local, state, national, and international. Start with local tournaments and work your way up as you gain competition experience.

Another way to enjoy archery competition is by shooting in an archery league. These are usually weekly competitions organized around teams; each archer has a handicap so that shooters of all levels, ages, genders, and any equipment classification can compete in the same program. Awards might be given for first-place team, most improved archer, or other distinctions.

For young archers, the National Archery in the Schools Program (NASP) provides a means of learning to shoot, practicing skills, and competing, as an individual or as a team. Regional, state, and national tournaments are often organized, as are international tournaments, sometimes as "virtual" tournaments wherein scores are submitted to a website by certified instructors.

To shoot competitively, you need to take several steps. First, you must learn how to score in a tournament. You also must know how to participate according to the rules of archery. You need to know how to shoot in wind and rain at outdoor tournaments and how to handle nerves during tournaments. Finally, you need to know about additional equipment appropriate for tournament shooting. This step reviews these topics, but remember, too, that your equipment needs to be in good working order to allow you to shoot competitively. You should get the best equipment you can afford and then tune it as discussed in step 8.

SCORING IN A TOURNAMENT

The first step toward participating in a tournament is learning the scoring procedures used in archery. To compare your performance with that of other archers, you must score your shots consistently. You would obtain very different scores if, for example, one time you gave arrows cutting two rings the higher value and another time you gave them the lower value. You must record the scores the same way as others are recording them, particularly in a tournament in which many people are shooting. Questions may arise regarding the accuracy of a score at the conclusion of shooting, and the scorecard is the official and permanent record of what really happened. Some tournaments break ties by counting the number of hits on the target, the number of bull's-eyes, the number of hits in a small tiebreaker ring, and so on. All archers must be aware of scoring procedures and must keep score accurately in order to compare their performances.

At tournaments, each archer is assigned to a target at check-in. Scorecards are either given to the archer or placed at the assigned target (figure 10.1a). Typically, four archers are assigned to a target (figure 10.1b). Depending on the shooting distance and equipment classification, all four archers might shoot at one target face, or each archer might shoot at their own target face. These archers perform specific scoring duties either by assignment of the tournament officials or by mutual agreement of the archers. One archer serves as target captain and calls out the value of each arrow on the target, archer by archer. If an archer disagrees with a call, a tournament official is called to make the final decision on that arrow (figure 10.1c). The tournament official might use a magnifying glass to decide. Two of the remaining archers keep score on independent sets of scorecards. They may cross-check each archer's end score and running score on each end so that discrepancies can be quickly rectified. The fourth archer retrieves any arrows that miss the target and may assist the target captain by checking the scores announced.

Figure 10.1 **SCORING IN A TOURNAMENT**

Scorecard

1. Obtain scorecard at check-in.
2. Obtain target assignment.

Roles

1. One archer calls arrow values.
2. Two archers write scores independently.
3. Any additional archers observe scores as called and retrieve arrows.

(continued)

Courtesy of Competition Archery Media.

Figure 10.1   *(continued)*

Rules

1. Arrows on lines get higher value.
2. Arrows are not touched until scored.
3. Highest value is dropped if too many arrows are shot.
4. Unshot arrows are scored zero.
5. Undecided arrows are called by tournament official.

The tournament officials usually provide a scorecard that is prepared specifically for the round being shot. Figure 10.2 shows an example. The value of each arrow is entered on the card in the appropriate area, as is the end score and, often, a running score. Although the two archers keeping score on each target cross-check the scorecards, the archer being scored is responsible for seeing that everything on the card, including the addition of the score, is correct before the scorecard is turned in at the conclusion of the day's shooting. In some tournaments, an archer can be disqualified for scorecard errors. When the archer is satisfied that the scorecard is correct, each scorekeeper and the archer sign the card before submitting it.

Each archery governing body and tournament can have specific rules for scoring, but the following guidelines are common to most sets of rules:

1. The traditional target face in archery consists of five concentric scoring zones: gold or yellow, red, blue, black, and white, from the center outward. Each color zone is divided into two equally wide zones by a thin line. This division results in 10 scoring zones of equal width. The innermost zone has a value of 10, the next 9, and so on through the outermost zone, which has a value of 1. The target face can be of various diameters, but the scoring zones must all be of equal width. An even smaller circle inside the 10 ring is sometimes used for tie-breaking purposes.

2. The lines dividing the scoring zones are considered to be entirely within the higher scoring area. Any arrow touching a dividing line even slightly is therefore assigned the higher value. An exception is a tournament or certain scoring ends designated for inside-out scoring. If an arrow touches a line in this type of scoring, it is considered to be in the lower scoring area. Inside-out scoring is sometimes used as a tiebreaker or in classifications for archers using mechanical releases. The competition in this category can be so close that only finer scoring will determine a winner.

						Hits	Score
Name							
Class							
50 yards							
Distance score							
40 yards							
Distance score							
30 yards							
Distance score							
Total score							

Figure 10.2 Scorecard prepared for a Columbia round. Compare this scorecard to the information about a Columbia round in table 10.1.

3. Arrows are scored by the positions of the shafts in the target face at the time that archers arrive at the target butt to score the arrows. Arrows sometimes enter the target at an angle or vibrate on impact, tearing into an adjacent scoring ring. These tears are ignored, and the arrows are scored as they are sitting in the target face. A subsequent shot arrow can strike an arrow in the target and push it slightly. Again, the arrows are scored as they are sitting in the target face.

4. You are not allowed to touch any of the arrows in the target or the target face itself until all the arrows are scored and any questionable scores are decided by the appropriate official.

5. Arrows that skip into the target after striking the ground receive a score of 0.

6. If an arrow passes through the target face but not the target butt, it can be pushed back through the butt and target face to determine which scoring zone it penetrated.

7. If an arrow passes completely through the target butt or bounces out of the scoring area and is witnessed by another archer or tournament official, it is scored as 7 points unless the procedure in the tournament is to mark the

target face at the impact point of each arrow during scoring. In this case, the pass-through or bounce-out arrow is scored according to the hole made in the target face.

8. If you shoot more arrows than the number specified to constitute an end in the round being shot, only the lowest-scoring arrows in the number constituting an end are scored. For example, if an end consists of six arrows and you shoot seven, only the lowest-scoring six arrows are scored.

9. If you do not shoot all the arrows allowed in an end and do not discover this fact before the signal to score or retire from the shooting line, you lose the chance to shoot those arrows, and you receive 0 points for them.

10. Any arrows you shoot into a target other than the particular target assigned to you are not scored.

11. An arrow that embeds itself in another arrow and does not therefore reach the target face is scored as the same value as the arrow in which it is embedded.

Generally, 40-centimeter targets are used for indoor archery rounds that are typically shot at 18 meters, or 20 yards. For outdoor shooting distances of 30 to 50 meters, 80-centimeter targets are used, and for shooting distances of 70 to 90 meters, 122-centimeter targets are used. With advancements in archery equipment and the use of compound bows and mechanical releases, it is common for multiple archers to shoot perfect scores. This has led to the use of a smaller ring inside the 10 ring (or inside the 5 ring on a field archery target face), often called the X-ring. The number of arrows in the X-ring is recorded and used in the event of a tie in score. In some cases, the X-ring is scored 10 and the remaining area of the gold is scored 9. The high quality of shooting, especially indoors, also has led to the use of multi-spot target faces (see figure 5.6) rather than the standard multicolor target face. Note that multi-spot targets feature only the inner rings (6-10), and arrows falling outside the 6 ring are scored zero. Three-spot target faces can arrange the targets in a triangle or in a straight vertical line. Some tournaments require compound bow shooters to use a multi-spot target, and some give recurve bow shooters the option to do so. Archers can shoot multi-spot targets in any order.

Some tournaments, including the Olympics, have two archers shoot against each other, and the higher scorer advances to meet the winner of another pair of shooters until eventually a winner is determined. Within each "minicompetition," a small number of sets of three arrows (usually five sets) is shot. The archer with the highest score in the set receives 2 points for winning the set. In the case of a tie, each archer receives 1 point. The archer with the most points advances to another round until a winner is determined. Sometimes archers qualify for this head-to-head shooting by competing for total score in a short tournament round, called a positioning round, and the scores are used to seed archers for the head-to-head portion. In the case of head-to-head shooting, the actual score is not important. The person with the higher score merely moves on in the tournament, but the scoring rules for arrows presented here still apply.

At the 2012 World Cup Finals, an automatic scoring system using optical lasers was tested. Automatic scoring in real time makes archery events more exciting for spectators and shooters alike. The system can identify the scoring value and exact position of an arrow as well as its distance from center, which is the tiebreaker in many competitions when archers are tied in head-to-head shooting after the required number of arrows. With the success of this system at the World Cup, automatic scoring has become more common, especially for medal rounds at the Olympics and shoot-off rounds in other tournaments. TV coverage of head-to-head shooting using an automatic scoring system is as exciting as any sport, with the value of each archer's arrow announced immediately after it strikes the target.

Scoring Exercise 1   Scoring by End

Figures 10.3 through 10.6 show four targets. Each target has the location of shot arrows marked by dots. Place the value of each arrow in the appropriate space on the scorecard shown in figure 10.7, with the arrows of greater value to the left. Also indicate the number of hits, or arrows striking the target face, as well as the total score for the end and the running score as additional ends are shot. Double-check your score by adding the column of end scores and comparing the result with the running score. The correct, completed scorecard appears at the end of this step.

Figure 10.3   End 1: One arrow missed the target.

Figure 10.4   End 2: One arrow bounced out of the scoring target and was witnessed by another archer.

(continued)

Scoring Exercise 1 *(continued)*

Figure 10.5 End 3: One arrow skipped into the 2 ring after striking the ground, and another is embedded in the arrow in the 9 ring.

Figure 10.6 End 4: Seven arrows are in the target face.

End	Scorecard						Hits	End score	Running score
1									
2									
3									
4									
Total									

Figure 10.7 Scorecard for the Scoring by End exercise.

Success Check

- If too many arrows are shot, the highest value is dropped.
- Arrows that bounce out count as 7 points. Arrows that skip in count as 0 points.
- Any arrow embedded in another arrow takes the same value.

Score Your Success

Complete accurate scorecard = 3 points

Complete scorecard with one error = 1 point

Your score _____

SHOOTING IN A TOURNAMENT

Before the day of a tournament, you have several responsibilities. One is to see that all equipment is in safe condition; another is to ensure that the equipment will provide the best possible shooting efficiency. Inspect your arrows and straighten them if necessary. Prepare a backup bowstring, and gather other spare parts such as arrow nocks and arrow rests (figure 10.8a). Inspect the nock locator and serving. Inspect the bowsight and tighten any screws. Inspect the arrow rest and cushion plunger. Take the time to see that the equipment is prepared to perform as expected. Furthermore, you must obtain sight settings for all distances that will be shot in the tournament. In contests that are important to competitors, such as the Olympics, archers typically have two identical bows, set up as identically as possible, in case there is a problem with one bow or any of its parts.

Figure 10.8 SHOOTING IN A TOURNAMENT

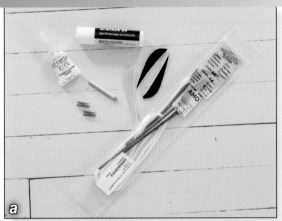

Preparation

1. Check equipment for safety and efficiency.
2. Gather spare parts for backup.
3. Get sight settings for needed distances.
4. Prepare food, drink, and clothing.

Procedures During Shooting

1. Follow signals of tournament official.
2. Retire from line when finished shooting.
3. Manage time to shoot all arrows if time is limited.
4. Raise bow if equipment fails.
5. Be courteous to other archers.

Prepare carefully for outdoor tournaments. In hot and humid weather, you should take the same precautions as any other athlete would. Although archery competition is not as intense as other sport contests, it can last longer, sometimes all day. Bring plenty of water and a hat. Use sunscreen, and consider bringing a chair and sun umbrella. You should also prepare for rain. Unless there is lightning, most tournaments continue in light rain.

Although it is important to prepare your equipment and accessories in the last days before a tournament, this is probably not the time to make drastic changes in your equipment setup or form. Even if a change will serve you well in the long run, it is best to save changes for posttournament practice. A change in form immediately before a tournament can result in you faltering under pressure, which will hurt your scoring. Because it is tempting to second-guess equipment changes if you do not score better immediately, last-minute changes can distract you from focusing where you should: on back tension and aiming.

A tournament official controls the shooting in a tournament with whistle signals. One whistle blast typically indicates that archers on the shooting line can begin shooting. Two blasts signal that archers can cross the shooting line to score. Three or more blasts mean that shooting should cease immediately because an emergency situation exists.

Large tournaments often have multiple shooting lines. Half the archers assigned to a target step up to the line to shoot their ends, and then they retire from the line while the remaining archers shoot, all before any arrows are scored (see figure 10.8b). In this case, another single whistle blast is used to indicate the end of shooting for one line and to call the second group to the line. Yet another single blast indicates that the second shooting line can begin shooting.

Tournament officials often establish a time limit for shooting the arrows within an end. The time limit chosen depends on the number of arrows shot in each end, but it also varies from tournament to tournament. Usually, a warning signal is given when only 30 seconds remain in the time period. Check to see whether a time limit will be in effect for the tournament you plan to enter and, if so, how long it will be. Practice shooting with a timer so that you can establish a good shooting rhythm and pace. In the tournament, then, you can shoot as you have practiced and avoid being distracted by the time limit.

Most tournament rules provide a time period during which you can repair or replace equipment that fails on the shooting line. If this should happen, raise your bow while on the shooting line to signal the tournament official. You will be given an opportunity to shoot missed arrows at a later time, provided you can make the necessary repairs in the time allowed.

Archery tournaments provide an opportunity to make new friends and renew old acquaintances. Between shooting ends, you can visit with other archers or friends or keep to yourself, as you prefer. It is common courtesy, however, not to disturb archers who are on the line shooting, either directly or indirectly, by talking loudly or creating distractions. You should never talk while on the shooting line, unless it is necessary for the purposes of the tournament. You should also avoid distracting fellow archers on either side of you by moving onto or off the shooting line while they are at full draw. Among some archers it is traditional to remain on the shooting line until the archer on either side has finished shooting all arrows so that no archer is left on the line alone to finish shooting.

The number of arrows shot in a scoring round, the size of the target, and the shooting distances vary from round to round. This variety often adds to the interest of target shooting. Each round provides its own challenge. Examples of the common scoring rounds are given in table 10.1. Though these are the established archery rounds, archers are always free to design their own or modify an established round, provided all participants are made aware of the rules beforehand.

The NASP provides tournaments for students in grades 4 to 12 if their school teaches an approved instructional and safety program to all students during the school day. NASP tournament shooting requires archers to use the Genesis bow and Easton 1820 aluminum arrows. No sights, stabilizers, or mechanical releases are allowed. Rather, good shooting form is emphasized. The round used in NASP tournaments is described in table 10.1.

Table 10.1 Popular Target Rounds

Round	Number of arrows per distance	Size of face	Number of arrows per end	Perfect score	Age group
FITA[a] Outdoor Target Archery round, men	36 at 90 m 36 at 70 m 36 at 50 m 36 at 30 m	122 cm 80 cm	6 (shot 3 and 3)	1,440	Adult
FITA Outdoor Target Archery round, women	36 at 70 m 36 at 60 m 36 at 50 m 36 at 30 m	122 cm 80 cm	6 (shot 3 and 3)	1,440	Adult
Olympic round, men Elimination round Finals round	18 at 70 m 12 at 70 m	122 cm	6 3	180 120	Adult (adapted for youth)
Olympic round, women Elimination round Finals round	18 at 60 m 12 at 60 m	122 cm	6 3	180 120	Adult
Olympic rounds, team Men Women	9 per archer 27 per team men 70 m women 60 m	122 cm	3 per archer	270	Adult
FITA standard round	36 at 50 m 36 at 30 m	122 cm	3	720	Adult
Metric 900 or FITA 900	30 at 60 m 30 at 50 m 30 at 40 m	122 cm	6 (shot 3 and 3)	900	Adult
Metric Easton 600	20 at 60 m 20 at 50 m 20 at 40 m	122 cm	5	600	Adult
Metric Collegiate 600	20 at 50 m 20 at 40 m 20 at 30 m	122 cm	5	600	Adult

(continued)

Table 10.1   *(continued)*

Round	Number of arrows per distance	Size of face	Number of arrows per end	Perfect score	Age group
American	30 at 60 yd 30 at 50 yd 30 at 40 yd	48 in., scored 9 to 1	6	810	Adult
Columbia	24 at 50 yd 24 at 40 yd 24 at 30 yd	48 in., scored 9 to 1	6	648	Adult
720 Collegiate	24 at 50 m 24 at 40 m 24 at 30 m	80 cm	6	720	Adult
Junior Metric 900	30 at 50 m 30 at 40 m 30 at 30 m	122 cm	6	900	12-15 years
Cadet Metric 900	30 at 40 m 30 at 30 m 30 at 20 m	122 cm	6	900	Under 12 years
Interscholastic Metric	36 at 50 m 36 at 30 m	122 cm 80 cm	6	720	14-18 years
Modified Collegiate, boys	20 at 50 m 20 at 40 m 20 at 30 m	122 cm 80 cm	5	600	14-18 years
Modified Collegiate, girls	20 at 40 m 20 at 30 m 20 at 20 m	122 cm 80 cm	5	600	14-18 years
Junior Metric	36 at 60 m 36 at 50 m 36 at 40 m 36 at 30 m	122 cm 80 cm	6 (shot 3 and 3)	1,440	12-15 years
Cadet Metric	36 at 45 m 36 at 35 m 36 at 25 m 36 at 15 m	122 cm 80 cm	6 (shot 3 and 3)	1,440	Under 12 years
Junior American	30 at 50 yd 30 at 40 yd 30 at 30 yd	48 in., scored 9 to 1	6	810	12-15 years
Cadet American	30 at 40 yd 30 at 30 yd 30 at 20 yd	48 in., scored 9 to 1	6	810	Under 12 years
Junior Columbia	24 at 40 yd 24 at 30 yd 24 at 20 yd	48 in., scored 9 to 1	6	648	Under 12 years
NASP[b]	15 at 15 m 15 at 10 m	80 cm	5	300	Grades 4-12
18 m FITA Indoor	60 at 18 m	40 cm	3	600	Adult
25 m FITA Indoor	60 at 25 m	60 cm	3	600	Adult
Modified FITA Indoor	30 at 18 m	80 cm	3	300	14-18 years

Round	Number of arrows per distance	Size of face	Number of arrows per end	Perfect score	Age group
NAA[c] 300 Indoor	60 at 20 yd	16 in., scored 5 to 1	5	300	Adult
Chicago Indoor	96 at 20 yd	16 in., scored 9 to 1	6	864	Adult
USA Archery/World Archery Indoor round	60 at 18 m	40 cm	3	600	Adult
Vegas round	30 at 20 yd	40 cm	3	300	Adult
Lancaster Classic	60 at 18 m	40 cm	3	660 (X-ring scored 11 pts)	Adult
NFAA[d] Indoor	60 at 20 yd	40 cm	5	300	Adult

[a]Fédération Internationale de Tir à l'Arc; [b]National Archery in the Schools Program; [c]National Archery Association (known today as USA Archery); [d]National Field Archery Association.

Tournament Exercise 1 Modified Metric 900 Round

Shoot a modification of the metric 900 round, using the distances of 40, 30, and 20 meters rather than the official metric 900 distances. Consult table 10.1 to find the target face size and the number of arrows shot at each distance. You can have the option of retrieving and scoring your arrows after shooting six arrows or after shooting three arrows. You can shoot your score alone or with a group of archers. If you shoot with a group, decide who will call the arrow values on a target, who will keep score, and so on. You should also follow the scoring rules listed earlier in the Scoring in a Tournament section. One archer can control the shooting line. Record your score on the scorecard shown in figure 10.9. If you are shooting indoors, substitute the USA Archery/World Archery indoor round.

TO INCREASE DIFFICULTY

- Shoot from 50, 40, and 30 meters.

Success Check

- Follow scoring rules.
- Record arrows of highest value first.

Score Your Success

Complete the modified metric 900 round = 6 points

Complete two-thirds of the round = 3 points

Your score _____

(continued)

Tournament Exercise 1   *(continued)*

Name						Hits	Score
Class							
						Hits	**Score**
40 meters							
Distance score							
30 meters							
Distance score							
20 meters							
Distance score							
Total score							

Figure 10.9   Scorecard for the Modified Metric 900 Round exercise.

Tournament Exercise 2   Interscholastic Metric Round

Shoot an interscholastic metric round from 40 and 30 meters rather than from 50 and 30 meters. Note that you need two different-sized target faces for this round (see table 10.1). Follow the scoring rules. Again, you can shoot alone or with a group. Members of the group should act as target captain, scorer, and tournament official as mutually decided. Record your scores on the scorecard shown in figure 10.10. If you are shooting indoors, substitute the Vegas round.

TO INCREASE DIFFICULTY
- Shoot from 50 and 30 meters.

TO DECREASE DIFFICULTY
- Use larger target face at both distances.

Success Check

- Have sight settings beforehand.
- Check equipment beforehand.
- Use personal mental checklist.

Score Your Success

Complete the interscholastic metric round = 6 points

Complete half of the round = 3 points

Your score _____

Name								Hits	Score
Class									
								Hits	**Score**
40 meters									
Distance score									
30 meters									
Distance score									
Total score									

Figure 10.10 Scorecard for the Interscholastic Metric Round exercise.

Tournament Exercise 3   **Head-to-Head Shoot**

Find three other archers and put everyone's name in a hat. Draw out two names; these archers should shoot against each other, as should the remaining two. Shoot four ends of three arrows each. The winners from each pair should then shoot against one another. The remaining archers can determine a third-place finisher.

TO INCREASE DIFFICULTY

- One archer in each pair, as determined by the flip of a coin, starts with a 2-point advantage. The next time you shoot, reverse who gets the point advantage.

TO DECREASE DIFFICULTY

- If the archers in the group would be in different equipment classifications, determine handicapping points so that everyone has an equal chance of winning.

(continued)

Tournament Exercise 3   *(continued)*

Success Check

- Relax hands.
- Focus on target and aim.
- Block out other shooters.

Score Your Success

Shoot two tournaments = 6 points

Shoot one tournament = 3 points

Your score _____

COMPETING IN RAIN AND WIND

Many archery tournaments, especially those held in the warmer months and those featuring long shooting distances, are held outdoors. Naturally, archers hope for sunny, calm weather, but they do not always get their wish. Rain, wind, or both can affect scoring. The 2012 Olympic competition featured downpours and swirling, gusty wind conditions. Those archers who are able to adapt, though, often gain an advantage over others who let the conditions detract from their performances. Naturally, the scoring might not be as high in inclement weather as in good, but because the conditions are the same for everyone, archers who adapt can have an advantage.

Archers should not shoot if there is lightning in the area. Standing in open or wooded areas with metal objects is never warranted. If there is no lightning and just rainy conditions, though, most tournaments go on as scheduled unless the rain is extremely heavy. Plan ahead by taking an outer garment that repels water and will keep you warm if the temperature is cool or cold. Always have a hat to keep the water out of your eyes and off your eyeglasses, if you wear them.

Carry a plastic bag to place over the arrows in your quiver. For outdoor tournaments, many archers use plastic vanes rather than feathers, even if they use feathers indoors. If you do not want to add the weight of vanes, be sure to waterproof your feathers with a spray intended for this use before the outdoor season. Try to keep your finger tab or mechanical release as dry as possible when you are not shooting. Also, have dry towels handy so you can periodically wipe off your equipment. You can place a towel over your peep sight and magnifying lens, if you use them, between ends.

Good archery equipment is very durable. Do what is logical to keep your tackle as dry as possible, but continue shooting as you would in good weather. Stay with your routine and focus on setting up good shots, aiming, and following through. Moisture in the air might cause your arrows to land slightly low, and in a downpour even lower, especially at longer distances. A small correction in your sight settings might be all that is required to adjust for these conditions.

Archers who can shoot as routinely as possible in the rain can often score close to their average on a particular round. Don't cancel a practice session just because it is raining. That practice can give you the confidence to shoot well at a rainy tournament!

Shooting in the wind is more problematic than shooting in the rain. The one thing you want to do on every shot is to settle your sight on the bull's-eye, and that is the very thing wind works against, especially a crosswind. The wind affects both the arrow in flight and your ability to hold steady. The effect is more pronounced at longer shooting distances. You need specific strategies for shooting in windy conditions.

First, consider your equipment. If you have not yet purchased a bow but plan to shoot outdoors, look for handle risers with cutouts that allow the wind to pass through (figure 10.11a). This reduces the wind resistance when holding on target. A heavier bow is easier to hold steady in the wind than a lighter one, so you might want to add stabilizers and heavier weights to those stabilizers. We will say more about this in the next section. Some archers carry heavier weights for their V-bar stabilizers or extra weights to add to the back of the bow in case of wind. If you adopt this strategy, be sure the total weight is still one you can handle (that is, that the extra weight does not, regardless of the wind, cause you to shake or drop your bow arm at release). It is wise to practice with the extra weight from time to time in good conditions. Also, within the set of possible arrow sizes for your draw length and weight, choose the smallest-diameter arrow because it will be least affected by wind.

Second, consider your aiming strategy. Some archers like to deal with a crosswind by aiming at nine o'clock or three o'clock, depending on the wind direction, and letting the wind carry their arrows into the bull's-eye (figure 10.11b). Before trying this strategy, practice in the wind several times to learn how far off to aim for a given shooting distance and the strength of the wind. Take notes on what works so you have a basis for what to do at a tournament. At outdoor tournaments, a small flag will be placed on top of each target. Check this flag for the wind direction and to estimate wind strength before each shot.

Many archers find it difficult to aim off center because this strategy counters the natural tendency to center things. They prefer to adjust their bowsights horizontally—that is, make a windage adjustment—to compensate for the drift of their shots due to the wind. This is effective in a constant rather than gusty wind. An alternative strategy is to cant the bow to compensate for the wind and continue to aim at the center of the target (figure 10.11c). Again, if you decide to use this strategy, practice in the

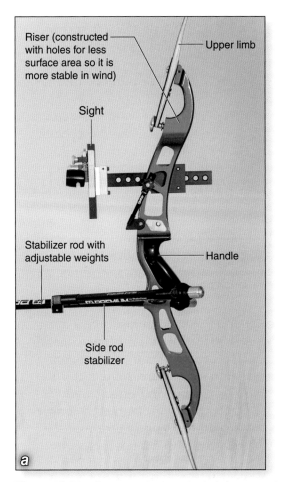

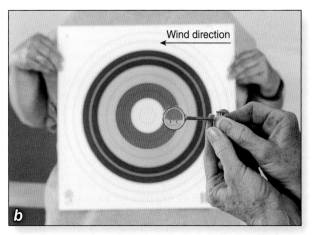

Figure 10.11 Shooting in the wind: *(a)* cutouts in the bow handle allow wind to pass through; *(b)* aiming off center; *(c)* canting the bow and attached sight aperture to compensate for wind.

wind several times to determine how much cant works for a given wind velocity and a given shooting distance. Probably the amount of cant will range from 3 to 5 inches (7.6-12.7 cm) or 5 to 15 degrees. If you use an aiming aperture with a level, you can use the bubble to keep track of the cant.

Third, monitor your timing when you shoot in a crosswind. Try to use nearly the same timing as you would use in ideal conditions. If you tend to get your shots set up and off in seven to eight seconds, extending much beyond this in windy conditions will probably be self-defeating. It would be better to let down once you have gone a few seconds beyond normal to set up your shot once again. Obviously, you need to consider any time limits that are in effect for the tournament. If the wind is gusty, you can begin your shot sequence as a gust starts to lessen so you are aiming during a lull.

Recognize that when you shoot in a crosswind, your aim will not be as steady as it is on a calm day. Attempting to force your bow arm to be still in a brisk wind increases the tension in your bow arm and hand, breaking down your follow-through. A better strategy is to stay relaxed and to continue focusing on the center of the target.

If the wind is along the direction of shooting rather than a crosswind, it might not be as difficult to aim. You might find that a tailwind results in high arrows and a headwind results in low arrows. A crosswind might also cause slightly lower arrows. Again, when you have an opportunity to practice in these conditions, note how much adjustment of your sight aperture is needed for a given wind strength and shooting distance.

Practice to find out how particular strategies for shooting in the wind affect your shots, but be careful. An excessive amount of shooting in a crosswind can be counterproductive, resulting in anticipating the release, which will cause you to punch the release if you are a release shooter or to pluck the bowstring if you are a finger shooter.

KEYS FOR SHOOTING IN THE WIND

1. Assume stance.
2. Set bow and draw hands (or mechanical release).
3. Check wind flag.
4. Draw to anchor.
5. Find aiming spot on target or cant bow.
6. Increase back tension.
7. Focus on aiming spot.
8. Allow release explosion to occur.
9. Follow through.

Wind Exercise 1   Aiming Off Center

On a windy day with a crosswind, practice aiming off center so you learn how far to aim off center for a given wind speed. Shoot two ends of six arrows at 20, 30, and 40 yards (18, 27, and 37 m). Aim at nine o'clock or three o'clock, depending on the wind direction. On the first end, pick a place to aim. For example, if you are using a five-color target, aim at the line between the red and blue rings. On the second end, adjust if your arrows aren't landing around the bull's-eye. Using the targets shown in figures 10.12 through 10.14, mark each of your arrows. Below each target, record where you aimed and make a note about the wind strength, such as "strong wind" or "light wind." Note what adjustments were required as you moved to longer shooting distances. According to this information, write your strategy for the next time you shoot in a wind of this strength (e.g., In a strong wind, aim at ____ from 20 yd or 18 m).

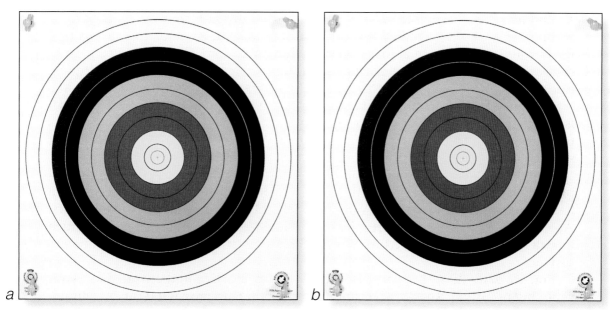

Figure 10.12 Shooting at 20 yards (18 m): *(a)* end 1; *(b)* end 2.

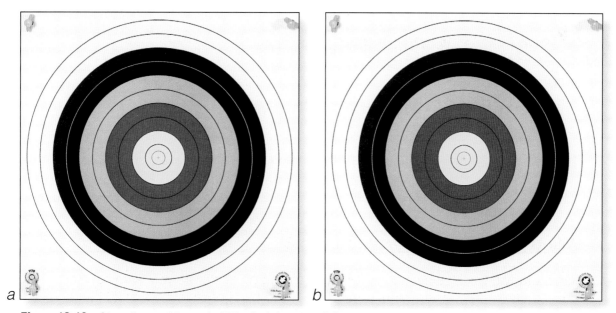

Figure 10.13 Shooting at 30 yards (27 m): *(a)* end 1; *(b)* end 2.

(continued)

Wind Exercise 1   *(continued)*

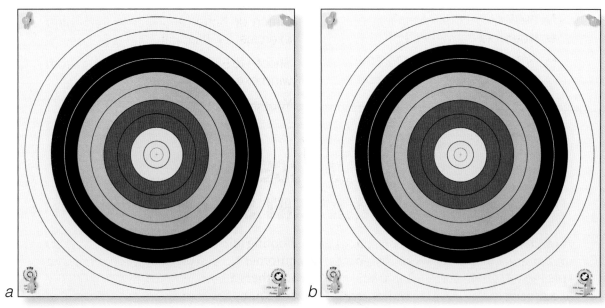

Figure 10.14   Shooting at 40 yards (37 m): *(a)* end 1; *(b)* end 2.

Success Check

- Aim at aiming spot.
- Keep bow arm relaxed.
- Shoot in a normal time frame.

Score Your Success

Determine a complete strategy for shooting in the wind by aiming off center = 6 points

Your score _____

Wind Exercise 2   **Water Bottle Shooting**

One way to simulate shooting in the wind is to shoot with a water bottle hanging from your front stabilizer. Put a little water or sand into a disposable water bottle and tighten the lid. Tie a string around the neck of the bottle, and then tie the string around your stabilizer. Use several feet of string, but allow the bottle to swing freely below your bow when you are at full draw. After you raise your bow, move it back and forth slightly to start the bottle swinging, then proceed with your shot. This simulates shooting in a crosswind. Shoot two ends of five arrows at 30 yards (27 m). Note your 30-yard (27 m) two-end score from wind exercise 1.

TO INCREASE DIFFICULTY

- Increase the swing of the bottle.
- Increase your shooting distance.

TO DECREASE DIFFICULTY

- Decrease the swing of the bottle.

Success Check

- Focus on the bull's-eye.
- Keep bow arm relaxed.
- Shoot in a normal time frame.

Score Your Success

Match or better your score from wind exercise 1 = 3 points

Shoot 1 to 5 points below your score from wind exercise 1 = 1 point

Your score _____

ADVANCED ACCESSORIES FOR TOURNAMENT SHOOTING

As archers become more serious about their shooting and decide to enter tournaments on a regular basis, they usually add more equipment accessories. Some of these are specific to certain shooting classifications, and others are not. We review some of the accessories here, but remember that you can acquire some of them over time. You don't need every accessory before you start participating in tournaments. Avoid falling into the trap of thinking that you can do well only if you buy an additional, or more expensive, piece of equipment!

Recall that competitive recurve bow shooters, such as those competing in the Olympics, use take-down bows with metal handle risers and limbs of the most expensive materials. They typically use long stabilizers in front with shorter back or V-bars attached and an extended sight that can be precisely adjusted. Compound bow target shooters tend toward compound bows with straighter handle risers and longer axle-to-axle lengths than compound bows used for hunting. They often use a similar stabilizer setup to recurve shooters and extended quality sights, but their sights might incorporate a magnifying scope, and they can use a peep sight. Compound bow target shooters have a choice between a finger release and a mechanical release.

Recall that stabilizer setups are intended to help you hold your bow still as you aim and to diffuse vibration. If you added a single stabilizer early in your shooting and now want to shoot in tournaments, consider a change. Stabilizer setups are individualized for shooters and for bows. It is typical to see tournament recurve and compound bow shooters with a long stabilizer extended to the target and two stabilizers extended back toward the archer at an angle forming a V, hence the name V-bars. Some archers use just one back bar. Front and back bars balance out one another.

Tournament-quality stabilizer rods today are made of carbon, so they are very light. They can be of a small diameter, yet they are very strong and can support whatever amount of weight an archer chooses to place at the end. Stabilizer mounts are available that angle the front stabilizer down. Some back or V-bar mounts are adjustable so that the bars can be wider or narrower and angled down various degrees. Dampeners, which deaden movement, can be added to the end of the stabilizer between it and the weights, while others are made to slide up and down the bar.

Tournament archers look for a combination of front stabilizer and back bar lengths and end weights that allow them to hold the bow steady by gradually increasing length and weight. If they get to a combination that results in more bow movement during aiming rather than less, they know they have lengths too long, weights too heavy, or both. It is a trial-and-error process to find the best combination for the archer and bow. A good starting point is a 30-inch (76 cm) front stabilizer with 4 ounces (113 g) of weight and two 12-inch (30 cm) back bars with 12 ounces (340 g) of total weight.

Many tournament shooters use a sight aperture that is actually a magnifying scope (see figure 10.11b in the Competing in Rain and Wind section). This makes the target picture bigger and can facilitate aiming. Typically, a level is built into these scopes, and some are available with a fiber optic aiming pin. Be sure you can use a magnifying scope in your equipment classification. Olympic-style classifications do not allow them, but most compound bow divisions do. Olympic-style recurve divisions do allow aiming apertures with a zero-power lens and a fiber optic sighting pin. Some of these apertures also allow archers to change the size of the aperture ring.

Magnifying scope apertures come in a variety of strengths, or magnifications. It is not necessarily the case that more is better in terms of magnification. Although six-times and eight-times magnifications can fill the sight picture entirely with the bull's-eye or the inner ring (sometimes called the X-ring) of the bull's-eye, they also accentuate the perceived movement of the bow arm. No one can hold the bow arm perfectly still, so the natural oscillation of the sight aperture through a scope can seem so great that archers eventually try to muscle the bow arm into a dead stop in the very center of the bull's-eye. This is counterproductive. Because an archer cannot hold the arm perfectly still, the tendency is to begin anticipating when the sight aperture will cross the very center of the bull's-eye, and punching a mechanical release or plucking the bowstring soon follows.

What Sport Science Says About Stabilizers

Stabilizers, rods attached to and extending away from the bow's handle riser, were first used in competition in 1960. Today it would be rare to see a bow without a stabilizer in competition, even bowhunting competitions. Stabilizers are an example of a basic principle in rotational mechanics. Distributing some of an object's weight away from the axis of rotation makes the object more stable—that is, less likely to rotate. Recall from our discussion of the basic archery shot that archers might have basic flaws that turn a bow on its long (vertical) axis. For example, squeezing the bow handle on release of the bowstring can cause the bow to turn to the left and create a horizontal error. A stabilizer distributes some of the bow's weight away from its long axis so that any shooting flaws that cause the bow to rotate are minimized. When a bow is equipped with stabilizers that extend in multiple directions (see figure 2 on page xii and figure 14 on page xxiv), movement around the bow's vertical axis also is minimized.

Few research studies have examined stabilizers. One group of sport scientists (Clarys et al. 1990) investigated the muscular activity of elite archers shooting at 70 and 90 meters with and without a stabilizer. They found no significant difference in the pattern of muscle use or in the precision of shooting with or without a stabilizer among these elite archers. They did find a difference in muscle intensity, suggesting that shooting without a stabilizer is less energy consuming. This finding confirms the importance of improving muscle strength and endurance so that the weight of a stabilizer or stabilizers is not a detriment to accurate shooting. It would be ideal to have newer studies of stabilizer use because the materials used today in stabilizers, such as carbon, result in 30-inch (76 cm) stabilizers weighing less than 6 ounces (170 g).

If you decide to try a magnifying scope sight aperture, a good strategy is to begin with a small magnification and perhaps a version with an open circle etched on the lens rather than a dot or crosshairs. The open circle facilitates a focus on the center of the target and follows an archer's natural tendency to center things.

Many tournament archers eventually invest in a good pair of binoculars or a tripod-mounted telescope. At long distances, archers can check where their arrows are landing so they can make small sight adjustments. A good investment is a bow stand to keep your bow off the ground, especially in wet conditions.

Many archers have two bows that are identically set up for important tournaments. Even if you do not have two bows, you might want to purchase extra arrows and a backup finger tab or mechanical release. Arrows should be fitted to your bow, draw length, and shooting weight. The finger tab or mechanical release you use probably reflects your preference. So it is unlikely you would shoot very well if you had to borrow someone else's arrows, tab, or release! If you are paying entry fees to shoot in tournaments, the purchase of some backup equipment can be a good investment in ensuring that you can finish any tournament you start.

Tournament Accessories Exercise 1   Magnifying Scope

Borrow a magnifying scope sight aperture if you do not have one. Use the scope to shoot two ends of five arrows from 20 yards (18 m). Remember to focus on aiming at the bull's-eye. Note the power of the scope. On a scale of 1 to 6, indicate how much greater you perceived your bow arm movement to be with the scope than without the scope (figure 10.15).

No additional movement					Much more movement
1	2	3	4	5	6

Figure 10.15 Rating scale for a magnifying scope.

Success Check

- Keep bow arm and hand relaxed.
- Allow sight to settle without trying to stop all movement.

Score Your Success

Shoot two ends with a scope = 3 points

Your score _____

SHOOTING WITH TOURNAMENT NERVES

In step 9, we discussed the ideal anxiety level for shooting archery—a relatively low level compared to that for many other sports and activities. We also discussed the ideal of focusing attention on aiming once the shot is set up and ready to be executed. In this section, we just briefly expand the discussion to deal specifically with tournament pressure.

Tournaments are not the same as shooting practice or even shooting in a weekly league. You might pay an entry fee for a tournament. Others know you entered and will ask you how you did. There might be spectators at the tournament. The results might be posted or printed in a newsletter or magazine. Because you are nervous, your bow arm probably won't be as steady as it is in practice. It is easy to see how you would be tempted to control your shooting in a tournament, even if you have practiced for hours by focusing on aiming and letting your subconscious execute the shot. As a result, you may switch from focusing solely on aiming to trying to attend to everything, including the symptoms of nervousness. The key to performing well, though, is trusting that your subconscious can execute shots while you focus on aiming.

It is important to practice tournament shooting. The more tournaments you shoot, the more you are practicing tournament shooting. If you have trouble shooting well in a tournament, look for ways to practice tournament shooting without actually being in one. Find ways to practice shooting under pressure.

Try using imagery to create a tournament atmosphere. Join fellow archers to create your own competitions. Designate a trophy that circulates among the group. As one person wins the trophy, assign everyone else handicap points for the rematch. The handicap points could simply be the difference between the winner's score and the nonwinning archer's score or the difference minus 1 or 2 points. Incorporate some head-to-head competition to practice the format.

Remember that if you create shooting conditions that increase your anxiety level, you also have an opportunity to apply the mental skills discussed in step 9.

Tournament Nerves Exercise 1   Pressure Shooting

Archers often place extra pressure on themselves in head-to-head shooting by focusing on the other archer's success, especially in tournament formats in which the archers shoot arrows alternately. A good practice for head-to-head shooting is to write the various values of 12 shot arrows on small pieces of paper. Make the total value of the 12 shots equal to your average score for 12 arrows. Now shoot four ends of three arrows each, but before each shot, pull out a piece of paper and read the number. Imagine that this number is the value of the arrow just shot by your opponent.

TO INCREASE DIFFICULTY

- Write higher arrow values on the 12 pieces of paper.

Success Check

- Use personal checklist.
- Block out distracting thoughts.
- Set up shot.
- Focus on aiming.

Score Your Success

Shoot your average or higher on the 12 arrows = 6 points

Shoot 1 to 2 points under your average = 3 points

Your score _____

Tournament Nerves Exercise 2 Time Pressure

Many tournaments establish a length of time during which archers must shoot all the arrows in an end. To prepare for the pressure of shooting against a clock, practice shooting 6 three-arrow ends in two and a half minutes each.

TO INCREASE DIFFICULTY

- Shoot with a two-minute time limit.

Success Check

- Relax hands.
- Focus on aiming.
- Maintain timing.

Score Your Success

Shoot all 18 arrows within the time limit = 6 points

Shoot 16 or 17 arrows within the time limit = 3 points

Your score _____

ANSWER KEY

SCORING EXERCISE 1. SCORING BY END

Compare your scorecard from figure 10.7 with the following correct, completed scorecard.

End	Scorecard						Hits	End score	Running score
1	10	7	5	4	3	0	5	29	29
2	9	7	6	5	4	1	6	32	61
3	9	9	6	6	5	0	5	35	96
4	8	8	6	6	5	2	6	35	131
Total							22	131	

SUCCESS SUMMARY

A natural progression for archers is to begin shooting in weekly leagues or local tournaments and later move to larger tournaments. Tournaments are a good test of your skills as well as your ability to shoot under pressure.

Prepare for competition by having your equipment in good order and having all of the equipment necessary, including spares of some equipment. Know the rules of scoring and the format of a tournament before you go to the event, and have sight settings for all distances you will shoot, including strategies for adjusting for the conditions on the day of the tournament. Practice in situations in which the anxiety level is higher than it would otherwise be in a practice session. Confidence is an important part of good shooting, and solid preparation should make you more confident.

For each of the exercises in this step, record the points earned to chart your preparedness for tournament shooting. If you earned at least 32 points, you are well on your way to shooting in target archery tournaments, and you can move on to the next step to try shooting activities related to bowhunting. If you earned fewer than 32 points or you want to prepare for an actual tournament, repeat the tournament exercises to earn additional points.

Scoring Exercise

1. Scoring by End   _____ out of 3

Tournament Exercises

1. Modified Metric 900 Round   _____ out of 6

2. Interscholastic Metric Round   _____ out of 6

3. Head-to-Head Shoot   _____ out of 6

Wind Exercises

1. Aiming Off Center   _____ out of 6

2. Water Bottle Shooting   _____ out of 3

Tournament Accessories Exercise

1. Magnifying Scope   _____ out of 3

Tournament Nerves Exercises

1. Pressure Shooting   _____ out of 6

2. Time Pressure   _____ out of 6

Total   _____ **out of 45**

Shooting in tournaments is a way to put your archery skills to the test. Your focus should be more on how you do in relation to your practice scores, your previous tournament scores, or your personal best and less on how you compare with others. Yet, how you place in a tournament also tells you how close you are to achieving the scores shot by the most proficient archers. This can motivate you to continue your practice routines and return to more competitions.

Target archers also enjoy the change of pace that some bowhunting activities afford. In step 11, you will see how archery equipment is adapted for hunting and learn some of the factors that come into play when shooting in field conditions.

Bowhunting

I t's early morning in the woods. The sun is coming up. The fall air is cool. Birds are beginning to sing. A lone bowhunter waits in a tree stand. A buck comes over the rise. The hunter's heart begins to pound. *Set bow hand,* the bowhunter thinks. *Set release.* The buck turns away, down the far path. No problem. There's always next week.

Archers who bowhunt enjoy it for many reasons. Probably all of them like the challenge of hunting, but some also like being in and around nature. They enjoy the peacefulness of the forest, perhaps because it is a contrast to their daily lives. Some appreciate the opportunity to observe wildlife. They look forward to hunting season all year long.

Humans have bowhunted for centuries, first out of necessity, but now for the challenge of hunting and to participate in a natural cycle of checks and balances on the world's animal population. Bowhunters enjoy preparing, testing their skills at judging distance, and executing one perfect shot when the right moment comes. Many have their game meat processed and feel part of an age-old tradition. They help control the size of game herds, many of which have lost their natural predators and would otherwise suffer the disease and starvation that accompany overpopulation. Bowhunters also enjoy being in the woods, away from the fast pace and pressure of daily life.

Bowhunting is far from a one-weekend-a-year hobby. Bowhunters must spend countless hours preparing their equipment and practicing for that one, all-important shot. Fortunately, there are several enjoyable ways to practice for bowhunting. Some archers make bowhunting a year-round activity by participating in indoor tournaments for archers with bowhunting equipment, in field archery events, and in 3-D target shoots. In fact, 3-D target shooting has become a special tournament circuit enjoyed by many archers. Archers might have a wider range of choices in equipment for field archery or 3-D target shooting, but a majority shoot with hunting equipment to practice for hunting. Our emphasis in this step is on hunting equipment; however, keep in mind that because broadheads damage targets so badly, many events require shooters to replace broadheads with field points or target tips on their hunting arrows.

The basic archery shot remains the same whether you are shooting at a paper target or at live game. When you execute the fundamentals of a shot well, you are more likely to experience success. A bowhunter who believes that one shot can be made at the critical moment without hours of repetitive practice and preparation is asking for failure. The preparation required for successful bowhunting is just as great as for target competition. Although the basic technique for the shot remains the same across all forms of archery, bowhunting requires some adaptations to the conditions under which you hunt. They are not as predictable as in target archery, and you usually get only one chance to hit your mark! This step addresses bowhunting equipment and adaptations in shooting technique related to bowhunting; information on how to hunt is left for other resources.

Generally, bowhunting equipment must be more durable than target equipment because it is used outdoors in the elements and must be carried, sometimes over rough terrain. You must dress for the elements and still be able to execute a clean shot. Adaptation to an uneven stance is often needed, in contrast to straddling a line on a flat floor. You might shoot from a tree stand (see figure 3 in The Sport of Archery) or a kneeling position. You must judge the distance to your target so that you know which sight setting to use without being fooled by the terrain or lighting conditions. The equipment setup must provide adequate penetration of game, and the timing of shots is more variable than in target shooting. The following sections address how to shoot under these circumstances.

CHOOSING HUNTING EQUIPMENT

A typical bowhunting setup consists of a compound bow, a short stabilizer, and a hunting bowsight (figure 11.1). Bowhunting changed dramatically with the advent of the compound bow. The compound has become the bow of choice for hunters, although some enjoy the challenge of hunting with traditional equipment. Some hunting jurisdictions even provide special hunting days on which only traditional equipment can be used.

As a rule, the compound bow allows you to shoot at a heavier draw weight than with a recurve bow, resulting in a faster arrow with less arc. The degree of let-off in poundage in newer compounds allows archers to maximize their poundage. A let-off of 80 to 90 percent is typical for hunting bows compared to 60 to 75 percent for target bows. Heavier draw weight makes judging distance slightly less critical and hunting more humane by producing fewer wounds without a kill. The compound bow makes it easier for smaller archers, children, and people with disabilities to hunt. The hunting compound bow is also shorter than a target bow, at 28 to 34 inches (71-86 cm) compared to 35 to 40 inches (89-102 cm), and easier to carry through the woods or shoot from a tree stand.

Compound bows have evolved greatly over the years since their inception. Generally, the trend has been toward faster bows that shoot

Figure 11.1 A hunting bow.

shorter arrows. Cams have replaced round eccentric wheels. Bow limbs are closer to parallel, and handle risers are the reflex shape, resulting in a brace height of 5 to 6 inches (13-15 cm) and allowing for a shorter arrow.

As with many aspects of archery equipment, there is often a trade-off between speed and accuracy with compound bows. Cams provide more arrow speed than round eccentric wheels do, but they tend not to be as smooth or as forgiving. The reflex handle riser shape makes it possible for you to use a shorter, lighter, and therefore faster arrow, but small errors of the bow hand upon release of the shot are magnified. Innovations in new compounds have addressed some of the disadvantages of designs with fast arrow speeds, but hunters are often easily convinced by advertisements that more is better when it comes to arrow speed. Remember, though, that if you cannot consistently shoot an arrow into an area the size of a kill zone from the distance you hunt, you are not likely to be a successful hunter. It makes little difference how fast your arrow sails past a deer! When choosing a hunting bow, do not assume that the fastest bow is always the best bow. Rather, look for a combination of speed and accuracy that will maximize your success, especially if the bow is primarily for hunting. Trading some forgiveness and accuracy for speed is reasonable, but keep your shooting goal in mind when choosing a bow. Most archers competing in target tournaments and hunting-type events have a bow for each type of shooting to best match the advantages of a bow to the goal of the event.

SELECTING A HUNTING BOW

1. Choose a recurve or compound bow.
2. Choose the type of release.
3. Choose the type of arrow rest.
4. Choose the type of bowsight.
5. Choose the type of stabilizer.

Bowhunters using traditional equipment use a finger release. Increasingly, bowhunters using compound bows with their short axle-to-axle lengths are using a mechanical release aid because the small angle formed by the bowstring at full draw makes a finger release both uncomfortable and difficult to smoothly execute. Hunting often does not provide the luxury of time that target shooting does, so if you decide to use a release, consider a type that can be drawn quickly. If it takes too long to set a mechanical release, you might miss your opportunity. This is why many hunters use releases that are quickly set. These would probably not be the best for precision target shooting, but they are acceptable for hunting. For example, releases triggered by back tension are probably preferable for target shooting. Caliper releases that can be clipped onto the bowstring or a D loop on a bowstring, though, can be set very quickly. Many archers choose these for hunting, especially models with a wrist strap. Not only does the strap prevent misplacing the release, but it also allows hunters to draw with a relaxed hand and fingers.

In earlier discussions, we acknowledged the tendency for release shooters to punch the release. Hunters, just like target shooters, can counter this tendency by adjusting the release to a heavy tension of 3 to 4 pounds (1.4-1.8 kg) and a very short travel of the trigger. This allows a bowhunter to squeeze the trigger with the finger with about half the pressure required and use back tension to produce the remaining force. This minimizes anticipation and punching the release.

Hunters use stabilizers that are shorter than those on typical target bows. This arrangement provides the benefits of a stabilizer without making the equipment setup too cumbersome to carry in the woods. Recall that you can achieve the same torque-dampening effect by using a heavier weight on a short stabilizer as you would by using a lighter weight on a longer stabilizer. Some bowhunters use a single, short back bar. Those who mount an arrow quiver on their bow often offset this back bar to the opposite side as a counterbalance.

Hunting sights are typically mounted on an extension bar, just like target sights, but most bowhunters prefer a short extension for ease of carrying and handling their bows in a wooded area. Hunting sights typically have three or four pin apertures that you can set for various, usually even, distances. A common setup would be for 20, 30, 40, and 50 yards (18, 27, 37, and 46 m). When you have an odd-distance shot, such as 35 yards (32 m), align the bowsight so that the 30- and 40-yard (27 and 37 m) pins are approximately equidistant around the kill zone. If you estimate your shooting distance to be 32 yards (29 m), you could aim your 30-yard (27 m) pin slightly above the kill zone. You can see why it is advantageous to hunt with heavier draw weight, faster arrows, and therefore, a lower trajectory. In fact, with today's bows, most archers can use one pin for any target 25 yards (23 m) or closer. The aperture on a hunting sight is typically larger than a target sight so that the bowhunter can better see game (compare figures 5.1a and 5.1c). Some archers choose hunting sights with fiber optic pins because some hunting areas can be so heavily forested and dark that it is difficult to see a regular sight pin. The longer the fiber, the more light is gathered and the brighter the sight pin, so the fiber is wrapped around the aperture in some designs.

Most bowhunters use a peep sight, but it is important for the peep sight to be turned with the opening toward the archer on the first draw when hunting (see figure 11.1). Some archers use flexible tubing attached to the peep sight and then to the limb or cables to properly orient the peep sight. Others choose a peep sight with a larger opening than a target archer would use. While aiming is not as precise with the larger opening, chances are the bowhunter can see through it on the first draw.

Bowhunters often use a quiver mounted on the side of the bow when they hunt with broadheads. Arrows are then handy, but the setup is still compact. The hunting quiver has a hood to shield the broadheads mounted on the arrows. We address arrows and broadheads in more detail later, but one thing all broadheads have in common is their sharpness. They must be handled with extreme care so as not to cut either the archer or the bowstring! Never climb or walk in the woods with an arrow or broadhead in hand because you might fall on it.

Hunters make other adaptations to their equipment setup to address extremes in temperature and moisture and the need for durability. Some use a heavier but less flexible arrow rest than target archers use; others use a shooting glove for a finger release rather than a finger tab. Most hunting equipment comes in dark colors or camouflage patterns; some bowhunters like to paint their own camouflage patterns on their equipment. Hunters frequently add string silencers to their bows, which come in a variety of types (some look like a ball of rubber strings). They muffle the sound of the bowstring at release so that game are not startled and move at the sound.

Bowhunters prefer to shoot a heavy peak draw weight. Even though today's compound bows have a high percentage let-off, the heavier the peak draw weight, the flatter the arrow's trajectory for any type of bow. Factors such as judging distance to game or being uphill or downhill have a larger margin for error with a flatter arrow trajectory. The stronger the archer, the heavier the bow peak draw weight (or draw weight for a recurve bow) the archer can shoot. Strength training is the obvious way that bowhunters and target archers alike can comfortably and accurately shoot heavier weights. In The Sport of Archery, we emphasized the importance of bilateral resistance training. What does sport science say about the importance of bilateral resistance training?

Schmitt and colleagues (2021) recruited competitive archers for a comparison study. They identified 50 archers who were training unilaterally and matched them to 25 archers who were training bilaterally. The match was for age, sex, and level. The scientists then measured the cervical spine range of motion, upper arm and shoulder (glenohumeral) rotation, upward rotation of the shoulder blade, and elevation of the arm in all the archers. None of the archers were experiencing pain. When the groups were compared, there was no difference in cervical spine range of motion, although the archers had a larger range than the general population. The archers training unilaterally, though, showed greater asymmetries in the other measurements—that is, they showed asymmetries in the general mobility of the shoulder. These asymmetries may put the archers training unilaterally at greater risk of injury. This finding reinforces the importance of bilateral training for archers, no matter what type of archery they enjoy.

CHOOSING HUNTING ARROWS

Hunting arrow shafts available to bowhunters today include aluminum, carbon fiber bonded to an aluminum-core tube, wrapped carbon, and carbon composite. Charts to help you select the appropriate hunting shaft spine are available from each manufacturer, just as for target arrows. Table 11.1 is a portion of an Easton chart. You find your compound bow peak weight (left column) or recurve bow weight at your draw length (right column), then read across to locate your arrow length column. Several spine sizes are provided. Note that the chart is based on a set of assumptions listed in the footnote, but you can adjust for different equipment. Generally, heavier poundage bows require a stiffer arrow spine. Heavier point weight, in effect, weakens the spine.

Multiple spine sizes might be provided for a bow weight and arrow length combination so that you can choose an arrow weight and diameter with that spine. Durability, type of broadhead, and need to penetrate the game being hunted are all factors in choosing arrow shaft weight. Arrow manufacturers provide a table that tells you which of their products are available in a given spine.

Recall that your draw length is not necessarily your arrow length. With bowhunting equipment, you must ensure your broadhead does not contact the bow hand or the handle riser. To determine the correct arrow length for shafts to be shot with broadheads, you must note whether your bow has a broadhead cutout sight window. If you're using a bow with a cutout window, your shaft for broadheads should be 1 to 2 inches (2.5-5 cm) longer than the point at which the shaft contacts the arrow

Table 11.1 Hunting Arrow Shafts

CARBON ARROW SPINE SELECTION				
Compound bow peak draw weight (lb)	26 in. arrow length	28 in. arrow length	30 in. arrow length	Recurve bow poundage at draw length (lb)
42-46	600	500, 480, 470, 460	400, 390	42-46
47-51	500, 480, 470, 460	400, 390	400, 390	47-51
52-56	500, 480, 470, 460	400, 390	340, 330, 320	52-56
57-61	400, 390	400, 390	340, 330, 320, 300	57-61
62-66	400, 390	340, 330, 320	330, 320, 300	62-66
ALUMINUM ARROW SPINE SELECTION				
Compound bow peak draw weight (lb)	26 in. arrow length	28 in. arrow length	30 in. arrow length	Recurve bow poundage at draw length (lb)
42-46	500, 2013, 2016	500, 2018, 2114	400, 2117, 2215, 2216, 2314	42-46
47-51	500, 2016	400, 2117, 2213	400, 2216, 2219, 2314	47-51
52-56	500, 2018, 2114	480, 2117, 2215, 2216, 2314	340, 2219, 2315, 2413	52-56
57-61	400, 2117, 2213	400, 2216, 2219, 2314	340, 2219, 2315, 2413	57-61
62-66	400, 2117, 2215, 2216, 2314	340, 2219, 2315, 2413	300, 2317	62-66

Selected columns adapted from the Hunting shaft selection chart, 2023, www.eastonarchery.com. *Note:* This chart assumes a bow speed rating of 301 to 340 feet per second (FPS), 100-grain points, a brace height greater than 6.5 inches (16.5 cm), and a mechanical release. The following adjustments can be made for other speed ratings or point weights:

Bow speed rating: Subtract 5 pounds of bow weight for a speed rating of 300 FPS or slower; add 5 pounds (2.3 kg) of bow weight for a speed rating of 341 to 350 FPS; add 10 pounds (4.5 kg) of draw weight for a speed rating of 351 FPS or faster.

Point weight: Subtract 3 pounds (1.4 kg) of bow weight for a 75-grain point weight; add 3 pounds (1.4 kg) of bow weight for a 125-grain point weight; add 6 pounds (2.7 kg) of bow weight for a 150-grain point weight.

Brace height: Add 5 pounds (2.3 kg) of bow weight for a brace height lower than 6.5 inches (16.5 cm).

Release: Add 5 pounds (2.3 kg) of bow weight for a finger release.

rest. If your bow does not, the shaft should be 1 to 2 inches (2.5-5 cm) longer than the front of the bow handle. Without a cutout window, a fixed-blade broadhead cannot be drawn past the back of the bow and could bump against the bow if the shaft is too short. Expandable broadheads provide more clearance and could allow the use of a shorter arrow.

Bowhunters should heed several precautions. First, bow manufacturers recommend a minimum arrow weight based on the peak weight of the bow and, if a compound, the wheel type or bow speed rating. Bowhunters and 3-D shooters should know this minimum arrow weight for their bows and choose arrow shafts and tips that at least meet the minimum. Second, bowhunters who choose carbon shafts must be aware that these shafts damage more easily than aluminum shafts do. They should be inspected routinely (see step 8) because a damaged arrow could break on release. They can also shatter when shot into a big game animal. Hunters should check for this possibility, avoiding broken segments and discarding any meat that could contain carbon splinters.

Bowhunters usually practice with heavy or field points that screw into inserts installed on their arrows (figure 11.2a). These points are closer in weight to broadheads than target points are. They can be easily replaced by a broadhead when hunting because both points screw into the same insert. Bowhunters can choose traditional fixed, two-blade, or multiblade broadheads that are exposed or expandable broadheads. Expandable broadheads create less air resistance in flight and are less likely to wind-plane, yet the blades expand on contact. When installing a broadhead on an arrow shaft, align the shaft of the broadhead (ferrule) with the arrow shaft. If it is crooked, the arrow may drift on its flight to the target and miss it.

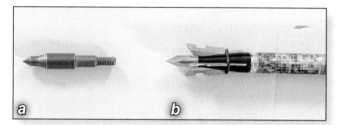 

Figure 11.2 Broadheads: *(a)* heavy screw-in point for practice; *(b)* expandable broadhead; *(c)* multiblade broadhead.

Most hunters find that a large fletching better stabilizes arrows, given the heavy broadhead. They also prefer plastic vanes to feathers because of the range of weather conditions encountered when hunting. Hunting arrows typically have offset fletching to cause the arrow to spin. If you buy arrows already fletched, the vanes are probably offset about one degree to the right. Experienced archers like to shoot a bare shaft to determine whether the arrow naturally spins left or right. They will then fletch their arrows with a right or left offset of approximately three degrees to match. This enhances arrow spin and therefore stability.

You still must tune and sight in your broadheads when installing them. A large piece of Styrofoam is good for sighting in because broadheads ruin target butts quickly and are banned on most ranges. Be sure to decide on your fletching before tuning, and if you change your fletching, retune your setup.

SELECTING HUNTING ARROWS

1. Determine arrow length.
2. Choose broadhead type.
3. Choose tip weight.
4. Determine arrow spine group.
5. Choose type of shaft.
6. Tune broadheads to setup.

The first step in tuning broadheads is to tune your setup with your hunting shafts equipped with field points. The field points should be as close as possible in weight to the broadheads you will use. Once you have tuned with field points, shoot a group of field tip arrows into your Styrofoam target from 20 to 30 yards (18-27 m). Be sure to ignore poorly executed shots. Using the same aiming spot, now shoot a group of arrows with broadheads installed. Never shoot broadheads with unfletched shafts, because the flight of such arrows is erratic and dangerous.

Compare your two groups of arrows. Make vertical adjustments first. Move the nocking point up if the broadhead group is above the field points and down if the group is below. Once your two arrow groups match vertically, make adjustments for any left-to-right differences. If the broadhead group is left of the field group, you can adjust by increasing the bow poundage, using heavier broadheads, decreasing the tension of the cushion plunger, if used, or moving the arrow rest (or cushion plunger) slightly toward the bow. If the broadhead group is to the right of the field group, adjust in the opposite way. It is best to try only one adjustment at a time.

Bowhunters use blunt rubber or metal tips when hunting small game such as rabbit or squirrel. These tips kill by impact force, usually instantaneously. A broadhead would destroy too much edible meat in small animals.

MISSTEP

Your field tips and broadheads are of different weights.

CORRECTION

Adjust your field tips to match the weight of your broadheads. With tips and broadheads matched in weight, you will be able to tune your setup and determine your sight settings.

Hunting Equipment Exercise 1   Selecting Hunting Arrows

Practice reading the arrow selection chart in table 11.1. For each combination of draw weight, tip (point) weight, and arrow length, indicate the spines recommended for the type of arrow shaft indicated. Assume the bow is a compound bow with a speed rating of 320 feet per second (FPS), a brace height of 6.5 inches (16.5 cm), and that a mechanical release is being used. (The answer key appears at the end of this step.)

1. Peak bow weight of 58 pounds, tip weight of 150 grains, and 30-inch length

   Aluminum shaft: _____

   Carbon shaft: _____

2. Peak bow weight of 48 pounds, tip weight of 100 grains, and 28-inch length

   Aluminum shaft: _____

   Carbon shaft: _____

3. Peak bow weight of 42 pounds, tip weight of 125 grains, and 26-inch length

   Aluminum shaft: _____

   Carbon shaft: _____

ANSWER KEY

HUNTING EQUIPMENT EXERCISE 1. SELECTING HUNTING ARROWS

1. Aluminum shaft: 300, 2317; carbon shaft: 330, 320, 300
2. Aluminum shaft: 400, 2117, 2213; carbon shaft: 400, 390
3. Aluminum shaft: 500, 2013, 2016; carbon shaft: 600

Success Check

- Identify draw weight.
- Identify arrow length and tip (point) weight.

Score Your Success

Identify all six recommendations correctly = 6 points

Identify four or five recommendations correctly = 3 points

Identify two or three recommendations correctly = 1 point

Your score _____

Hunting Equipment Exercise 2   Tuning Broadheads

If you have a set of hunting arrows, tune them for your bow. Shoot a group of arrows with field tips from 20 yards (18 m) at a Styrofoam target with an aiming spot marked on it. Then, shoot a group of arrows with broadheads installed from the same distance. Compare the two groups and answer these questions:

- Compared to the field points, was your broadhead group higher or lower? What adjustment would you make?
- Compared to the field points, was your broadhead group left or right? What adjustment would you make?

ANSWER KEY

HUNTING EQUIPMENT EXERCISE 2. TUNING BROADHEADS

If broadhead group is:	Your answer should have been:
Higher than field point group	Move the nocking point up
Lower than field point group	Move the nocking point down
Left of field point group	• Increase bow poundage • Use heavier broadheads • Decrease cushion plunger tension, or move arrow rest or cushion plunger closer to handle riser
Right of field point group	• Decrease bow poundage • Use lighter broadheads • Increase cushion plunger tension, or move arrow rest or cushion plunger out from handle riser

(continued)

Hunting Equipment Exercise 2   *(continued)*

Success Check

- Adjust vertical before horizontal.

Score Your Success

Identify the correct vertical and horizontal adjustments = 3 points

Identify the correct vertical adjustment only = 1 point

Identify the correct horizontal adjustment only = 1 point

Your score _____

MAXIMIZING HUNTING SUCCESS

We have discussed that bowhunters sometimes trade some precision in shooting for arrow speed and equipment durability. The basic hunting shot, though, has much in common with the basic target shot. Archers who can execute good shots repetitively with good T-form are likely to be successful hunters; those who merely hope everything will fall into place when the time comes are likely to be disappointed.

A difference between target shooting and hunting is the environment. In target shooting it is relatively constant, whereas in bowhunting it is always changing. First, you must adapt your stance to the terrain. Your feet might have to be farther apart or closer than ideal. You might have to straddle a fallen tree. One foot might be higher than another. You might have to crouch or kneel to get a clear shot under a branch. If you hunt from a tree stand, you might even be sitting rather than standing. As best they can, successful bowhunters start a shot by establishing a stable body position (figures 11.3a and 11.4a) and then turning or bending at the waist as necessary to align their shoulders to the target.

You will usually wait for game with your arrow nocked. Anytime you must change locations, though, place your arrow with its broadhead in a hooded quiver. Injuries from falling on a broadhead can be life-threatening! Containment arrow rests contribute to safety, but it is still better to store a hunting arrow when changing locations.

As your game comes into view, begin to estimate its distance from you. You should take a shot only if the distance is one with which you are comfortable and confident. When the game stops, estimate the distance. Later, we discuss how to adjust this estimate for the conditions and take into account the game's angle of orientation. As with target shooting, set your bow hand and your draw hand or mechanical release, and then draw and anchor (figure 11.3b). Leveling your bow is particularly important because slopes, hills, and shadows can cause you to unknowingly cant your bow. Locate your aiming spot and concentrate on it. Difficult as it may be, relax your hands as you aim.

After releasing the bowstring, keep your arm up (figure 11.3c). Following through is as important in hunting as it is in target shooting. When hunting large game, wait 30 minutes to an hour before trailing your game. If a wounded animal senses it is being pursued, it may run, covering a long distance and making it more difficult for you to track.

Figure 11.3 **BOWHUNTING**

Stance

1. Stabilize body position.
2. Nock arrow.
3. As game moves within range, determine whether shot is possible.
4. Wait for game to stop.
5. Estimate distance.
6. Adjust estimate of distance for conditions.
7. Decide whether angle of game affords a good shot.

Draw and Aim

1. Set bow hand.
2. Set draw hand or mechanical release.
3. Draw and anchor.
4. Align string and shaft and level bow.
5. Locate aiming spot and concentrate on target.

(continued)

Figure 11.3   *(continued)*

Release and Follow-Through

1. Maintain back tension.
2. Keep hands relaxed.
3. Relax draw hand or trigger release.
4. Keep bow arm up.
5. Wait 30 minutes to an hour to trail game.

MISSTEP

The arrow sails over the back of the target.

CORRECTION

Adjust your estimate of distance to a shorter shot if shooting more than 15 degrees uphill or downhill or down from a tree stand.

MISSTEP

The arrow tails off downhill on a side-of-hill shot.

CORRECTION

Maintain follow-through on a side-of-hill shot. You can also aim slightly higher in the kill area.

Judging Distances to Prey

A unique challenge of bowhunting compared to target shooting is having to judge your distance from your target. Compound bowhunters have the luxury of being able to use the same sight setting for short distances, but traditional archery hunters must develop their skill at judging distances. To be a successful hunter, you cannot rely on a lucky guess of distance. Rather, you should establish a system for judging distance and practice using it, just as you practice shooting. At least some of your practice should be in the same terrain as where you hunt.

One system you can use is to spot a reference point 20 yards (18 m) away. Do this by spotting 5-yard (4.6 m) increments from your location to the reference point. You can then estimate the distance to a farther or nearer target from this point. Many archers find 20 yards (18 m) to be a natural reference point because it is common to practice indoors at this distance. You can double-check your estimate by picking a point halfway between your location and the target and estimating your distance to this target. If twice this distance is too different from your first estimate, repeat your judgments.

You should also get to know how many of your normal walking steps correspond to a known distance. When practicing judging distances, take a shot at a target based on your estimate. Then walk the distance to see how accurate your estimate was. If your shot is off the mark, you will know whether your error was in estimating your distance from the target or in executing your shot.

Some archers realize that they tend to over- or underestimate yardage consistently. They then build this tendency into their decisions. To see a pattern, you should keep a log when shooting at 3-D or other unmarked distance shoots and in practice. Record the distance you estimated the target to be and whether your shot was higher or lower than where you aimed. Obviously, it takes some time to accumulate enough shots to see a pattern. The pattern might not be the same for all distances. For example, you might overestimate short yardages and underestimate long yardages.

Some hunters use a range finder, a device that measures the distance to a location for you. Others enjoy the challenge of estimating distances and consider this a fundamental part of the hunting experience. To check on your judgments, you can use a range finder when you practice. Range finders are usually prohibited in competitive tournaments for archers practicing hunting skills.

Finally, some archers use a framing system, although perhaps more often for 3-D shoots than for hunting. Framing is aligning some part of your bow or sight, or even your fingers or hand, to a known distance on your target. An example might be the distance between the top of the back and the belly of a particular deer target. If you find a reference on your hand or equipment that exactly matches this known distance, then you know the target is a particular distance away. To work properly, the two points creating the gap on your hand or equipment must be held at a constant distance from your eye. An archer using a framing system might come to full draw, find the two points on the bowsight (such as two of the pins or a pin and the guard around the bowsight) that frame the known distance on the target, and then let down. The archer then draws again, using the sight setting for the distance that she has previously determined corresponds to that particular gap.

Some archers have been known to have as many as 14 gaps to use for reference on a five-pin bowhunting sight with a pin guard. Of course, it takes considerable time and a good memory to develop so many references. Most shooters who use such a system first estimate their distance and then use the framing system to check or adjust their estimate, usually more for longer distances than for shorter ones. Before using a framing system in competition, check the rules of the competition to see whether it is allowed.

Shadows in wooded areas sometimes make it difficult to judge distance accurately. Some hunters report that they overestimate distance in the shadows (especially if they are standing in a well-lit area and the target is in the shadows) and underestimate distance when shooting from the dark to a well-lit target. Practice in shadows to find out what your tendencies are. Shadows also make it difficult to maintain your aim on game because the natural coloring of game animals creates a camouflage effect. Hunters commonly report that their aim tends to drift low or toward a patch of sunlight on the animal's back. Practice with paper animals or 3-D targets in shadowy conditions to learn your tendencies so you can overcome or compensate for them.

Hunters tend to overestimate distance if they cannot see the ground between them and the target, such as when shooting across a valley or small hill. Shooting over water or an open field tends to make hunters underestimate distance. Again, try to practice in such conditions, and keep a log of your tendencies so you can compensate.

Shooting on Hillsides

Shooting on hills affects your shot alignment and your shooting distance. When you shoot up and down hills, especially steep ones, your bow must be pointed acutely up or down. Learn to bend from the waist to shoot so you can maintain the best alignment of your upper body, keeping your shoulders level and your arms in line (figure 11.4).

The sight setting you use for an up- or downhill shot of approximately 15 degrees or more is slightly off the linear distance from you to your target. You will need to use a sight setting for a shorter distance (about a yard shorter). Exactly how much you adjust depends in part on your arrow velocity, the weight of your arrow, and the angle to the target. Because gravity acts to slow an uphill shot or speed a downhill shot, the arrow does not travel in the near-perfect parabolic trajectory as it does with a horizontal shot (figure 11.5).

How much should you adjust for hills? If you shoot light poundage or are taking a long shot, you will need a larger adjustment. Long downhill shots, in particular, call for an adjustment in your sight setting. To learn how much to compensate for this effect on uphill and downhill shots, you must practice these shots regularly. Remember that if you later make an equipment adjustment that affects your arrow speed, you should test the effect of this change on your sight-setting adjustment.

In addition to the actual effect on arrow trajectory, shooting uphill and downhill can affect your distance judgment when the distance is unknown. Hunters tend to overestimate distance when the target is downhill and underestimate it when the target is uphill.

Sometimes you will have shots across the side of a hill. Side hills do not change your distance judgment to the target, but they create illusions that cause many shooters to let the bow drift down the hill during aiming and follow-through. To avoid this drift, aim on the uphill side of your ideal hit zone or use a bowsight with a level. (The rules of competitive tournaments for those with bowhunting equipment often preclude the use of a level in competition.) If you are standing on the side of a hill, gravity tends to pull you downhill. When you come to full draw and then attempt to force your bow upright, you can unintentionally torque the bow. It is better to compensate before drawing by leaning slightly into the hill.

Figure 11.4 *(a)* Bend from the waist when shooting on hills; *(b)* keep your bow vertical when shooting on a side hill; *(c)* bend from the waist when shooting on a tree stand.

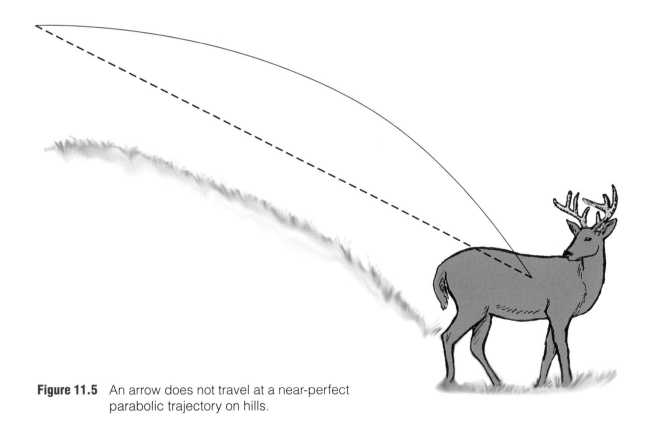

Figure 11.5 An arrow does not travel at a near-perfect parabolic trajectory on hills.

Aiming

The goal in hunting is to kill rather than wound game animals so they die as quickly as possible and can be retrieved. Know the anatomy of the game you are hunting, especially the location of the heart and lungs. The most effective kill shots are those through the heart and lungs, although shots through major arteries, the liver, stomach, or kidneys can cause severe bleeding and result in a kill. You should also know the location of major bones to avoid shots that would strike bone rather than the chest cavity or vital organs.

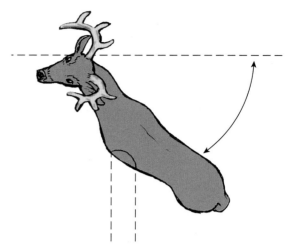

Figure 11.6 The kill zone shrinks when the game is angled.

One way to learn the locations of the vital organs of the game you want to hunt is to practice with paper animal targets, silhouettes, or 3-D targets that have these organs marked. Practicing with 3-D targets also helps you learn which positions of the animal afford a good shot. If you cannot aim at the vital organs without hitting a major bone, you are better off passing up the shot until the animal changes positions or waiting for another opportunity altogether. Working with 3-D targets will also make you realize that when the game is angled rather than broadside to you, the kill zone shrinks (figure 11.6).

Practicing

Although hunting involves few shots, you must be well practiced to ensure success. You can practice for hunting in a variety of ways. First, indoor practice at a short distance is an excellent way to practice shot execution. You can more easily judge whether your shot execution is good when you are indoors than you can when you are outdoors, where there are more variables to influence your performance. You know that your scores reflect your shooting and not the elements or a poor estimate of distance. Conditions are better controlled, too, for trying new equipment and tuning equipment.

For a change of pace indoors, hunters use paper animal targets for practice. Some indoor ranges sponsor bowhunting leagues in which shooters take shots that simulate hunting. For example, some shots may be from a sitting or kneeling position, and shooting distances may vary from shot to shot or end to end.

Outdoor target practice can also contribute to your bowhunting skills. You can practice at longer distances and obtain good sight settings. You can practice using your bowsight at odd distances, such as 23 yards (21 m) or 37 yards (34 m). Most bowhunters practice at a maximum distance of 50 yards (46 m). At longer distances, even a small error in judging distance can result in your arrow being far off its mark. The risk of wounding rather than killing your game is not worth taking a shot over 50 yards (46 m).

Field archery is an effective and fun way to practice for bowhunting, in addition to being an enjoyable form of archery in its own right. There are two governing bodies for field archery events in the United States. One is the National Field Archery Association (NFAA), and the other is World Archery. NFAA field ranges are typically 14 targets set out in golf course fashion, usually in a wooded area. Targets of varying sizes are set at various distances and on varying terrain. Distances are marked. You can practice uphill and downhill shots; shots in the shadows; shots in the sun, rain, and wind; and shots with level and unlevel footing. You can shoot field archery with the exact equipment setup you would use for hunting, except with field tips in your arrows rather than broadheads. Target archers enjoy field archery, too, and tend to shoot field events with their outdoor target equipment. There are three possible rounds that can be used in NFAA events: one with distances that are multiples of five, another with odd distances (such as 32 yd, or 29 m), and a third with paper animal targets. World Archery includes a round with unmarked distances.

Three-dimensional (3-D) rounds are the type of competitive shooting closest to actual hunting. The 3-D refers to the targets, usually foam animals of various sizes placed in natural settings in the woods. You are given a location from which to shoot, but the distance is unmarked. Most 3-D competitions are shot with field tips, too, but occasionally broadhead rounds are held. Three-dimensional targets are helpful when you're learning where to aim at various game animals standing at various angles. They also help you practice maintaining your aim on the dark coat of a game animal, which is quite different from aiming at a gold bull's-eye!

If you will be hunting from a tree stand, practice shooting at targets you place around the tree stand. This particularly helps with distance judgments. If you must practice away from the woods, consider using an elevated platform. Some outdoor ranges provide elevated platforms and 3-D targets to practice shooting from a tree stand or hill (see figure 11.7). A key to shooting from a tree stand, just as when shooting downhill, is to bend at the waist rather than just lowering the arm.

Although repetitive practice is beneficial for hunting, you should also practice taking single shots at various distances. This type of practice

Figure 11.7 Practice for shooting from a tree stand. *(a)* Platforms at various heights and *(b)* 3-D targets downrange from the platform.

disciplines you to put together one critical shot perfectly the first time. You otherwise may find yourself getting lazy with multiple practice shots from the same location.

Because your footing may be unlevel or awkwardly positioned in hunting or you may be seated in a tree stand, simulate these conditions in practice. You must learn to draw with good upper-body alignment even if you cannot position your lower body as you prefer.

Hunting Success Exercise 1   Indoor Practice

Indoor practice allows you to perfect your shot without dealing with some of the elements outdoors. You can also simulate hunting conditions to some extent. Obtain five animal targets like the one in figure 11.8 of various types and sizes. Take four shots at each target from different body positions: standing, kneeling, standing on a stable platform or chair, and standing with an open stance. If you can, also vary your distance from the

Figure 11.8   Animal target for indoor practice.

target. Score 5 points for each arrow in the kill zone on the target, 3 points for each arrow in the wound zone, 1 point for hitting somewhere else on the animal, and 0 points for a miss. Total your score.

TO INCREASE DIFFICULTY

- Use smaller targets.
- Change the distance for each shot.
- Change the angle of each shot.

TO DECREASE DIFFICULTY

- Use larger targets.
- Take all shots from a standing position.

Success Check

- Square shoulders to target.
- Maintain alignment.

Score Your Success

Score 90 points or more = 6 points

Score 70 to 89 points = 3 points

Score 50 to 69 points = 1 point

Your score _____

Hunting Success Exercise 2 Field Archery

Locate a field archery range (figure 11.9) and shoot a field archery round. Field ranges typically have 14 targets varying in shooting distance from 20 feet (6 m) to 80 yards (73 m). One end of four arrows is shot at each target. A shooting stake marks the specified distance for each target. If you do not have the equipment or sight settings to allow you to shoot long distances, you can shoot these targets from a shorter distance. A sign at each target tells you what to do because field ranges do not have to be arranged with targets in any particular order. Field target faces are black and white. Score them with 5 points for the bull's-eye, 4 points for the two white rings, and 3 points for the two black rings. Total your score for the 14 targets.

TO INCREASE DIFFICULTY

- Use 5, 4, 3, 2, 1 scoring for each of the five rings.

TO DECREASE DIFFICULTY

- Use youth shooting distances.
- Use animal targets.

Figure 11.9 Field archery target.

Success Check

- Maintain upper-body alignment despite footing.
- Adjust for hills.
- Double-check sight setting for marked distance.

Score Your Success

Score 200 points or more = 10 points

Score 150 to 199 points = 6 points

Score 100 to 149 points = 3 points

Score 50 to 99 points = 1 point

Your score _____

Hunting Success Exercise 3 **Animal Round**

On the field range you located for exercise 2, shoot an animal round. Bring a pair of binoculars. The shooting stakes for an animal round are at uneven distances, such as 23 or 32 yards (21 or 29 m), but the distances are marked. Paper targets of game animals are used. Each target is marked with a kill zone and wound zone and is usually the outline of the animal (figure 11.10). Shoot an initial arrow. If it lands in the kill zone, record 20 points. If it lands in the wound area, record 18 points. If your first arrow misses, shoot a second arrow. The target might be labeled to move up to a closer stake for the subsequent shot. For your second arrow, record 16 points for a kill or 14 points for a wound. If your second arrow misses, shoot a final arrow. For this final arrow, record 12 points for a kill and 10 points for a wound. If your third arrow misses, your score is 0 for the target. Shoot a second or third arrow only if you do not score with the previous arrow. Total your score for the 14 targets.

Figure 11.10 Animal targets for an animal round on a field range.

TO INCREASE DIFFICULTY

- Use the bonus X-ring on each target: 21 points (first arrow), 17 points (second arrow), or 13 points (third arrow).

Success Check

- Locate ideal area for aiming.
- Adjust for hills.
- Follow through.

Score Your Success

Score 250 points or more = 10 points

Score 200 to 249 points = 6 points

Score 150 to 199 points = 3 points

Score 130 to 149 points = 1 point

Your score _____

Hunting Success Exercise 4   3-D Animal Round

Find out from a local bowhunting club when a 3-D round will be held and whether field tips or broadheads will be used. Go through the round on the indicated day and record your score. The center vital scoring area of the animal model is worth 10 points, the outer vital area is worth 8 points, and the remainder of the animal's body is worth 5 points (figure 11.11).

Figure 11.11   A typical 3-D animal target.

Success Check

- Estimate shooting distance in 5-yard (4.6 m) increments.
- Double-check estimate of distance.
- Adjust for conditions.
- Maintain aim until steady on target.

Score Your Success

Score 90 points or more on 14 targets = 10 points

Score 70 to 89 points on 14 targets = 6 points

Score 50 to 69 points on 14 targets = 3 points

Score 30 to 49 points on 14 targets = 1 point

Your score _____

Hunting Success Exercise 5   Tree Stand Practice

If you will be bowhunting from a tree stand, practice from an elevated position so you learn to judge your distance, taking into account the downhill angle. You can shoot from a platform or from a ladder. Swimming pool ladders with a platform at the top are well suited for this exercise. Place the ladder about 20 yards (18 m) from a target butt. Use an animal target. Shoot four arrows, and then score your shots: 5 points for the inner zone, 3 points for the outer zone, and 1 point for an arrow hitting any part of the animal. Reposition the ladder closer to the target and shoot four more arrows. Repeat this exercise until you have shot 20 arrows; total your score.

(continued)

Hunting Success Exercise 5   *(continued)*

TO INCREASE DIFFICULTY

- Mix up shooting distances.
- Include distances up to 30 yards (27 m).

Success Check

- Adjust shooting distance for down-hill shots.

Score Your Success

Score 80 points or more = 10 points

Score 60 to 79 points = 6 points

Score 40 to 59 points = 3 points

Your score _____

BOWFISHING

Bowfishing is yet another way to enjoy archery. While it is tempting to think of bow-fishing as simply bowhunting for fish, there are important differences, especially in equipment. Bowfishing equipment is less complex than bowhunting equipment. Shots are much shorter than in hunting, but fish are usually moving. A line is attached to the arrow so that it can be reeled back in after a shot, whether successful or not.

You can bowfish in waters that are shallow and relatively clear. This can be in freshwater rivers, canals, streams, lakes, and reservoirs. Saltwater shallow flats, bays, and estuaries also are good for bowfishing. Bowfishers can walk the shore or wade into the water, or they can bowfish from a kayak, canoe, or shallow-hull boat. Some of these flat boats have platforms and downfacing lights for night fishing.

Bowfishing is likely regulated in your area, so you must be familiar with the species you are allowed to catch. Freshwater fish that are commonly taken include carp, gar, tilapia, drum, catfish, and buffalo. Saltwater fish include flounder and sheepshead.

Bows

Both recurve and compound bows are used for bowfishing, but remember that bow-fishers shoot at short range. A draw weight of 30 to 40 pounds (14-18 kg) is sufficient. Compound bows still provide the advantage of a lighter holding weight because bowfishers must sometimes hold at full draw to get a shot at their moving target. A type of compound often seen in bowfishing is a lever bow (figure 11.12). You might think it looks like a combination of a recurve and a compound. The limb tips move back as the bow is drawn and then forward on release. The risers of both the familiar compound bow and the lever bow feature the same cutout riser design as target and hunting bows.

The important addition to the bow used in bowfishing is a reel, from which the line attached to the arrow plays out as the arrow travels to its target. There are three types of reels: hand reels, bottle reels, and spincast reels. The traditional reel is a hand reel. It looks like a disk mounted vertically on the bow. After the shot, the archer grabs the line and winds it back onto the reel. Hand reels are economical and durable. Archers should wear a glove to protect the hand working the line. Traditional bowfishers using a recurve bow typically use a hand reel.

The second type of reel is a bottle reel (figure 11.13). The bottle holds the line. It is mounted on the side of the bow and has a handle. The archer winds the handle to reel in the arrow and fish. A spincast reel, just like those used on fishing rods, is the third option (figure 11.14). Line can be reeled in quickly, and thinner line can be used, facilitating the arrow's movement through water. Spincast reels are the most expensive of the three and require maintenance. A single arrow quiver also can be mounted on the bow.

The arrow rest on a bow for fishing is simple. Without fletching, all a bowfishing arrow requires is a trough to hold the arrow steady. There is a type of rest that features a roller (revolving cylinder) with a trough. It provides smooth forward travel for the arrow when

Figure 11.12   A lever-type compound bow used for bowfishing.

Figure 11.13   Bottle reel.

released. Many bowfishers put a finger protector on their bowstrings so that they don't have to use a finger tab or glove. The finger protector consists of two pieces of rubber, one the width of the top finger of the bow hand that is positioned above the nocking point, while the other is the width of the two fingers positioned below the nocking point.

Most bowfishers shoot without a sight. Distances are typically short, and with some aiming practice, bowfishers can be very accurate without a sight. Light waves bend when they hit water because water is denser than air. As we look into the water, objects are not actually where they appear to us—they are lower. Bowfishers must aim below where a fish appears to be. Beginners can do well using the simple rule of aiming 6 inches (15 cm) lower than the fish. With practice, bowfishers develop an instinct for how to adjust their aiming for the varying distances and depths of the fish.

With this configuration of equipment, there are a few important keys to shooting form. First, your target is below you, so you will need to bend at the waist but maintain T-form with your upper body. A side-of-face anchor, as described in step 6, is likely to be your preferred anchor since you are not using a bowsight and want to set your anchor quickly to be ready for a shot.

Ike Carasquillo

Figure 11.14 A compound bow used for bowfishing and equipped with a spincast reel.

Arrows

The arrows used in bowfishing are made especially for this purpose. A fletched hunting or target arrow will not fly true once it enters the water. So, a bowfishing arrow is simply a shaft without fletching made of fiberglass, carbon, or a combination of materials, such as a carbon core with fiberglass wrapped around it. All types of arrow shafts work well for most conditions, but archers shooting large fish typically choose a carbon shaft. Bright colors are traditional for bowfishing shafts so that they can be seen in the water. A recent innovation is a translucent fiberglass shaft used with a glow stick. These arrows are ideal for night fishing. One glow stick can be used for 24 hours. Bowfishers take one shot at a time, so they don't need many arrows.

Arrow points all have barbed tips that set as a fish is being reeled in (figure 11.15*a*). Tips are replaceable and can vary depending on the fish species sought. Arrows are removed from fish by being pushed all the way through the fish, if they are not already through, unscrewing the tip so that the barbs reverse, and then pulling the arrow back out (figure 11.15*b*). Nocks are like those used in target shooting, but some bowfishers use lighted nocks.

A danger in bowfishing is getting the fishing line tangled in the bow or cables as the arrow is shot. If this keeps the line from playing out, the arrow could snap back toward the archer. It is very important to use a safety slide on bowfishing arrows (figure 11.15c). The line is attached to the slide, and the slide is pushed forward, keeping the line forward of the bow.

Figure 11.15 *(a)* The point of a bowfishing arrow (this tip is recommended for gar); *(b)* with the tip loosened or removed, the barbs can be reversed and the arrow pulled back out of the fish; *(c)* a safety slide, which the fishing line is attached to.

Timing

The spring and summer are particularly good seasons to bowfish and allow for fishing throughout the day. Still, many archers prefer fishing in the early morning or at dusk, when fish are more active. The best bowfishing is done in calm winds so that visibility is good. Using specialized boats with downfacing lights, some bowfishers enjoy hunting after sundown.

At any time, approaching fish quietly and without stirring the water too much is important. If you are on the shore, move quietly and step softly, as fish can feel vibrations from heavy steps and be spooked.

It is easy to see that bowfishing is yet another way you can enjoy archery. Beginners can see success rather quickly if they keep in mind the fundamentals—the keys to a successful shot.

Bowfishing equipment is relatively economical. An entire bowfishing package can cost less than a hunting bow alone.

Bowfishing Exercise 1   Aiming in Bowfishing

Since bowfishers typically do not use sights, practice and experience aiming at fish in water are needed to develop the instinct for aiming quickly and accurately. While experience bowfishing helps in this process, it is possible to use a practice setting for additional experience. Take a gallon (4 L) plastic milk jug and weight it with some sand so that it will sink in the water. Attach a light rope to the handle and anchor it on shore or in your boat. This will allow you to retrieve the jug if your last shot misses. In shallow fishing water, throw the jug into the water and take a shot, remembering to aim below the jug. Your arrow might go all the way through the jug, so avoid pools and decorative fishponds with liners. Take six shots and record the points earned for the number of hits. If you hit the jug, reel it in, remove your arrow just as you would with a fish, and toss the jug into the water again.

TO INCREASE DIFFICULTY

- Throw the jug into water of varying depths.
- Throw the jug varying distances from your position.

TO DECREASE DIFFICULTY

- Use a shallow area approximately 12 inches (30 cm) deep.
- Toss the jug just a few feet away from your position.

Success Check

- Relax your bow hand.
- Anchor consistently.
- Bend at the waist.
- Aim lower for farther and deeper shots.

Score Your Success

Hit the jug five or six times = 4 points

Hit the jug three or four times = 2 points

Hit the jug one or two times = 1 point

Your score _____

SUCCESS SUMMARY

Most archers can hardly resist the many ways to enjoy archery. Some target archers never hunt live game but enjoy field and 3-D rounds. Some who intend to only hunt eventually take up target archery. Adapting your equipment and your shot for the conditions is part of the challenge of shooting archery.

In this step, you learned how to adapt your shot and your equipment for hunting, and you learned ways of practicing for bowhunting. If you are planning to bowhunt, you will probably want to read more about hunting techniques, including camouflaging, calling game, trailing game after a successful shot, and field-dressing your kill. You also learned about bowfishing equipment and how to practice aiming at fish in the water.

Check to see how far you have progressed in taking up bowhunting, the various forms of shooting that simulate hunting, or bowfishing. For each exercise in this step, record the points you earned. If you earned more than 41 points, you did well in your initial preparations for bowhunting. If you earned fewer than 41 points or you plan to hunt for the first time soon, repeat the exercises. You can continue to use these exercises for practice even after you reach a level of proficiency.

Hunting Equipment Exercises

1. Selecting Hunting Arrows _____ out of 6

2. Tuning Broadheads _____ out of 3

Hunting Success Exercises

1. Indoor Practice _____ out of 6

2. Field Archery _____ out of 10

3. Animal Round _____ out of 10

4. 3-D Animal Round _____ out of 10

5. Tree Stand Practice _____ out of 10

Bowfishing Exercise

1. Aiming in Bowfishing _____ out of 4

Total _____ **out of 59**

Congratulations on reaching the top of the staircase for the steps to success in archery! You have come a long way. You know how to select equipment that is matched to your size and strength and is appropriate for your interests. You have established solid T-form adapted to your body shape and strength. You know how to analyze your performance so you can correct flaws in your shooting. With solid form and tuned equipment, you should be able to score well and improve with additional practice.

Now that you're armed with the information presented in these last two steps, all that remains is to get involved in archery activities. Remember that you can use many of the exercises in this text for practice, even as you become a proficient shooter. Varying your practice activities keeps your practice sessions interesting! After all, archery is a sport for a lifetime, and you want to enjoy it for years to come.

Glossary

3-D round—An archery shoot in which the targets are three-dimensional, lifelike foam animal shapes and are placed at unknown distances to simulate hunting.

3-D target—A lifelike foam shape of an animal, decorated to look like that animal, often with the ideal kill zone marked.

actual draw length—The arrow length needed by an archer, measured from the bottom of the slit in the arrow nock to the back of the bow.

actual draw weight—The energy (expressed in pounds) required to draw the bow to the actual draw length.

address—To assume a stance while straddling the shooting line.

aim—To visually place a bowsight aperture over the target center; if a bowsight is not used, to place the arrow tip over a particular point.

aiming aperture—The extension of the bowsight into the bow window that the archer aligns with the bull's-eye or target; literally, a circle in which the bull's-eye is centered but could be generalized to all sight pins.

alignment—With regard to the bowstring, the relationship between the string and sight aperture; with regard to shooting form, the relationship of the trunk to the arms.

anchor—To draw the bowstring to the anchor point.

anchor position—A fixed position against the body to which the draw hand is brought.

archer's paradox—The way the arrow clears the bow upon release by bending around the bow handle.

arm guard—A piece of leather or plastic placed on the inside forearm of the bow arm to protect it from a slap of the bowstring upon release.

arrow rest—A projection from the bow window, above the arrow shelf, on which the arrow lies when drawn.

arrow shelf—A horizontal projection at the bottom of the bow window on which the arrow can lie in the absence of an arrow rest.

backstop—See string stopper.

back tension—A key feature of good shooting form, wherein the archer draws the bow using the back muscles and then maintains or increases this tension through the aiming and release phases of the shot.

barbed tip—The type of arrow tip used on bowfishing arrows with barbs that spring out as a fish is being reeled in, preventing the tip from slipping out of the fish; a fish point.

barebow—A type of shooting that does not allow the use of bowsights, stabilizers, release aids, or other shooting aids.

bare shaft—An arrow shaft without fletching of any kind.

blunt—An arrow with a flat tip that is used to hunt small game.

bounce-out—An arrow that strikes the scoring area of the target face but rebounds away; also called a rebound.

bow arm—The arm of the hand that holds the bow.

bow efficiency—The ratio of the kinetic energy received by the arrow to that stored by the bow.

bow hand—The hand that holds the bow.

bow scale—A mechanical device that measures the draw weight of a bow at any stage of the draw.

bowsight—Any device mounted on the bow that allows an archer to aim directly at the target or a mark.

bow sling—A strap attached to the bow through which the archer slips the bow hand, thereby preventing the bow from being dropped upon release.

bow square—A device that attaches to the bowstring and lies on the arrow rest to measure brace height and nocking point location.

bowstring—The string on the bow, usually made of Dacron or Kevlar.

bowstringer—A device used for bracing, or stringing, a bow.

bow window—The recessed area above the grip; the sight window.

brace height—The distance between the bow (measured at the pivot point) and string when the bow is strung; string height.

breakover—The point in the draw of a compound bow at which the draw weight reaches its peak and then begins to decrease.

broadhead—A multiedged, sharp arrow point used in hunting game.

bull's-eye—The area on the target face with the highest scoring value, usually in the center.

butt—A backstop for arrows; typically made of grass, excelsior, straw, cardboard, polyethylene foam, or fiber; target butt.

cable guard—An adjustable rod mounted on a compound bow that holds the cables away from the bowstring, ensuring that the arrow's fletching does not contact the cables as the arrow travels forward upon release of the bowstring.

cam—An elliptically shaped eccentric pulley mounted on one or both tips of a compound bow that provides an advantage in draw weight let-off compared to a round eccentric pulley.

cant—To tilt the bow to the right or left, as indicated by the top limb tip, at full draw.

cast—The ability of a bow to project an arrow; the distance and speed a bow can shoot an arrow.

center serving—The wrapping thread over the center of the bowstring where the arrow is nocked.

center-shot bow—A bow design wherein the sight window is cut out so that the arrow, sitting on the arrow rest, is at or very near the centerline of the bow.

chest protector—A piece of nylon netting or vinyl worn over the clothing to prevent the bowstring from catching.

clicker—A device attached to the bow or sometimes to the cables of a compound bow that indicates by sound that the arrow has been drawn a certain desired distance; most archers use the sound of the click as an indication to release.

closed stance—A shooting stance in which an imaginary straight line to the target intersects the toes of the rear foot and middle of the front foot.

clout shooting—A type of shooting wherein archers shoot to a large, ringed target laid out on the ground, usually from a long distance.

cock feather—See index feather.

compound bow—A bow that uses a cable system attached to cams mounted at the limb tips; this system produces peak resistance at mid-draw and then drops off to a holding weight that is less than the draw weight.

creeping—Allowing the draw hand to move forward immediately before or during release.

crest—A decoration painted on arrows, often a colored band, to help archers identify their set of matched arrows.

crossbow—A type of bow that has a barrel and trigger release, similar to a gun; the limbs are short and oriented horizontally rather than vertically.

cross-dominant archer—An archer with a dominant hand and a dominant eye on opposite sides of the body.

crosshair sight—A sight with a circular aperture in which two fine lines cross at right angles; the intersection of the lines is aimed at the target.

cushion plunger—A spring-loaded button mounted horizontally through the bow above the handle pivot point to absorb force as the arrow pushes against it upon release.

dead release—A bowstring release in which the hand stays locked in its anchor position and the fingers extend to release the string; back tension is not used to release.

deflex bow—A bow whose handle riser is somewhat C-shaped toward the archer; it provides an advantage of forgiveness but a disadvantage of speed.

D loop—A short length of string (about 1/2 in., or 1.3 cm) attached to the bowstring above and below the nocking point to which a mechanical release is attached, instead of attaching the release directly onto the bowstring.

dominant eye—The eye preferred by an archer for sighting or visually fixating on an object.

draw—To pull the bowstring.

draw check—A device attached to the bow to indicate that full draw has been reached.

draw hand—See string hand.

draw length—The distance between the nocking point and the grip of the bow at full draw; at one time, draw length was measured to the back of the bow.

draw weight—The amount of force measured in pounds required to draw any bow a given distance.

drop-away rest—An arrow rest designed to drop as the bowstring is released and the arrow begins to move forward so that any contact with the arrow and its fletching is eliminated or minimized.

dry-fire—To draw and release a bowstring without having nocked an arrow; also, to draw and release a bowstring after an arrow has come off the bowstring.

eccentric pulley or wheel—A round wheel with an off-center axle mounted at the limb tip of a compound bow that decreases the amount of weight held on the bowstring at full draw.

end—A specified number of arrows shot before archers go to the target to score and retrieve their arrows.

expandable broadhead—A broadhead whose blades are designed to lie down until they open at impact with game.

face—The paper or cardboard with a target printed on it; see target face.

face walking—A technique used in barebow or instinctive shooting that involves raising or lowering the anchor point to adjust the distance of a shot.

field archery—A type of competitive archery shot outdoors in a wooded area with targets of varying distances and sizes; archers walk from target to target.

field point—An arrow point that is heavier than a target point and similar in weight to a broadhead; it can be unscrewed from a mounting insert in aluminum arrows so a broadhead can be installed.

field round—A competitive round, usually of 14 ends, each shot to a different target from a different distance; it is similar to golf in that archers walk the round, but it is typically in a wooded or field setting.

finger protector—Two cylindrical pieces of rubber that mount onto the bowstring lengthwise above and below the nocking point, allowing archers, especially bowfishers, to forgo a finger tab or glove.

finger sling—A piece of leather, plastic, or rope looped at each end through which the archer slips the thumb and a finger after taking hold of the bow; it enables the archer to maintain a loose grip.

finger tab—A piece of leather or plastic worn over the draw fingers to protect them and to ensure a smooth release of the bowstring; tab.

fish point—An arrow point used for bowfishing, usually with movable barbs that open after entry to prevent the arrow from pulling out of the fish; a barbed tip.

fishtailing—A back-and-forth motion of the nock end of an arrow on its flight to the target.

fixed pins—The sight pins on a bowhunting sight; in competitive rounds for archers with bowhunting equipment, the pins must be set before competition and remain fixed in position until the end of the round.

fletching—The turkey feathers or plastic vanes mounted on an arrow to stabilize it in flight.

flight shooting—A form of archery in which the object is to shoot an arrow for the greatest distance possible. Flight bows are designed with maximum cast so as to shoot maximum distance without great accuracy. Flight arrows are small in diameter with small fletching so they can fly as far as possible.

flinching—A form error in which the archer suddenly moves, often the bow arm, immediately before or during the release, thus disturbing the flight of the arrow as it clears the bow.

flu-flu—A type of fletching that is high and wide, often mounted in a spiral; it is designed to slow an arrow and limit its flight because it is used in aerial shooting or hunting small game.

follow-through—The archer's position after release of the arrow; ideally the body, head, and bow arm positions are held steady and the string hand recoils over the string shoulder as a result of continuous back tension.

foot markers—Anything used to mark the exact position of the feet in addressing the target so that the archer can duplicate the position and distance of the stance from the target on subsequent shots.

force-draw curve—The graph created by plotting draw weight (vertical axis) against draw length (horizontal axis) for a bow as it is drawn to full draw.

freestyle—A competition classification that typically allows archers to use bowsights, release aids, and other mechanical devices and shooting aids.

freezing—An aiming difficulty encountered by some archers wherein they get "stuck" aiming at a point on the target face other than the center and cannot easily move to aim at the center.

full draw—The position wherein the bowstring is moved back and the draw hand anchors with respect to the head and neck.

gap shooting—An aiming technique used when no bowsight is used; the archer focuses on and adjusts the gap or distance between the target and the tip of the arrow to hit the target.

glove—A leather covering that slips over the fingertips of the string hand and attaches to the wrist to protect the string fingers and permit a smooth release; an alternative to a finger tab.

gold—The center area of the multicolored target often used in target archery.

grip—The part of the bow handle where the bow is held. Also, the removable plastic piece that allows a change in the shape of the bow where it is held.

ground quiver—An arrow holder that sits on or sticks into the ground; some also hold a bow.

grouping—The pattern of an archer's arrows in the target.

handle riser—The middle section of the bow exclusive of the limbs.

hard cam—A cam designed to accelerate an arrow very quickly, providing an advantage of speed but a disadvantage in smoothness and forgiveness.

heeling—A shooting flaw in which the archer pushes forward suddenly with the heel of the bow hand at release.

high anchor—An anchor position in which the draw hand contacts the side of the face.

high wrist—The bow hold position in which the top of the wrist is held level with the top of the bow arm.

holding—Maintaining a steady bow position at full draw during aiming.

holding weight—The weight measured in pounds held by the archer at full draw; with recurve bows, the holding weight increases with the length of the draw, whereas with compound bows, the holding weight is less than the peak weight. For this reason, holding weight is often reported as part of a compound bow's specifications.

hunting arrow—An arrow used for hunting that is typically longer and sturdier than a target arrow to accommodate a broadhead.

hunting round—A competitive round that mimics hunting conditions. Archers typically walk from target to target; the targets are pictures of animals or three-dimensional foam animals, positioned at various, sometimes unmarked, distances.

index feather—The feather mounted on an arrow shaft at a right angle to the nock slit, often of a distinct color; also called the cock feather.

instinctive shooting—A shooting style wherein no bowsight is used and archers aim by instinct and experience to shoot targets of various distances.

kisser button—A small disk attached to the bowstring that is meant to contact the lips in the anchor position to ensure proper anchor and head positions.

launcher—A shoot-through arrow rest.

let-down—A return to the ready position without releasing the bowstring.

let-off—The weight reduction from peak weight to holding weight on a compound bow (sometimes reported as a percentage).

level—A device attached to the sight or the bow to help the archer maintain a vertical bow position.

lever bow—A type of bow commonly used in bowfishing with limb tips that move back when the bow is drawn—that is, they move as levers.

limb bands—Pieces of rubber mounted on compound bow limbs to dampen vibration and make the bow quieter.

limbs—The energy-storing parts of a bow above and below the handle riser section.

longbow—A bow style popular in England in the Middle Ages; long limbs without a recurved shape are characteristic of longbows. Although not as efficient in design as a bow with recurved limbs, the longbow does not require the bonding of materials, which was especially difficult in the past in the damp weather of England.

loose—An older term for releasing the bowstring.

low wrist—The bow hand position wherein the hand is flat against the bow handle and the pressure during the draw is through the forearm bone.

minnowing—Side-to-side movement of an arrow in flight that is smaller and more rapid than fishtailing; typically caused by the arrow's fletching contacting the arrow rest after release.

nock—The removable piece, usually plastic, on the end of an arrow with a slit for the bowstring.

nocking—Placing the arrow on the bowstring in preparation for shooting.

nocking point—The location on the bowstring where the nock locator is positioned.

nock locator—A stop on the bowstring against which the arrow is placed.

no glove finger protectors—Cylindrical pieces of rubber attached to the bowstring above and below the nocking point so that a finger tab or glove is not necessary.

open stance—A position on the shooting line wherein a straight line to the target passes through the middle of the rear foot and the toes of the front foot.

outsert—An arrow attachment that is mounted over an arrow shaft rather than inside it, usually when the arrow shaft is made of carbon. Some outserts are adapters that allow nocks made to fit inside a shaft to be used and changed more easily.

overdraw—To draw an arrow so that the point passes the face of the bow; also, a device that permits the use of arrows shorter than the archer's draw length.

overnock—An arrow nock designed to fit over an arrow shaft so that it is slightly wider in diameter than the arrow shaft.

overstrung—A condition in which a bow is strung with a bowstring that is too short, making the brace height too high.

pass-through—An arrow that penetrates completely through the target face and target butt.

peak weight—The heaviest draw weight achieved during the draw of a compound bow.

peeking—A shooting flaw wherein the archer moves the head at release to watch the arrow in flight.

peep sight—A plastic or metal piece that has a small hole and is tied into the bowstring so that an archer can look through the hole to line up the bowsight and target.

perfect end—An end in which all arrows land in the highest scoring area.

pinching—Squeezing the arrow nock with the draw fingers during the draw.

pin sight—A sight using one or more sight apertures similar to a pinhead.

pivot point—The place on the bow's grip that is farthest from the string.

plucking—A shooting flaw in which the string hand is pulled away from the face and body upon release instead of recoiling over the rear shoulder.

point—The arrow tip.

point of aim—A method of aiming in which the arrow point is aligned with some point in front of and below the target. Natural point of aim refers to the use of a naturally occurring object, whereas artificial point of aim employs a stake, cloth, or other device placed by the archer.

porpoising—Up-and-down movement of an arrow in flight, typically caused by a mispositioned nocking point.

post sight—A bowsight with an aperture that has a metal piece projecting vertically up or down, the tip of which is aligned with the bull's-eye.

pressure point—The place on the arrow plate against which the arrow pushes upon release of the bowstring.

pull—To remove shot arrows from the target; also, to draw the bow.

punching—A release error encountered by archers using a mechanical release, usually one with a trigger. The archer anticipates triggering the release and moves the draw hand and arm forward (hence, the term *punching*) instead of maintaining back tension.

push–pull draw—A method of reaching full draw by pushing the bent bow arm away from the body while the string is drawn by the string hand.

quiver—A holder for arrows that may be worn, placed on the ground, or mounted on the bow, particularly when hunting.

range—The place where archery shooting takes place; also, the distance to be shot.

rebound—An arrow that hits the target face but bounces back toward the archer rather than penetrating the target; also called a bounce-out.

recurve bow—A bow with limb tips that are curved forward.

reel—A spool that holds the line attached to an arrow for bowfishing. There are three types of reels: the hand reel, the bottle reel, and the spincast reel.

reflex bow—A bow whose handle riser section is C-shaped away from the archer, resulting in a short brace height; this provides an advantage of speed but a disadvantage of forgiveness.

release—Letting go of the bowstring, ideally by opening the string finger hook; also used to describe a particular style of holding the string. For example, the Apache release uses three fingers under the arrow, and the primary release uses the thumb and forefinger to pull the arrow itself.

release aid—A handheld device attached to the bowstring; it is used to draw and release the string, minimizing the string deflection otherwise seen with a finger release.

ring sight—A bowsight with an aperture that is an open circle; the bull's-eye is centered in the ring to aim the arrow.

riser—The center handle portion of the bow exclusive of the limbs.

Robin Hood—To shoot an arrow into the end of an arrow in the target, named after the legendary character; also called telescoping.

round—The number of ends shot at designated distances and target sizes to obtain a standard score.

roving—A form of practice wherein the archer walks woods or fields and randomly chooses targets such as tree stumps; the origin of formal field and hunting rounds shot today.

safety slide—A movable cylinder that slides up and down a bowfishing arrow, allowing the line to be attached to it and slid forward toward the tip, minimizing chances of the line tangling in the bow or its cables.

scoring area—The part of the target face made up of scoring circles.

selfbow—A bow made of a single piece of wood.

serving—A heavy thread wrapped around the bowstring at its center and on the loops to protect the string and add strength.

set—A group of three arrows shot alternately with a competitor in head-to-head shooting tournaments; points are awarded based on high score, and the archer with the highest score after a maximum of five sets advances.

set arm draw—The method of reaching full draw by first extending the bow arm and then drawing the string.

shaft—The body of an arrow.

shelf—A horizontal projection at the bottom of the bow window upon which the arrow can lie in the absence of an arrow rest.

shooting glove—A leather covering that slips over the fingertips of the string hand and attaches around the wrist, protecting the string fingers and allowing a smooth release; an alternative to a finger tab.

shooting line—A marked line parallel to the targets from which all archers shoot.

shoot-through rest—An arrow rest mounted away from the bow handle so that on release the arrow does not have to bend around the bow handle but rather can travel straight to clear the bow on its way to the target.

sight—Any device mounted on the bow that allows an archer to aim directly at the target or a mark.

sight aperture—The part of the bowsight that extends into the archer's view and is aligned with the center of the target. Apertures can be of many styles, such as rings, posts with a ball, or dots mounted on glass that may or may not magnify the target; they can also be lighted posts.

sight bar—The part of the bowsight to which the aperture assembly is attached.

sight extension—A bar that allows the bowsight to be extended from the bow toward the target.

sight pin—A bowsight aperture that is a straight piece of metal with a dot or ball at the end.

sight window—The recessed area above the grip; the bow window.

silencer—A clump of yarn or rubber bands attached to the bowstring to reduce vibration and therefore noise; usually used for hunting.

sling—A strap attached to the bow or to the hand holding the bow that prevents the bow from dropping to the ground upon release.

snap shooting—A shooting flaw wherein the arrow is shot immediately as the bowsight crosses the bull's-eye.

soft cam—A cam designed to accelerate an arrow more gently than other designs; it maintains some forgiveness and smoothness while still providing arrow speed.

spine—The measured deflection or bendability of an arrow shaft, established by hanging a 2-pound (1 kg) weight at the center of the arrow.

springy rest—A small spring with an arrow rest extension substituted for a cushion plunger.

stabilizer—A rod-and-weight assembly mounted on either the face or back of the handle riser to help eliminate the torque of the bow around its long axis upon release.

stacking—A rapid, disproportionate increase in draw weight in the last few inches of draw in some recurve bows.

stance—The foot position taken to address the target.

standard draw weight—The draw weight of a bow at the standard distance of 26-1/4 inches (66.7 cm) from the pivot point or 28 inches (71 cm) from the far side of the bow handle.

stick bow—Another name for a recurve bow, as opposed to a compound bow; sometimes a selfbow made of one piece of wood.

stops—A term used in the expression *drawing to the stops* to describe drawing a compound bow equipped with cams past the point of maximum let-off, at which the force needed to continue drawing rises sharply. Some archers use it as a draw check.

straight-limb bow—A bow with relatively straight limbs.

string—The bowstring; also, to attach the bowstring to the limb tip by bending the bow limbs and placing them under tension.

string alignment—The relationship between the bowstring and the sight aperture.

string fingers—The fingers that hold the bowstring in shooting the bow.

string hand—The hand that holds the bowstring; the draw hand.

string height—The distance between the bow (measured at the pivot point) and the string when the bow is strung; brace height.

string loop—See D loop.

string pattern—The relationship between the bowstring and the sight aperture.

string silencer—A piece of rubber attached to the bowstring to muffle its sound as it moves forward on release, especially if it strikes the limbs.

string stopper—An extension with a rubber end mounted on the handle riser below the grip to stop the bowstring's forward movement, causing the arrow to leave the string sooner and making the bow more forgiving and quieter.

string walking—A style of shooting wherein the archer moves the position of the fingers on the string to adjust the vertical displacement of the arrow; no bowsight is used.

tab—A piece of leather or plastic worn over the draw fingers to protect them and to ensure a smooth release of the bowstring; finger tab.

tackle—An archer's equipment.

take-down bow—A bow with detachable limbs.

target butt—A backstop for arrows, typically made of grass, excelsior, straw, cardboard, polyethylene foam, or fiber; butt.

target captain—The person at each target during a tournament who is designated to call the scoring value of all arrows on that target.

target face—The paper or cardboard scoring area mounted on the target butt; see face.

target panic—Anticipating the release, which results in the disruption of a smooth and accurate shot; involves one or more symptoms including, but not limited to, flinching, punching, freezing, and snap shooting.

telescoping—See Robin Hood.

T-form—Good shooting form; named because an archer's body looks like a T when the arms are level and properly aligned with the body, which is erect and straight.

tiller—A measure of even balance in the two limbs; on a compound bow, a tiller is adjustable through the limb bolts, thus varying the distance between the base of the limb and the string.

tip—The end of a bow limb; also, an arrow point.

torque—A rotation of the bow about its long axis upon release of the bowstring.

toxology—The study of archery.

toxophily—The art and craft of archery.

tree stand—A platform in a tree that allows a shooter to hunt from an elevation.

tuning—Adjusting the arrow spine, arrow rest, pressure point, cushion plunger, string height, tiller, and nocking point; used for achieving the truest arrow flight possible.

understrung—The description of a bow with a string that is too long, resulting in a low brace height and reduced efficiency.

valley—The point of lowest holding weight reached near full draw on a compound bow.

vane—A plastic fletching that is more windproof and weatherproof than feathers but often heavier.

V-bars—Short stabilizers attached near the long, main stabilizer, forming the shape of a V with the point toward the target.

weight—The force measured in pounds required to draw the bowstring a given distance.

windage—Horizontal correction of the bowsight setting to compensate for drift caused by wind.

wrist sling—A strap that wraps around the archer's wrist and the bow, thereby preventing the bow from falling to the ground at release.

X-ring—A small circle at the center of the bull's-eye; the number of arrows landing in the X-ring is often used as a tiebreaker among archers achieving identical scores in competition.

References

Clarys, J.P., J. Cabri, E. Bollens, R. Sleeckx, J. Taeymans, M. Vermeiren, G. Van Reeth, and G. Voss. 1990. "Muscular Activity of Different Shooting Distances, Different Release Techniques, and Different Performance Levels, With and Without Stabilizers, in Target Archery." *Journal of Sports Sciences* 8: 235-57.

Ertan, H., B. Kentel, S.T. Tümer, and F. Korkusuz. 2003. "Activation Patterns in Forearm Muscles During Archery Shooting." *Human Movement Science* 22: 37-45. https://doi.org/10.1016/S0167-9457(02)00176-8.

Ertan, H., A.J. Knicker, R.A. Soylu, and H.K. Strüder. 2011. "Individual Variation of Bowstring Release in High Level Archery: A Comparative Case Study." *Human Movement* 12: 273-76. https://doi.org/10.2478/v10038-011-0030-x.

Gonzalez, C.C., J. Causer, M.J. Grey, G.W. Humphreys, R.C. Miall, and A.M. Williams. 2017. "Exploring the Quiet Eye in Archery Using Field- and Laboratory-Based Tasks." *Experimental Brain Research* 235: 2843-55. https://doi.org/10.1007/s00221-017-4988-2.

Horsak, B., and M. Heller. 2011. "A Three-Dimensional Analysis of Finger and Bow String Movements During the Release in Archery." *Journal of Applied Biomechanics* 27: 151-60.

Kim, Y., T. Chang, and I. Park. 2019. "Visual Scanning Behavior and Attention Strategies for Shooting Among Expert Versus Collegiate Korean Archers." *Perceptual and Motor Skills* 126: 530-45. https://doi.org/10.1177/0031512519829624.

Laborde, S., F.E.M. Dosseville, P. Leconte, and N. Margas. 2009. "Interaction of Hand Preference With Eye Dominance on Accuracy in Archery." *Perceptual and Motor Skills* 108: 558-64. https://doi.org/10.2466/PMS.108.2.558-564.

Martin, P.E., W.L. Siler, and D. Hoffman. 1990. "Electromyographic Analysis of Bow String Release in Highly Skilled Archers." *Journal of Sports Sciences* 8: 215-21. https://doi.org/10.1080/02640419008732147.

Miyazaki, T., K. Mukaiyama, Y. Komori, K. Okawa, S. Taguchi, and H. Sugiura. 2013. "Aerodynamic Properties of an Archery Arrow." *Sports Engineering* 16: 43-54. https://doi.org/10.1007/s12283-012-0102-y.

Pellerite, B. 2001. *Idiot Proof Archery.* Gahanna, OH: Robinhood Video Productions.

Quan, C., and S. Lee. 2016. "Relationship Between Aiming Patterns and Scores in Archery Shooting." *Korean Journal of Sport Biomechanics* 26: 353-60. https://doi.org/10.5103/KJSB.2016.26.4.353.

Sarro, K.J., T. de Castro Viana, and R.M. Leite de Barros. 2021. "Relationship Between Bow Stability and Postural Control in Recurve Archery." *European Journal of Sport Science* 21: 515-20. https://doi.org/10.1080/17461391.2020.1754471.

Schmitt, M., L. Vogt, J. Wilke, and D. Niederer. 2021. "Unilateral and Bilateral Training Competitive Archers Differ in Some Potentially Unhealthy Neck-Shoulder Region Movement Behaviour Characteristics." *BMC Sports Science, Medicine and Rehabilitation* 13: 44. https://doi.org/10.1186/s13102-021-00272-6.

Simsek, D., A.O. Cerrah, H. Ertan, and R.A. Soylu. 2018. "Muscular Coordination of Movements Associated With Arrow Release in Archery." *South African Journal for Research in Sport, Physical Education and Recreation* 40: 141-55.

Simsek, D., A.O. Cerrah, H. Ertan, and A.R. Soylu. 2019. "A Comparison of the Ground Reaction Forces of Archers With Different Levels of Expertise During the Arrowing Shooting." *Science & Sports* 34: e137-45. https://doi.org/10.1016/j.scispo.2018.08.008.

Spratford, W., and R. Campbell. 2017. "Postural Stability, Clicker Reaction Time and Bow Draw Force Predict Performance in Elite Recurve Archery." *European Journal of Sport Science* 17: 539-45. https://doi.org/10.1080/17461391.2017.1285963.

Wada, Y., and N. Takeda. 2020. "Postural Stability Against Full-Field Dynamic Visual Disturbance in Archery Players." *Journal of Medical Investigation* 67: 67-69.

Wise, L. 2004. *Core Archery: Shooting With Proper Back Tension.* Mequon, WI: Target Communications.

About the Authors

Kathleen M. Haywood, PhD, is a professor emerita in the College of Education at the University of Missouri–St. Louis. The lead author on the previous editions of *Archery: Steps to Success*, she is a former competitor who has taught archery at several universities, both for the general student body and for teacher preparation students. Haywood has a background in motor learning and motor development, which lends itself to implementing instructional models for participants of all ages. She resides in St. Charles, Missouri.

Catherine F. Lewis, MEd, was the coauthor on the previous editions of *Archery: Steps to Success*. She is a former amateur and professional competitor who has participated in tournaments at the local, state, regional, and national levels. Lewis has taught archery to people of all ages, especially children in school physical education and camp settings. She is a retired physical education teacher from the Riverview Gardens School District in St. Louis County, Missouri. She resides in St. Peters, Missouri.

Steps to Success Sports Series

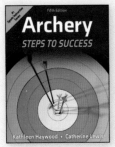

The *Steps to Success Sports Series* is the most extensively researched and carefully developed set of books ever published for teaching and learning sports skills.

Each of the books offers a complete progression of skills, concepts, and strategies that are carefully sequenced to optimize learning for students, teaching for sport-specific instructors, and instructional program design techniques for future teachers.

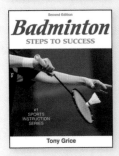
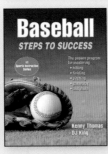
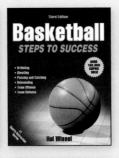
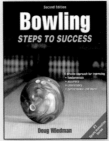
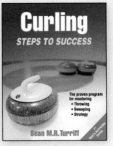
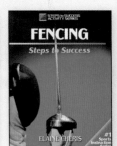

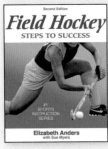
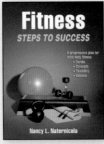
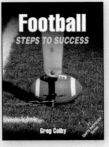

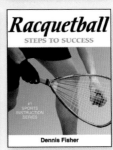
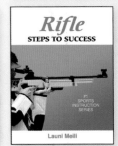

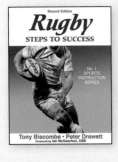
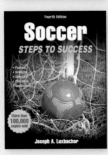
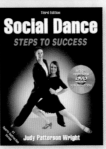
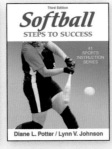
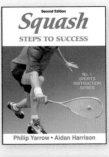
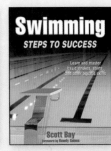

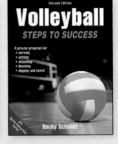
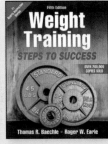

To place your order,

US and International:
(800) 747-4457
(217) 351-5076
US.HumanKinetics.com

Canada:
(800) 465-7301
Canada.HumanKinetics.com

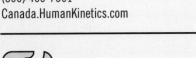

Nearly all the titles from the *Steps to Success Sports Series* are available through a subscription service. With the *Steps to Success Ebook Service*, you will receive full access to all the included titles for six months so that you can master every sport you wish.

Scan to find out more